Slow Train Coming

Slow Train Coming

Bob Dylan's *Girl from the North Country* and Broadway's Rebirth

Todd Almond

methuen | drama

LONDON · NEW YORK · OXFORD · NEW DELHI · SYDNEY

METHUEN DRAMA
Bloomsbury Publishing Plc
50 Bedford Square, London, WC1B 3DP, UK
1385 Broadway, New York, NY 10018, USA
29 Earlsfort Terrace, Dublin 2, Ireland

BLOOMSBURY, METHUEN DRAMA and the Methuen Drama logo are trademarks of
Bloomsbury Publishing Plc

First published in Great Britain 2025

A catalogue record for this book is available from the British Library.

A catalog record for this book is available from the Library of Congress.

ISBN: HB: 978-1-3504-0738-1
       ePDF: 978-1-3504-0740-4
       eBook: 978-1-3504-0739-8

Typeset by RefineCatch Limited, Bungay, Suffolk
Printed and bound in Great Britain

To find out more about our authors and books visit www.bloomsbury.com
and sign up for our newsletters.

CONTENTS

List of Illustrations vi
Prologue vii

Part 1

1   Heaven 3

2   Lafayette 57

3   Downtown 115

Part 2

4   42nd Street 153

5   44th Street 173

6   Hospital 190

7   The Real World 194

8   The New World 219

Epilogue 241
Afterword 245
Works Cited 248
Permissions 252
Acknowledgments 254
Index 255

ILLUSTRATIONS

1 Jeannette Bayardelle and cast sing "Pressing On" at the Tony Awards. Courtesy Mare Winningham

2 John Schiappa spinning in the Legacy Robe. © Rachel Stern

3 Ovation at the Belasco. Courtesy Mare Winningham

4 Marc Kudisch and Jeannette Bayardelle, in her Covid cab, as I called it. © Chiara Trentalange

5 Dressing-room roommates, Austin Scott and Todd Almond. © Bruce Glikis

6 Daily pre-show testing. © Rachel Stern

7 Closing night party. © Chiara Trentalange

8 Pre "Duquesne Whistle" selfie for my husband. © Todd Almond

9 First week of rehearsal, Public Theater, August, 2018. © Tom Nelis

10 The new world. © Todd Almond

11 Anthony Edwards steps into the show at a moment's notice, has one rehearsal. © Tom Nelis

12 Austin Scott, here rehearsing with Kimber Elayne Sprawl, joins the Broadway company. Conor with his guitar. Courtesy Kimber Elayne Sprawl

PROLOGUE: FLOWERS

I stood there in shock or like someone dissociating mid-crime; a thick, contractor-size garbage bag in my left hand and still-living flowers in my right. There wasn't time to think—we had thirty minutes to get out before they locked the building, so I stuffed the flowers, roses, head-first into the bag, snapping their stems to make room for the dozen or so other bunches that also needed to go. *This is wrong,* is all I could think as I grabbed the white peonies my husband had sent me and shoved them in next, destroying them. *I should take these home.* But I'd come by bike, I couldn't manage flowers, and even if I could, wouldn't the petals just rip away one by one? Either way, the streets outside were starting to feel chaotic and end-of-the-world dangerous around the edges; I needed to throw away every living thing in this room and just get myself home.

Once the garbage bag was full, I tossed it onto the growing pile in the hallway outside my dressing room, an upsetting stack that even in the frenzied moment struck me as the perfect metaphor for the frenzied moment: my castmates and I *were* these just-bloomed flowers not allowed to live. I could hear similar activity to mine in the neighboring dressing room: snapping stems, frustrated sighs, a panicky zipper closing on a backpack after it had been stuffed full—like mine, I imagined—of personal items: books, a sweater, cards that read "Happy Opening!"

Just days before, we had been dancing at a party in Bryant Park. Toasting each other with the Heaven's Door whiskey that Bob Dylan himself had sent us.

Just days before, our faces were on the front page of the *New York Times'* Arts section—above the fold—our names singled-out and celebrated; the two-page full-color ad was still, at this moment, lying open on my dining room table at home.

Just days before, all of these flowers now choking to death in plastic bags arrived fresh at the stage door, wrapped in colorful ribbons and with break-a-leg wishes.

We were on the upswing. It was 2020. The *roaring* twenties, everyone had joked. We were on Broadway. At last. An open-ended run, a hit show. Heaven. Ahead of us, a year to come of sold-out performances.

On opening night, not even a week past, I declared that I would keep the dressing room filled with fresh flowers for our entire run. "Every week,"

I vowed to my dressing-roommate Austin, "on my way to the first of our eight shows, I will stop at my favorite flower shop to *re-stalk*." And he laughed at my corny joke and over-abundant plans. Why not? We were finally *here*. We'd made it.

And then came the crash.

PART I

1

Heaven

Circus

My first encounter with Bob Dylan and Conor McPherson's *Girl from the North Country* was on an escalator in London. It was 2018, and I was on a tour of the UK with a folk singer, as her guitarist.

It was a stressful tour, mostly due to the fact that I do not play the guitar. And it's not as if I was a guitarist in a band with other musicians who could cover for that fact—I was the entire band.

This sort of thing happens to me all the time; when I first moved to New York City in 1999, for example, I was hired to install windows in a factory that was being repurposed as condominiums. I did not know how to install windows.

I still do not know how to install windows.

But I did it. And to this day, I sometimes wake up in the middle of the night in a panic—*did those windows all fall out one day?* The owner of the building had shown me how to do the job, and I did it exactly as he instructed, step by step. I'm an A-plus student. And since the police have never shown up to arrest me, I have to believe that the windows stayed in place just fine.

The same was true with the guitar. The folk singer showed me exactly where to put my fingers on the frets, which pick was best for each groove, etc. And I'm a musician—piano is my main instrument—so I do have an innate sense of how things *should* sound. I said yes to the tour and hoped for the best.

I rationalize these things like this: my childhood took place in a small town in western Nebraska where my working-class parents instilled in me, by their example, strong work ethic and rule-following. But I'm an artist, so there's something additional guiding me, a *third* influence. Whatever we want to call it. Inspiration. Creativity.

On my lunch breaks at the factory, I would go up to the rooftop to rehearse the sixteen-bar audition material my acting agent sent me for my *Les Misérables* callback. I was determined to play Enjolras—the student leader of the doomed revolutionaries—on Broadway. It's all I wanted. So I practiced. Five stories up, on top of the world, I would belt out the climactic high Ab toward the Manhattan skyline, the lyric underlining my resolve: *They will come when we call!*

Whatever force it was, whatever we name that third influence that got me onto that rooftop half believing in my big dreams and half accepting cold reality, it is the same force that got me on that UK tour years later and onto the very escalator that gave me a supernatural peek at my coming fate.

There I was in London, having just stepped off the tube, guitar case in hand, standing on the escalator that carried me past advertisements for very British things—biscuits, Kylie Minogue.[1] One ad really caught my eye. It was for a piece of theater playing on the West End called *Girl from the North Country.* On the poster was a woman in sunglasses hugging an old-fashioned microphone and next to her, on either side, were two names: Conor McPherson and Bob Dylan.

Bob Dylan? Wow. Bob Dylan. I love Bob Dylan.

I laughed a little to myself, wondering what Bob Dylan's entrance to the London folk scene must have been like in 1962, and what he would think of mine, with my charlatan-guitarist ways more than fifty years later. We were both born Midwesterners, me and Bob—Nebraska for me, Minnesota for him—and music had carried us both very far from home. All the way to New York and now London.

And the other name on the poster, *Conor McPherson?*, sounded familiar. *Oh, right,* I'd seen two of his plays in New York. And I'd loved them. They had ghosts in them. They were very Irish, his plays.

Yes. Conor was Ireland's great contemporary playwright.

Fascinating. Conor McPherson and Bob Dylan, the Irish playwright and the iconic American songwriter. What on earth could they have made together for the stage?

Sounded intriguing, but I didn't have time to investigate, let alone see the show. I was in London just for the night, and I had a show of my own.

As a professional guitarist.

Without a further thought from me, the poster receded into the background as the escalator carried me past it, further and further up to the world above, finally depositing me into the manic swirl of Piccadilly Circus and its surrounding streets. The chaos and the noise and crowds of London's theater district, the West End, made me think of New York's theater district, Broadway.

Broadway.

I got a chill. It was a cold, February day in London.

But there was no time to linger. Sound check was starting in five minutes, and I had to rush off to the venue to see if anyone there knew how to change a broken guitar string because I sure didn't.

---

[1]Kylie Minogue is Australian but huge in England.

Just a few months later I would get a phone call back in America that would set me on a four-year journey with Conor McPherson, Bob Dylan, Broadway, and *Girl from the North Country* itself.

Because after its run in London, the show was to travel across the pond to Dylan's home turf, *America*.

My home turf, too.

To make its entrance into America's great theater city, New York.

That's where I was.

To play on *Broadway.*

That's where I always wanted to be.

Exit

Girl from the North Country was my Broadway debut. The show opened on March 5, 2020, six days before the world shut down.

We were meant to have what's known in the industry as an "open-ended run"—meaning the show was to play eight performances a week for as long as the seats stayed filled. I had signed a year-long contract, so it was a real rug-pull to get only six performances in and then . . . *lights out.*

Typically, a show opens in New York City *one* time, most often for a "limited run." Like *Girl from the North Country* did when it opened off-Broadway at the Public Theater down in the East Village. You rehearse for a few weeks, you perform some "preview" performances to work out the kinks, and then you invite the press and you "open" the show. The show then runs its predetermined schedule, maybe a month or two of performances, and then it "closes." And everyone moves on to something else.

Sometimes, if you're lucky, you get to open the same show a *second* time in New York City, because it transfers to Broadway, like *Girl from the North Country* did when it "moved uptown" to the Belasco Theater in Times Square. And you do it all again, the rehearsing, the previewing, the press, the opening. Only this time, once you've opened, you run the show for as long as you can.

In March of 2020 I was ready to run my Broadway debut as long as I could. My one desire was to fulfill that one-year contract. And then maybe sign up for more. I was never more prepared for anything. This was the moment I had been waiting for.

But then, boom, we closed after only six performances. Because of Covid. And eighteen months later we opened again. And then we closed again because of Omicron. And then we opened again. And then we closed again.

Girl from the North Country opened *four* times in New York City. Once Off-Broadway, and three times *on* Broadway.

I'm not 100 percent certain, but I think that must be a record.

Broadway is an industry whose ". . . attendance for the 2018–2019 season topped those of the ten professional NYC Metro-area sports teams combined

(Mets, Yankees, Rangers, Islanders, Knicks, Liberty, Giants, Jets, Devils and Nets)."[2]

Broadway doesn't *shut down*. It can't. It is a major artery for the life-blood of the city. But for eighteen months it did shut down, the life-blood stopped flowing. Broadway lay unconscious, near-death.

It would never be the same again. How could it be?

We would never be the same again. As a community.

After *Girl from the North Country*, I would never be the same again.

But, strangely, it wasn't the pandemic that changed me. At first, anyway. Something else had already happened.

While we were performing *Girl from the North Country* in our off-Broadway run at the Public Theater, a full two years before the pandemic, I had a recurring, sustained religious experience.

It had to do with my character in the play. It happened onstage. Every night.

Here's the setup: my character, his name is Elias Burke, is a resident in a boarding house in Duluth, Minnesota, in 1934. It's the Great Depression. There are many other characters in the boarding house including Elias's parents, and they're all struggling. The whole country is.

Near the end of the play—or "musical," *Girl from the North Country* has been called both—Elias dies.

I die.

When he dies, when *I die*, the stage goes bright white with light and is cleared of all furniture and set pieces, making room for a full-company, gospel arrangement of Bob Dylan's song "Duquesne Whistle" performed in a kind of everywhere/nowhere liminal space.

I sing:

Listen to that Duquesne whistle blowin'
Blowin' like it's gonna sweep my world away[3]

That's how the music works in the show—it sweeps in and takes over. The play stops and Bob Dylan's music begins. Back and forth, over and over, play, then song. Play, then song. McPherson, then Dylan. Like awake, then dreaming. Or like sermon, then hymn.

Staging-wise, my death is simple: after I sing this enormous gospel song, I turn to my left, and as the music transitions to Dylan's "Señor," I walk to my mother, take her hands in mine, and sing:

Where she held me in her arms one time and said, "Forget me not."[4]

[2]Roger Sands, *Forbes* magazine, January 20, 2023.
[3]"Duquesne Whistle," Bob Dylan, *Tempest*, 2012.
[4]"Señor (Tales of Yankee Power)," Bob Dylan, *Street-Legal*, 1978.

I then turn away from her and walk upstage to a waiting, empty chair and sit. The lights shift, and just like that, Elias is gone.

We have died.

But there I am, the audience can still see me sitting upright in a chair (the furniture has returned), my eyes are open, I'm breathing, and singing backup harmonies for my mother and father, played by Luba Mason and Marc Kudisch, as they wail their heartbreaking duet about marriage.

I don't *look* dead. Theater is an art form of suggestion.

This was the moment it happened. In our first performance in 2018 at the Public Theater. The religious experience struck.

Sitting in that upstage chair, still physically in the play but no longer living, my body was angled in such a way that I could look into the darkness of the stage-right wing, the wing being the area just off-stage where actors go whenever they leave the play.

There was a door back there in the wing, a swinging door that led to the dressing rooms; one easy push of that door would take you from the world of the play to the world beyond the play. *Backstage.* Above the door, the word "Exit."

There I was, as Elias, having just died; onstage but looking off. I could see two of my castmates back there in the darkness—I couldn't quite make out who it was, they were silhouetted. They stood near that swinging door, the exit to the world beyond the play; shadow-figures hovering between worlds, like ghosts or angels or whatever you believe. Dust. I could tell by their shifting feet that they were ready to exit, anxious, but they couldn't go just yet, because they still had work to do; they had to sing harmony parts from offstage.

Once they finished that task, it was as if they were released, and they walked right through that door marked "Exit," disappearing into the bright light of the hallway just beyond.

I knew that I should also go toward the light, I should follow the others to the hallway beyond, because I was dead. This is the way. This is the exit. Come, follow.

Now, the audience was not aware that any of this was happening to me, right in front of them. They were watching the play continue on, Luba Mason had them by the throat with her big solo:

Well I've been to the mountain and I've been in the wind,
I've been in and out of happiness . . . [5]

I wasn't drawing attention to myself. To the observer, I was sitting perfectly still. The mystical stuff transfixing me was all happening offstage,

---

[5] From "Is Your Love in Vain," Bob Dylan, *Street Legal*, 1978.

in the dark wing. I was simply watching it. And besides, it was nothing special, really. It was just actors doing their job—standing where they were told to stand, singing their assigned parts, and then walking through an exit so they could go to their dressing rooms and change costumes or, more likely, check their phones.

But I had died. So I saw things differently now. That door was oblivion. Transcendence. And dammit if I wasn't compelled to walk through it.

Still onstage and "acting," my next move was to stand up, take one final look at my parents, and leave the stage, which I did, by simply walking into the wing with the rest of the cast following behind me in what was writer/director Conor McPherson's subtle take on a funeral procession. In the darkness of the stage-right wing, I hovered around that door the same way the two silhouettes had done earlier, ready to go through it, anxious even, but before I could, I still had some work to do; three final "ooh"s to sing under my mom and dad's duet. A ghost or angel or bit of dust myself now.

> Can you cook and sew, make flowers grow, (ooh)
> Can you understand my pain? (ooh)
> Are you willing to risk it all, or is your love in vain? (ooh)[6]

And then it was time. I was released and could now make my exit through that easy, swinging door to the world beyond.

The moment I did, Elias was gone, along with him Duluth, the Great Depression, and the sensation of death. I was me again, Todd, an actor in a backstage hallway of a theater in New York City, a man who now had to quickly change out of his white linen burial suit and back into his everyman coat, scarf, and hat for the finale of the show.

Every night I died. That was in the script, so no surprise there. But what was a surprise was that every night I would forget that it was coming. As soon as I turned away from my mother and walked to that chair upstage and sat facing the dark wing only to see the word "Exit," I was struck: *Oh, right. I've died. And as soon as I pass through that door, I will be reborn.*

Guesthouse

When we started rehearsals for *Girl from the North Country*, the idea of Americans struggling en masse through a terrible time—the Great Depression—was something unknowable to me first hand. I would have to research that kind of struggle and approximate the feeling for myself.

But in 2020, when the pandemic struck, the real world began to feel a lot like the world of the play.

---

[6]Ibid.

As I've said, *Girl from the North Country* was my first Broadway show, and, though I hope not, maybe my last; I don't know, it's always proved elusive to me, getting to be on Broadway. Even while singing and dying nightly on one of her stages, I looked at Broadway as something I *longed* for, like a character in Madame Bovary might long. Not Emma Bovary, who always longed for what she didn't have, but Charles Bovary, who finally had what he wanted in Emma, but still could never stop longing for her.

As an outsider, however, I realized that I had a unique vantage point. Theater was not new to me, I've been making theater professionally my entire adult life, but Broadway was. RuPaul Charles famously said that *Hollywood is an idea and not a place.* But that ain't true of Broadway. Broadway is a very specific place: between West 40th Street and West 57th Street in midtown Manhattan, New York City. There are forty-one theaters within that area (plus one outlier, the Vivian Beaumont at Lincoln Center on 65th) that qualify as "Broadway" houses. If you're not performing in one of those houses—and until *Girl from the North Country* I had never—then you're not on Broadway.

As a cast member of this particular Broadway show, a show battered by bad timing, a show ultimately defined by a once-in-a-century worldwide catastrophe, I had arguably one of the most unique debut experiences possible on Broadway.

My first time out was a doozy.

Girl from the North Country was rare, it was polarizing, and it was both gone-too-soon and old news by its closing. If I may: it was the best of times, it was the worst of times.

And I was a part of it.

I was so changed by the experience that I decided I wanted to investigate it now that some time has passed since we officially closed on June 19, 2022. What happened? What changed me? Why? What was *Girl from the North Country* anyway? A play or a musical, that's the surface question. There's something deeper I'm after. This is Bob Dylan. And Conor McPherson. Artists both known for sounding the fanfare of the common man who together made a most uncommon piece of theater. How did it happen?

Plus, I'm just having a hard time letting *Girl from the North Country* go. I think about it every day, about how I encountered death, about the cast that I grew to love, about our parties and our Hanukkah prayers, about our terrible struggles through the great depression of the Covid pandemic, about the thrill I felt in finally performing on Broadway after decades of trying, about opening and closing the same show again and again. About Mare Winningham, about Artie Gaffin, about our brunch feasts and about how scared I was playing the harmonica for Bob Dylan himself. About Jeannette Bayardelle's eerie prophecies and what we lost and all the harmonies we learned and relearned, and about the ghost in the theater, the lingering fear and the anger, the triumph, the heartbreak, the violence we had to practice daily and the day we had to throw away all of our opening night flowers because we didn't know when or if theater itself would ever come back.

This book is the story of all of that, and all of those people and all of those questions untangled.

Since theater is by its nature a collaborative art form, I decided the best approach would be to interview everyone involved in the show's creation.

I flew to London and talked to Matthew Warchus, artistic director at the Old Vic theater in London where *Girl from the North Country* premiered in 2017, to Sheila Atim and Shirley Henderson, original cast members who both won Laurence Olivier Awards for their performances in the show's West End transfer. I sat with the show's commercial producer Tristan Baker, and with the entire London creative team, playwright and director Conor McPherson, choreographer Lucy Hind and musical arranger/orchestrator Simon Hale.

And then I flew back home to New York to talk one-on-one with the Broadway cast, musicians, swings, understudies, and more.

I wanted to know everyone's experience, since mine had been so life-altering.

Back in the early summer of 2022 when *Girl from the North Country* was still running on Broadway, though running its final lap, my castmate Kimber Sprawl and I were chatting after an early morning performance we had just given for some out-of-town producers who were in town for the Tony Awards. "Can you believe everything we've been through?" she asked. We laughed, heading out into a gorgeous New York City morning, realizing how like our characters we had become. How like the past the present felt. How like the play, reality.

The characters, as written by Irish playwright Conor McPherson, are American, and they are all strangers who find themselves for various reasons living temporarily in "a fair sized family house, which is now serving as a guesthouse in Duluth, Minnesota, winter 1934." They struggle just to get through each and every day. There's a national crisis. Life is hard, and sometimes the characters just stop moving and sing. And while this feels so Irish—everyone suddenly singing, everyone knowing all of the words—the hymns themselves feel American, *quintessentially* American, and being songs from Bob Dylan's deep catalog, they are.

"And there's a slow, slow train coming up around the bend," the characters would sing in harmony,[7] a lyric from Dylan's born-again phase.

"Slow train coming," we'd repeat, some of us onstage, some of us in the wings.

That's what *Girl from the North Country* felt like. A slow train coming. Inexorable. Fated.

---

[7]"Slow Train," Dylan, *Slow Train Coming*, 1979.

We waited for that train together, singing in the guesthouse. Strangers, actors, and characters.

"There's a slow training coming . . ." A blessing and a warning. Something to long for and something to fear. Something you wait for your entire life and something you can't stop from coming.

Something that's going to happen because it was always going to happen.

Girl from the North Country came at me, as history came at us all, like a slow train.

Reading at the Public

Chris Highland, my then stage-acting agent at United Talent Agency, called me on a Friday in April, 2018, and asked me if I was available for a reading of a new musical for the Public Theater that would rehearse on Monday and perform on Tuesday.

"Excuse me?" I said.

I've been involved in theater for most of my life at this point, so I've done plenty of readings of new musicals both as an actor and as a writer. One thing I know about these readings is that, even though they are simple presentations (actors sitting at music-stands reading the play and singing the songs), they can't possibly be rehearsed in one day and performed the next. There's too much to learn.

But I had heard Chris correctly: the offer was to rehearse the entire show Monday and perform it on Tuesday. He assured me that Heidi (Griffiths) and Jordan (Thaler), the casting directors from the Public Theater, were confident that I was up to the task—the role of Elias Burke was mostly physical (not relevant in a reading) with only "one big song."

The Public Theater is one of the most important institutions in American theater; *Hair, Fun Home, A Chorus Line,* and *Hamilton* all started there. I couldn't take this offer lightly.

My history with the Public extends to last century. When I first moved to New York City in the fall of 1999, I pieced together a living however I could manage; I had to. Window installation, for instance. I had no money, and my plan of immediately being cast in a Broadway musical had flopped. I wouldn't get to Broadway for another twenty-three years, which makes me wonder: would I have stayed and struggled the way I did had I known how difficult it would truly be?

One of my sources of survival income was as a music director and accompanist for singers; I fell almost immediately into playing the piano for "downtown" gigs at Joe's Pub, the cabaret space at the Public Theater named for the institution's founder, Joseph Papp. "Downtown" gigs are often transgressive and edgy, distinguishing themselves from the more traditional "uptown" cabaret scene. Think Kiki & Herb. Burlesque. And this was the early days of Joe's Pub, when we would do all-night shows with downtown mainstays like John Cameron Mitchell, Mx. Justin Vivian Bond, and Bridget Everett, to name a few.[8]

It was thrilling. There was very little pay, and I often had to chase down the promoter who'd hired me for the lousy fifty bucks he owed me, but these were proper artists I got to work with, who had great taste in music. Yes, I was living on popcorn and peanut butter because that was all I could afford; and, yes, I was auditioning for every Broadway musical I could with little (*no*) success; but also, yes, I was receiving a music education from future legends, so I didn't notice how miserable I was.

And I *was* miserable. All I wanted to do was be on Broadway, and all I heard was "No." which I interpreted as "You're not good enough." Rejection is part of the job, you have to just keep showing up in spite of it. Absorb all of the "No, you're not good enough"s and try again. And again and again. For decades, in my case. Because . . . *eventually*, "no" turns to "yes."

Or so you hope.

I remember being at a party back then with some working actors. I'd lived in the city for several years at that point, and I found myself in a one-on-one conversation with a guy *currently* starring in a big Broadway show. He said to me, "Oh, I struggled for a long time before I got my first show." Buoyed by this shared experience and looking for guidance, I asked, "How long did you struggle?" And he cocked his head and squinted to really think about it. "Like, almost a *month*," he said.

Maybe I should have gone to church or something. Found a place to protect my easily bruised heart. But I never liked church. Instead, what I did was write songs. Most of them were about God, or loneliness, and I would write them as I walked the city, often on my way to the Public Theater to play a gig. This was, in its way, my church—I was the organist at a place called Joe's Pub.

Here are the lyrics to a song I wrote back then, while walking the city.

I forget that there's a sky above Manhattan
Until it does something like start to snow
And suddenly I'm trying to jump across the street
In one single bound
And I smile as I pass many strangers
I put my headphones on and I just
Go.
And I let the streetlights lead me
And I swear the streets that lead me

---

[8]John Cameron Mitchell wrote and starred in the original *Hedwig and the Angry Inch*; Mx. Justin Vivian Bond co-created "Kiki & Herb"; Bridget Everett blazed a singular trail with "Bridget Everett and the Tender Moments" and would go on to create the series *Somebody Somewhere* for HBO.

Are holy.
Holy.
Holy.

And I carried my heavy little soul this way into the Public, always believing in the streets' holiness.

In 2013, with director Lear deBessonet,[9] I would help create a new program for the Public Theater called "Public Works" which, according to the Public's website, is "a major artistic program of the Public Theater, aim[ing] to restore and build community by connecting people through the creation of extraordinary works of art."

For Public Works, I wrote the book, music, and lyrics for, as well as music-directed and acted in, pageant-style musical-theater adaptations of classic texts (Shakespeare, Homer). These musical pageants were performed on Central Park's Delacorte stage by a handful of select professional actors like Norm Lewis, Laura Benanti, Lindsay Mendez, and others; specialty ensembles like marching bands, children's choirs, taiko drummers, stilt-walkers, etc.; and a chorus of over 100 everyday New Yorkers from every corner of the city.

So, when my agent Chris said that the offer for the reading was coming from the Public Theater, all of this personal history surfaced, and with my quiet conviction that the holy streetlights have been leading me down the proper path all these years now confirmed, I said, "Sounds good, I'll do it."

It wasn't until then that I thought to ask: "What *is* the musical, anyway?"

"*Girl from the North Country.*"

The title instantly pulled up the escalator and poster memory from a few months back in London. I blushed head to toe, *Oh, god. Why haven't I been arrested yet for impersonating a folk guitarist?*

I told Chris that I'd heard of the show, but I didn't quite know what it was. It had music by Bob Dylan . . . was it new music? And Conor McPherson is a playwright . . . but this is a musical? . . . or is it more like a play? . . . something *other?*

I had homework to do. I love homework.

That weekend I read the script and I downloaded the original London cast recording of *Girl from the North Country* to get a sense of the show, and, more urgently, to learn my part. I admit that I jumped straightaway to the track "Duquesne Whistle," which was the "one big song" Heidi and Jordan mentioned my character Elias would sing. After peeling myself off the ceiling, having been blasted there by Jack Shalloo's roaring rendition, I listened from the beginning of the album to the end. Several times.

---

[9] Lear deBessonet would go on to receive a Tony nomination for her 2022 revival of Sondheim's *Into the Woods.*

This didn't feel like "Broadway" music. It wasn't, it was Bob Dylan, but it didn't feel like Broadway's version of Bob Dylan. It felt closer to the music I used to play downtown; it was melancholy, it was "other." It was right up my alley and I couldn't believe my luck.

Monday morning, April 16, 2018, my mother's birthday, I walked into Gibney Studios at Union Square (890 Broadway) for my one day of rehearsal. I would never be the same.

Marc Kudisch, the Tony Award-nominated, barrel-chested Broadway baritone from many, many shows including *Thoroughly Modern Milly* and Michael John LaChiusa's *The Wild Party*, was also cast in the reading; he remembers walking into the rehearsal room and seeing me.

MARC KUDISCH   I walked in and saw you there and thought, "Oh, good, you're music-directing!"

Marc and I had just collaborated on the revival of the Suzan-Lori Parks play *Fucking A* at Signature Theater on 42nd Street, where, as music director, I had Marc playing electric bass guitar onstage while acting in his scenes with Elizabeth Stanley, playing a tuba.

But I wouldn't be music-directing Marc this time, I would be acting with him, playing his son though I'm not even ten years younger than Marc. He howled when I called him "Papa." The role of Music Director fell to Or Matias, fresh from his run as music director and conductor of Dave Malloy's revolutionary Broadway musical *Natasha, Pierre, & the Great Comet of 1812*.

Or is like an entire music library inside a hip, handsome librarian. You meet him, and you wish to be only half as interesting as he is.

OR MATIAS   Oskar [Eustis] called me and he said, "So I have this thing, it's onstage musicians. I think you would be perfect for it. We want to do it in a day and a half." And I thought, *it's two days. Fuck it. Why not? Let's do it.*

Oskar Eustis, the captain-like Artistic Director of the Public Theater, is just like the spelling of his first name suggests: political, leftist, outspoken. A half-lion who calls people *comrade*. If you ever find yourself at an opening night of Shakespeare in the Park in New York, you'll hear Oskar give a speech that will make you believe that theater is the only thing that can save our divided world. Rousing speeches are his specialty; after each and every one I hear, I wonder if someone had the forethought of transcribing it for posterity.

OR MATIAS   I read the script and I was like, *what is this thing?* It's a Bob Dylan show, but it's not a jukebox musical, and it's *some* of his known songs, but all revamped and not his greatest hits. What is this? This is kind of crazy. There's no way that this can be a thing.

Jeannette Bayardelle, who would go on to be nominated for a Tony award for her performance in *Girl from the North Country,* almost turned the reading down.

JEANNETTE BAYARDELLE   I was on Long Island with my family at my sister's house, and I get a call from my agent, "Hey, are you interested in doing this reading of a Bob Dylan musical?" And I'm like, *Bob Dylan. I've heard of Bob Dylan, but I don't know his songs.* I said to my agent, "I don't know. I don't think so," because I was with my family, I didn't feel like going over music.

In an inspired bit of casting, Jeannette was offered the role of Mrs. Neilsen, the beautiful, forward-thinking, finance-savvy widow who foresees all of the troubles coming and is the only one making practical plans to deal with them. Minus the widow part, those are exactly the words I would use to describe Jeannette herself. She day-trades on her iPhone.

JEANNETTE BAYARDELLE   My agent said, "Jeannette, you need to do this." So I spent the weekend trying to spend time with my family, but at night I was going over the songs and just trying to make sense of the script.

The script, like the boarding house that serves as its setting, is chock-full of characters in survival mode. These people hide themselves in order to protect themselves. They obscure personal details by giving as little information as possible, and who knows if the information they do give is in any way true? They exist between the lines. This can be difficult to make sense of on the page. My character Elias, for example, has *two and only two sentences* of dialogue in the entire script, yet he's a major character whose death is the climactic moment of the piece.

As people are in life, the characters are contradictory, morally ambiguous, and imperfect.

While Jeannette spent the weekend finding her "Mrs. Neilsen" hidden in the subtext, I was busy obsessing over something different: *why is my song so high?*

JEANNETTE BAYARDELLE   And then on Monday, we walked into that space downtown, a little box space.

Large rehearsal studios in Manhattan, the room we found ourselves in at Gibney being no exception, have just enough room for a couple of folding tables, an upright piano, and a milling group of New York actors-who-sing. I find these rooms comforting and familiar.

OR MATIAS   And then we got into the room and I remember being on the rollercoaster—who knows what this is going to be?

JEANNETTE BAYARDELLE   And I just remember meeting everybody, like, "Oh, hi, this is Marc Kudisch . . ."

Most actors have a Marc Kudisch story because Marc Kudisch has worked with most everyone. He's a character, my *papa*; gregarious and striking, he could be a cowboy, only he talks a lot, he's emphatic, so *not* a cowboy, and his operatically resonant speaking voice carries to every corner when he opines about anything from politics to Sondheim. I always thought that if someone made a musical version of *The Mary Tyler Moore Show*, he would be the perfect Ted Baxter.

In addition to Marc, I was acquainted with Danny Jenkins, who was playing the doctor, Judy Kuhn and David Pittu, but I didn't know everyone in the room, so there were a lot of *hellos* over paper-cup coffees . . .

OR MATIAS   That first day, we were in that narrow long room and there was that long table. And Marc Kudisch was sitting at the end and talking to me about all his guitars and what he likes playing on guitar.

JEANNETTE BAYARDELLE   And then as we were going over the music—I'm happy that I was pretty prepared!

. . . and though it was exciting to be in the room with all of these great actors, many of whom I'd admired from afar for years, I remained certain that there was absolutely no way we could learn and perform the entire show in just two days.

JEANNETTE BAYARDELLE   I knew there was something about why I didn't want to do this reading—it was only two days!

OR MATIAS   Jin Ha was in that first reading, right?

Jin Ha, fresh from the *M. Butterfly* revival on Broadway, *was* in that reading. Along with other Broadway stalwarts including Samantha Ware, Michael McKean, Alma Cuervo, and of course Marc Kudish, Daniel (Danny) Jenkins, and Judy Kuhn. I've been listening to Judy Kuhn since I was a freshman in High School. She's a Broadway legend, the voice of Disney's *Pocahontas,* and she's still creating new roles like Helen in *Fun Home*, but most importantly to me, she is Cosette on the Original Broadway Cast Recording of *Les Misérables*, which I listed to obsessively in Nebraska. We're friends now and collaborators, me and Judy. Together we recorded an album celebrating the dynastic musical theater family of Richard Rodgers, his daughter Mary Rodgers-Guettel, and her son Adam Guettel.[10] I admire

---

[10]Richard Rodgers was one half the writing team Rodgers and Hammerstein; Mary Rodgers-Guettel wrote the music for *Once Upon a Mattress*; Adam Guettel wrote the music and lyrics for *Light in the Piazza.*

Judy's ever-inquisitive artistry, but I must admit, sometimes my husband and I beg her to sing "In My Life"[11] to us over FaceTime.

Typically, getting actors together to learn and present a new musical would require a producer to follow the union guidelines of what is known as a "29-hour reading."

OR MATIAS So, a "29-hour reading" is the framework of an Equity[12] reading in which you get a group of actors together, you get a director, typically a music director, a stage manager, and you have a total of twenty-nine hours to put a piece together. There are certain guidelines: you're not allowed to stage certain things; you're not allowed to ask people to memorize certain things. Props are usually very limited. And the goal of it is to use those twenty-nine hours, which is inclusive of the presentation, to really just be able to hear a piece of art from top to bottom. And so typically that process, from my experience, is very, very music driven, because usually it will take most of that time just to learn the music.

This was not a 29-hour reading, more like 10-hour. For the entirety of our one-day rehearsal, Or Matias sat at the piano, we actors hunched over our three ring binders stuffed with music and the script, and Conor McPherson, the Irish playwright and director, stood with his guitar in his arms, looking less like our leader and more like a friendly, red-headed musician who'd accidentally wandered into our rehearsal from somewhere else and decided to stay and play along.

JEANNETTE BAYARDELLE [Conor] had his guitar out. And I thought, *okay, that's odd.*

OR MATIAS Conor was sitting with his guitar and kind of playing along and I thought, *Oh, this is a visionary.*

He was mysterious. He didn't seem worried, this "Conor McPherson," though the following afternoon, after not a lot of preparation, we would be performing his script *in front of people.* Important people. He should be nervous, right, this "Conor McPherson"? Panicking, even?

OR MATIAS All the readings that I had ever done—there is always this element of stress, we're just rushing through everything, everything is going to be slapped together and haphazard. For whatever reason, this one did not feel stressful.

---

[11]From *Les Misérables*, music by Claude-Michel Schönberg, lyrics by Alain Boublil.
[12]Actors' Equity Association, AEA, the union for stage actors and stage managers.

Maybe Conor's non-stress, which translated into a roomful of non-stress, thankfully, had something to do with the stakes of this reading? Maybe the stakes were low. I didn't know the purpose of this reading—actors are never privy to what's happening behind the scenes—but I assumed it was some sort of audition for the Public Theater. Often readings like this are put together so that producers or investors can decide if they want to move forward with the project, to take on the financial risk. A reading can be an audition for the show *itself*. Is that why we were doing this? I didn't know.

> OR MATIAS   I know for me in past 29-hour readings, because there isn't that much time to talk to the actors, you get a really good sense of what an actor's first impulse is with material and whether it's something that their instincts are actually right for. And so it's usually a great litmus test—what is the baseline of how this actor delivers this material? And then is that somebody who we would want to continue working with?

No one ever told me why I was there, and I didn't have time to wonder. I was busy thinking about that *one big song*. "Duquesne Whistle" was high, and it was loud, and it started a cappella with one attention-demanding word: "LISTEN!" like some bossy angel shouting "All eyes on me!" For the record, the highest note I'll ever sing full-voice in front of people is an A flat. If a song has one A flat, I'm a little stressed. "Duquesne Whistle" had forty-two A flats, I counted.

So, although I was unclear whether the watchers watching the performance would be scrutinizing the play itself or my performance in it, all I could think was, either way, each one of those forty-two A flats was going to feel like an audition.

But an audition for *what* exactly? What was this show? I thought it already had a successful life in London? Americans typically swoon over transfers from London with the original British cast, why were a bunch of Americans learning it, and so quickly, and for an off-Broadway, not-for-profit theater? I was falling in love with the material we were cramming in, but just *what the heck was it?*

History of the Production

I. The idea

Tristan Baker is the co-founder of Runaway Entertainment, a production company based in London. He and his producing partner Charlie Parsons, one of the creators of the ubiquitous television hit *Survivor*, have been with *Girl from the North Country* from its outset.

Tristan is tall and friendly and canny. In arranging our interview, he told me that his office in London sits right across the street from the West End's "Sondheim Theater," which is where *Les Misérables* still plays.

Les Misérables is going to figure into this story quite a bit. In many ways, it is the stylistic antithesis of *Girl from the North Country* and is perhaps anathema to Dylan fans, but we're going to have to get comfortable with the dissonance the two titles create when rubbed together. It haunts me, *Les Miz*. I love it, I always have, I always will. I love the novel by Victor Hugo, I read every new translation that is published. If *Les Misérables* were the Bible, I would go to church. My husband and I travel to London frequently for his work, and sometimes I'll say, "While you're working, I'm going to go do some writing at that one cute coffee shop I like." He knows that I really mean "crying" not "writing" and "at *Les Misérables*" not "at that one cute coffee shop I like."

So I knew exactly where Tristan's office was.

Tristan smiles wide while he speaks, like he's been gazing upward at something wonderful just before talking to you, and he's eager to share it with you, and though I won't put them everywhere here, his sentences all end in exclamation points.

TRISTAN BAKER   I was doing a project with a guy called Steve Lappin, who was working for Sony Music at the time. Sony Music was based in South Kensington, and we were doing various bits and pieces and things. We looked at the Sony catalog and highlighted all the people that we thought would be fun to work with. And one of them was Bob Dylan. Steve said, "Oh, I think Bob's manager, Jeff Rosen," who's been his manager for thirty-five years, "is coming to London next week. Shall we see if he wants a cup of tea?" And like all of these things, you never say *no*. You will say *yes*.

Record companies and film studios (or their parent companies) have seen great success in recent years with "jukebox" musicals and film-to-stage adaptations (*Beautiful: The Carole King musical*; *Jersey Boys*; *Beetlejuice*), so they often invite producers and writers to peruse their catalogs of intellectual property (I.P.). As a writer/composer, I've done this, once with 21st Century Fox in a conference room at their NYC offices. They invited me to flip through a thick binder of their movie titles to see if anything caught my eye as a potential stage musical. I selected *The Magnificent Ambersons* even though I'd never seen the film (or read the book), and I'm not sure why I did that. I think I was nervous.

TRISTAN BAKER   And so we had a cup of tea with Jeff Rosen. It literally was a cup of tea. Ten minutes. Bob had done the Twyla Tharp dance piece . . .

Choreographer Twyla Tharp's 2002 dance musical *Movin' Out* used the songs of Billy Joel to great success. The show ran for three years on Broadway and won Tharp a Tony and a Drama Desk Award for Best Choreography; her follow-up dance-musical *The Times They Are a-Changin'* in 2006 used the songs of Bob Dylan less successfully. The show closed after only twenty-eight performances and largely negative reviews.

> TRISTAN BAKER   . . . I said, "Would Bob allow his music to be used in a . . ." and then I used the term *traditional musical. Girl from the North Country* is *not* a traditional musical. I said, "Would he allow it?" And Jeff said, "Yeah, great, great, yeah." And I said, "Oh, this is fantastic. Let's do it."

Although Dylan's representative Jeff Rosen said "Yes" (in so many words), it was unofficial. Tristan would need to send Jeff a proper pitch that Bob Dylan would then need to approve. Tristan had a long way to go to secure an official *yes*.

> TRISTAN BAKER   We were not going to get any rights or any permissions or anything until they knew exactly what it was [we wanted to do]. So we were in this very strange world where we were commissioning something which we didn't have the rights for.

I experienced something similar to this several years ago. A producing team that had the rights to the George Michael catalog reached out to a few writers to pitch ideas. I was one of those writers. My idea was a gay version of Madame Bovary, set in upstate New York and New York City. A provincial young guy falls in love with a country doctor and they set up house upstate, but the allure of the city is too strong; the young guy completely destroys his own life as well as the doctor's in the foolhardy, eternal search for more and more happiness. I didn't get the job.

> TRISTAN BAKER   So we asked ourselves *Who is Bob Dylan? What is it about Bob Dylan?* The storytelling, the poetry. He hadn't won the Nobel Prize for literature at that point, but he would.[13] There's a very short list of British writers that could match [him]. And at the top of that list is Conor McPherson. But I absolutely ruled out Conor McPherson because I thought, *There's no way that Conor McPherson is going to pitch*, because that's what we had to do, we had to pitch "the Bob Dylan musical." So we didn't go down that road to start off with.

---

[13]Bob Dylan won the Nobel Prize for Literature in 2016.

Conor McPherson and I sat in a quiet corner of a hotel restaurant on London's Dorset Square to talk about all of this. My iPhone sat on the table between us, and I kept dripping water on the screen accidentally every time I lifted my glass, which made me nervous that I would accidentally stop the recording.

How did he remember the beginnings of this project?

CONOR MCPHERSON   [The producers] went out to a few writers. I don't know who they were.

Conor works a lot in London, but he lives with his family in Dun Laoghaire, Ireland.

CONOR MCPHERSON   . . . an old sea port town on the outskirts of Dublin City's south side.

He grew up just on the other side of Dublin, in Raheny, and he wears his working-man poet aura humbly. If you met him on the street in his jeans and earth-tone long-sleeve shirt, you wouldn't assume he is a man with an Olivier Award, an Evening Standard Award, a Critics Circle Award, let alone numerous Tony Award nominations as both a playwright and a director, nor would you recognize him as the man the *New York Times* called, "The finest playwright of his generation."

CONOR MCPHERSON   My day begins around 7:00 a.m. when [my wife and daughter and I] get breakfast and we usually bring [our daughter] to school nearby. Then we walk Bluey in a nice place near us called Killiney Hill park, where dogs can walk off lead.

He would be a fantastic character in a murder mystery, Conor. With his muted red hair, a guitar in his arms; he'd be the guy you identify with because he's just like your good friend back home, back in your hometown, you have the same music references—"You like *Matthew Sweet*? Me, too!" Plus he's got that great Irish accent where he says "tanks" instead of "thanks."

And then at some point in the murder mystery you'd think *he's too friendly, I don't trust it, he must be the murderer. He did it.*

TRISTAN BAKER   I was on the phone not with Conor's agent,[14] but with another agent in the building about another project, and I said, "By the way, does Conor like Bob Dylan?"

It's a good question, so I asked Conor over our dinner (I had the fish) what he thinks about Bob Dylan.

---

[14]Nick Marston at Curtis Brown agency.

CONOR MCPHERSON   [Dylan] is a real writer. Like James Joyce or W. B. Yeats. It's powerful, unconscious, mythical stuff in there. Deep and full of humor, full of wisdom. And ignorance! It's all delivered with a kind of shrug, like, *don't ask me.*

TRISTAN BAKER   I asked, "Does he like Bob Dylan?" "*Yeah.*" "Would he be interested in a Bob Dylan project?" And Alastair Lindsey-Renton, who was the agent [I was talking to], put the phone down, ran down the hall to [Conor's agent] Nick Marston and said, "There's a Bob Dylan musical, Tristan's doing a Bob Dylan musical. Conor should do it. Conor should do it!"

Nick called Conor immediately.

NICK MARSTON   I rang Conor and said "This is a bit of a kind of crazy idea; you've never, never done a musical before."

CONOR MCPHERSON   My agent Nick [Marston] said, "Would you have any ideas of how to do something with Bob Dylan's music in the theater?"

Conor's lack of musical theater experience was a question.

NICK MARSTON   Conor's actually used music beautifully in his plays before . . . he adores music and he's always played guitar, as you know . . .

Tristan and Nick thought Conor was a great idea for the project, but what did Conor think?

CONOR MCPHERSON   I mean, I think I initially thought *definitely.*

NICK MARSTON   . . . and Conor then went away and I think genuinely walked along the seafront . . . as he does . . .

Not unlike Dylan, there is some mystery around Conor as a person. He's approachable and open—if he won the Nobel Prize he would certainly show up for the ceremony—but there are deep wells in the man. Nick's image of Conor walking along the seafront and thinking, feels accurate. Add to it a light fog and a boatman's ghost.

At some point in the process of writing this book, someone—I can't remember who—said to me, "I think Conor maybe studied to be a priest or something." I could ask Conor if this is true, I *should* ask him. One quick email is all it would take, but this is a rumor I like as a rumor. Did he or didn't he *maybe* study to be a priest? Neither answer matters. The conjecture perfectly describes the man and the way he speaks, whether in rehearsal or one-on-one across a dinner table: He speaks like someone who maybe studied to be a priest or something. His face is a fixed expression of both empathy and awe, with a big laugh always ready to pop through.

Conor's initial reaction to the question of whether or not he could imagine Dylan's music in a theatrical setting was "definitely."

CONOR MCPHERSON But the other side of me was the fatalistic, pessimistic side . . . *That's not ever going to happen.*

Conor is a pragmatist.

CONOR MCPHERSON And also if [a Bob Dylan musical] did happen, it would probably be horrible. And if it was me and it was horrible, I'd have to own that.

TRISTAN BAKER And so we said to Conor, "Please, could you pitch what you would do if you had the Bob Dylan musical?"

Conor told his agent Nick that he did, in fact, have an idea for what such a show could be, even though he was certain it would "not ever happen."

CONOR MCPHERSON I immediately thought, *well, it's not going to be what they want.* And I expressed that to [my agent Nick]. But he said, "Who knows? Maybe you should write it out anyway."

This was a shrewd move by Nick Marston. Conor drafted a message to Tristan, laying out the idea.

TRISTAN BAKER Conor sent a three-line email.

CONOR MCPHERSON (*email*) Hi Tristan,

I'm thinking of an expansive Eugene O'Neill type play with Bob Dylan's love songs intertwined. Perhaps set in a depression era boarding house in a US city in the 1930's with a loose family of thrown-together drifters, ne'er do wells and poor romantics striving for love and understanding as they forage about their deadbeat lives. We could have old lovers, young lovers, betrayers and idealists rubbing along against each other. And at the heart of it all, these songs that emerge out of the folk tradition and lead the way into something more individually expressive and timeless.

Many thanks,
Conor

Without changing a word, this three-line pitch perfectly describes what *Girl from the North Country* would end up being.

NICK MARSTON It's remarkably consistent with what came out.

TRISTAN BAKER   And this was his idea in 2013.

CONOR MCPHERSON   Funnily enough, the idea of setting it in the 1930s was the key for me because it suddenly felt like, in a way, it was a world that I could control, because then it didn't have to be about "Bob Dylan" and so forth.

TRISTAN BAKER   I said, "This is brilliant. I love it. I've got goosebumps." I cried, I still cry reading it. And I said, "Bob's going to need more than three lines. Will you write this up into a page or two?"

Conor's fear that this was "not ever going to happen," turned into something slightly more hopeful.

CONOR MCPHERSON   So I wrote a little one-and-a-half page treatment and we sent that off.

TRISTAN BAKER   He sent it through. That was October. Bob [Dylan] was performing at the Royal Albert Hall in November in the UK.

Here's where a mythical bit of the show's origin-story crops up, as seems often to happen with Bob Dylan stories. Clinton Heylin, in his exhaustive biographies of Dylan, catalogs these countless "tall stories," including Paul Nelson's, who noted that Dylan " . . . had a strong streak of dishonesty and strong streak of honesty . . . right together, almost inseparable it seemed."[15]

As with Conor's characters in *Girl from the North Country*, it's hard to know what is actually true about the character "Bob Dylan." He exists between the lines.

CONOR MCPHERSON   The way it was told to me, subsequently, by his management, was that they read [the treatment] to Bob . . .

If you conjure an image of "Bob Dylan" in your mind, he's likely not answering a work email at his kitchen table or sitting on hold with an airline like the rest of us.

CONOR MCPHERSON   I think they told me that they read [the treatment] to him backstage after one of his shows. He was in London at the time . . .

"Bob Dylan" in quotes doesn't sit at a kitchen table answering work emails or wait on hold with airlines because "Bob Dylan" in quotes is a mythical figure who doesn't have a kitchen table or a phone. "Bob Dylan" is

---

[15]Heylin, Clinton, *The Double Life of Bob Dylan*, Back Bay Books; Little, Brown and Company, 2022.

confined to a realm called *the stage*, like the Minotaur is confined to the Labyrinth.

CONOR MCPHERSON . . . and he was playing at the Albert Hall, I think.

And so the story goes that "Bob Dylan" read, or had read *to* him, Conor's full one-and-a-half page treatment of a musical based on his music. And this happened in the only place where the myth of "Bob Dylan" happens . . .

TRISTAN BAKER Bob got it when he came off-stage.

. . . *backstage*. It's the only place he exists: in some relationship *to the stage*. Either on, or just-off.

CONOR MCPHERSON They read it to him . . .

NICK MARSTON There must've been something in those pages that connected with Dylan in some funny, deep way.

CONOR MCPHERSON . . . and he said, "Let's go with that one." And that was it.

TRISTAN BAKER And about two in the morning I get a text message from Jeff [Rosen] saying "Bob loves it. We're in."

CONOR MCPHERSON Once we got that go-ahead, it was kind of shocking.

The entire journey of *Girl from the North Country* with its extreme ups and downs feels fated to me. Conor offering up his idea for the show through a note passed *backstage* is the blessed/cursed moment that set the whole thing in motion. This exchange, like some powerful rune that, once passed, cannot be returned was the only encounter between the two men; Conor McPherson and Bob Dylan have never met, still to this day, but they shared this fateful handshake "backstage" that set *Girl from the North Country* on its inexorable way.

BOB DYLAN (*Interview with Bill Flanagan*) I was born in Duluth—industrial town, shipyards, ore docks, grain elevators, mainline train yards, switching yards. It's on the banks of Lake Superior, built on granite rock. Lot of foghorns, sailors, loggers, storms, blizzards.[16]

Dylan's Duluth is where Conor's script begins, as if the play enters from the wing just as the songwriter bows and exits, the last chorus of the encore still reverberating as the first lines of the script are spoken by the narrator, Doctor Walker:

---

[16]"Q&A with Bill Flanagan," March 22, 2017, exclusive to bobdylan.com.

DR. WALKER: Good Evening. Tonight's story begins and ends at a guesthouse in Duluth, Minnesota, in November 1934. Duluth is an iron ore shipping town built on a rocky cliff that tumbles down into Lake Superior where each and every winter feels seven months long.

This would be the setting, then, Dylan a kind of ghost forever hovering.

In a conference room at his offices near *Les Misérables*, Tristan Baker takes a breath, his first since starting his rapid-fire recounting of events. He smiles at me as if he's just read the creation gospel to a congregation.

As that congregation of one, I confess I *was rapt.*

TRISTAN BAKER   So, that was November, 2013. And we were off. We said to Conor, "Write it."

II. The experiment

"This doesn't work" is a common phrase in the entertainment industry—I've used it, and I've heard it used, usually in hushed tones at some opening night where it means something close to, "I like the people involved with this show we just saw, I think they're talented, and I do wish them well, but I hate this."

A writer can start with every element necessary for success—a star, a beloved bit of I.P., a producer *with money*, the perfect slot at the perfect theater, etc.—but in the end their show could very well . . . *not work.*

Of course, this is all subjective. Maybe a show "doesn't work" but it runs for twenty years. Irrespective of financial success, some shows do just seem unanimously to *work.* The question for Tristan Baker and Conor McPherson, et al., was "Would *this* show work?"

Some of Conor's initial choices, when compared to other, successful rock-star catalog musicals, seemed to indicate *no, this will not work.*

Let's look at *Beautiful: The Carole King Musical,* which opened on Broadway in 2014, and followed the "bio-musical" format of tracing the career highlights and personal ups and downs of the songwriter, in this instance Carole King. According to the show's current website,[17] these are just a few of the titles from Carole King's catalog in the show: "(You Make Me Feel Like) A Natural Woman," "You've Got a Friend," "I Feel the Earth Move," "It's Too Late," "One Fine Day," and "You've Lost that Lovin' Feeling."

In other words: *hits.*

CONOR MCPHERSON   [Dylan's management] sent me all his albums. That's what happened. And that was really the moment of anointing. It was a box of CDs . . .

---

[17]As of writing this in 2023.

And maybe the creators of *Beautiful: The Carole King Musical*, had the right idea. Audiences who know and love King's hit songs, would certainly be expecting to hear them in a Broadway musical of her catalog. The producers must have felt justified; here's what *Variety* said on September 15, 2014: "'Beautiful,' the Carole King bio-musical that has posted million-plus weeks since April, has moved over to the hit column, recouping its $13 million capitalization costs, according to producers."

So, by all measures, a hit.

CONOR MCPHERSON   A huge thing for me was coming across [Dylan's] Christian era. That knocked me for six. I loved that. I just loved the passion of his music around that time.

Conor McPherson didn't look to *Bob Dylan's Greatest Hits (vols. 1, 2, or 3)* for inspiration.

CONOR MCPHERSON   He had an album called *Saved*, from 1980, which is one of what people call his "Born Again" phase—albums along with *Slow Train Coming* and *Shot of Love*. And *Saved*, to me, really is one of the best albums.

No, what inspired Conor was Dylan's trilogy of Christian albums, the opposite of Dylan's greatest hits.

CONOR MCPHERSON   There's no irony on those albums. He really, really cares about what he's writing about. He's writing about this one subject, which is redemption from sin by Jesus Christ. And that's what he's determined to write about.

Conor laughs, incredulous.

CONOR MCPHERSON   And the songs are so well crafted! Old school classy songwriting—with intros and verses and middle eights and breaks. And they're so kind-of neatly . . . he's really done a . . . what's the word? When something is very complete? A comprehensive, accomplished, treatment of every idea.

> I was blinded by the devil
> Born already ruined
> Stone-cold dead
> As I stepped out of the womb
> By His grace I have been touched
> By His word I have been healed
> By His hand I've been delivered
> By His spirit I've been sealed[18]

---

[18]"Saved," Bob Dylan, from *Saved*, 1980.

So, *not* the Carole King approach then.

> CONOR MCPHERSON   It's almost like he's in the service of something else. And what I love, too, is that energy, that gospel energy. He's bringing in that beautiful color of religious, Baptist, revivalist music, which suits him.

When I told friends that I had been cast in the "Bob Dylan" musical, the first question they inevitably asked was: "Are you playing Bob Dylan?" It's a fair question if you ignore the fact that I'm six-foot-six-inches tall, don't play the guitar, and neither look nor sound anything like Bob Dylan. But given the success of shows like *Beautiful: The Carole King Musical* and *Jersey Boys* and *Tina: The Tina Turner Musical*, they had a valid point: *someone* must be playing "Bob Dylan." The bio-musical featuring the highs and lows of the artist's life and the attendant hit songs from the radio is, at this point, a sub-genre of the Broadway musical.

But just as Conor did not look to Dylan's greatest hits for content, he did not look to the man's biography for plot. There would be no "Bob Dylan" in Conor's script, and you wouldn't hear "Blowin' in the Wind," or "Knockin' on Heaven's Door," or "Don't Think Twice It's All Right," or "The Times They Are A-Changin'," or "Tangled Up in Blue."

It would take a couple of workshops to convince everyone, including the playwright himself, that this was going to "work."

> CONOR MCPHERSON   So we went and we did a workshop for just two days, with Matthew Warchus directing. And I'll never forget, we had some actors around a table. There were perhaps ten performers and a little group of musicians. Shirley Henderson was there reading the role of Elizabeth.

Shirley Henderson, the Scottish actress known for playing "Moaning Myrtle" in the *Harry Potter* film series, but for my money is at her exquisite best in the Todd Solondz film *Life During Wartime*, was cast as Elizabeth Laine in the initial workshop. She would go on to win the Laurence Olivier Award[19] for Best Actress in a Musical for her performance.

> SHIRLEY HENDERSON   I'd never met Conor.

Shirley sits on our Zoom call with her knees folded up under her chin, and she has a reflective cadence when she speaks, a kind-hearted, Scottish rhythm.

---

[19]The West End theater awards, analogous to Broadway's Tony Awards.

SHIRLEY HENDERSON   I'd seen [Conor's play] *The Weir* years ago but I didn't know what Conor looked like. I had no picture in my head of him. The Old Vic sent me the script . . . and at that stage it was just to do a two day workshop. I think it was the summer as I remember wearing a white blouse.

The purpose of this workshop was for Conor to hear his draft of the musical, then titled *Hard Tale of Winter*, out loud.

CONOR MCPHERSON   We started reading some stuff—just as they might for a straight play but then, of course, people would start singing.

A writer sitting alone at his desk and reading his work on the page is not the same thing as that writer sitting in a room listening to others read his work aloud.

CONOR MCPHERSON   And I mean, I just could feel myself going gray. I just thought, *this is awful.*

My personal experience is that workshops like this, where actors sit under fluorescent lights and read aloud from photocopied pages, are humiliating for the writer. All of your bad ideas are spoken out loud in front of you and God and many witnesses. *It sounded so good in my head!*

I remember an early workshop of a play that I'd written. At the first read-through, by the third line on the first page I knew my play was just terrible and that I needed to rewrite the whole thing from word one, but I couldn't very well stand up and say to the actors, who had given up their afternoons for my sake, "Stop! Never mind!" no matter how badly I wanted to, and I badly wanted to. Ninety-three pages of torture ensued. One of the actresses hated every line I'd written for her character and kept telling me as much throughout the reading. She would stop and tell me all of the reasons each line was bad. I agreed with her and begged her, "Whenever we come to a moment when your character speaks, just say whatever you want. Literally say anything at all, anything, it doesn't even have to relate to the play."

SHIRLEY HENDERSON   I remember being a little nervous because I hadn't been on stage for a long time.

As painful as it is, as "gray" as Conor turned, this first step is necessary. Actors do a great service for the writer by participating, especially actors like Shirley Henderson, who sense the gold buried in the early draft and dig for it.

SHIRLEY HENDERSON   But there was something about this script. When I read Elizabeth's last speech it sent shivers up me. It was so haunting.

Conor's script had veins and veins of buried gold. Here is that speech, exactly the same in that first reading as it would be on closing night:

> Elizabeth: Well mister. You done it. You got 'em all out. I don't know how. But you did it.
> *She comes to him and takes the revolver. She looks at it.*
> I know. You start off—it's a love story. You wait outside the drug store where you said you'd meet her, searchin' in the eyes of everyone passing by. You can't believe it when she steps out of the crowd. Her face, perhaps plain to everybody else, well it uncloaks its beauty just for you. And you know you're gone. You're her hostage. And she takes you down into a world of plans and dreams you could never have sustained on your own.
> And then one day in the midst of the exhilaration and the worry and the children and the fighting and the whole damn shebang, one day you realize you're just about scraping through. And you look up and you see her again and you may as well be looking at a baby giraffe in the zoo.
> She's alive and she sees you but her world is not your world. You don't want to live in her world and she doesn't want you there anyhow. But you know you're too weak on your own. The children look to you. "What are you looking at me for?" you say. And they hate you and you're glad they hate you. 'Cos they stop coming to you.
> And then one day she turns round and says, "I don't love you anymore either" and you think, "What the fuck does that have to do with anything?!" Except you know she's just knocked you out cold. And you realize "Oh shit, I'm really on my own here now. Okay, okay, that's alright. I can drink myself to death in some room somewhere—it's alright."
> *She opens the revolver.*
> Until she loses her mind. And then you have her forever. You have her forever.[20]

For this first workshop, Matthew Warchus, artistic director of the Old Vic Theatre where the reading of *Hard Tale of Winter* took place, served as director.

MATTHEW WARCHUS   We organized a workshop with me as director and about eight or nine performers. And Conor came along with his guitar . . .

The Old Vic Theatre, a London theater mainstay for over 200 years at this point, is

---

[20]McPherson, Conor, *Girl from the North Country*, Nick Hern Books, pp. 101–2.

MATTHEW WARCHUS   . . . an independent not-for-profit theater with a strong social mission. That's how we write about ourselves.

One could say that the Old Vic is in many ways similar to the Public Theater in terms of its place in the industry as a non-commercial incubator of "downtown" theater that often transfers "uptown."

MATTHEW WARCHUS   And what that means is we don't have any regular subsidy, so we have to cover two-thirds of our costs through ticket sales and a third through donors and sponsorship. And unlike some of the most exciting producing theaters in London, we are a large theater. So the other producing theaters, I'm thinking of anything like the Donmar, the Royal Court, the Young Vic, the Hampstead, the Almeda, have 300, 400 seats. We have a thousand. So we are also sort of populist, that's become a bit of a dirty word. But basically my internal modus operandus is for brainy entertainment. Entertainment is really important for the Old Vic, we've got a large theater, we've got to fill it. We've got to have popular appeal whenever possible. But I don't want it to be empty entertainment. I like it to be thought-provoking, adventurous, groundbreaking, and with some social mission on some level.

With Matthew directing the workshop, Conor could sit and listen to his play.

SHIRLEY HENDERSON   At first I didn't know that Conor was the man sitting at the end of the table not saying anything. He was just sitting there really quietly.

MATTHEW WARCHUS   The first workshop was with Shirley Henderson and John C. Reilly, whom I'd worked with in *True West* in New York.

SHIRLEY HENDERSON   I kind of just kept my head down. I remember being nervous and thinking *I don't quite know what this is yet but try and keep it together*. I was aware of people coming and going over the two days. In and out of the rehearsal room.

MATTHEW WARCHUS   We spent a couple of days just working through and selecting songs, arranging the songs, teaching them, and Conor doing little bits of tweaks to the script here and there.

Just like the experience I would have at the two-day reading at the Public, Shirley noticed official-looking people observing the proceedings.

SHIRLEY HENDERSON   They may have been production people watching what we were doing. They were all just in my peripheral vision as I tried to just focus on what we were doing.

Conor sat silently. What was going through his head as he listened?

CONOR MCPHERSON   I think in my mind, I still probably thought in some way, *this needs to work as a traditional musical*. And I hadn't quite realized yet that there was another way that it could work. So I just thought, *oh my God, this just feels so strange* . .

Most musical theater playwrights (we call them "book-writers") focus obsessively on the transitional moments that lead from "book scenes" into songs—the on-ramp moments that go from speech to song. Speech and song, traditionally, should feel seamlessly connected. Think of Mama Rose in *Gypsy* leading up to "Rose's Turn": "With what I have in me, I coulda been better than any of you! What I got in me, what I been holding down inside of me, oh if I ever let it out there wouldn't be signs big enough. There wouldn't be lights bright enough! Here she is boys . . . "[21] Thanks to that perfect on-ramp, there's no other choice than for Rose to stop shouting and start singing. The scene would not exist without the song and vice versa.

CONOR MCPHERSON   I'd never had it where people were doing a play and then suddenly they started singing a song.

This is where Conor's script starts to differentiate itself from a typical "musical." For Conor, song isn't a seamless extension of speech. His transitions from scene to song are nothing like those by Arthur Laurents for Mama Rose in *Gypsy* because Conor's scenes don't bleed into song. His transitions are blunter. Harsher. Stranger. Scene and song abut one another as two distinct entities. They stand on their own and relate to each by mere proximity, sometimes they contradict each other, like collage art.

CONOR MCPHERSON   I thought, *What is this? What's going on?*

"Is this a 'musical' or a 'play'?" The music in *Hard Tale of Winter* wasn't functioning the way music functions in *Gypsy*. Or *Les Miz*. Maybe that's why it felt strange, because it wasn't a musical. But does music need to function in a particular way for a piece of theater to be a *musical*? Does it matter? Did *Hard Tale of Winter* even want to be called a musical? The questions would be asked again and again and never really answered.

CONOR MCPHERSON   I was confused, myself . . . But then Matthew [Warchus] then was kind of a bit more, I suppose, in control of the thing, he was the director at that point. And he was quite calm.

---

[21]Arthur Laurents, *Gypsy*, Theatre Communications Group, reprint edition, 1994.

Matthew Warchus, who in 2014 succeeded Kevin Spacey as artistic director of the Old Vic, won a Tony Award for his direction of Yasmina Reza's *God of Carnage*, and is perhaps best-known for his direction of the international musical hit *Matilda: the Musical.*

MATTHEW WARCHUS   I realized [Conor's script] was off-beat in a way. It was not mainstream in its identity, it's not trying to be mainstream, anyway. It was just trying to be what it is. And one had to allow it to be what it is. So there'd be no point in coming in and saying, "We need an opening number." It wasn't that kind of thing.

CONOR MCPHERSON   I just thought, *oh my God, this just feels so strange.*

If it was strange, and if strange was wrong, then what did it need to be right?

SHIRLEY HENDERSON   Matthew said "You all have to give it more, speak louder."

Maybe it just needed confidence.

SHIRLEY HENDERSON   I needed him to say that. Sometimes you need to be told you have to free up. Let more out. I could feel the production team watching us. I just thought to myself "focus, focus, focus." I suppose it was a little scary.

Dylan himself had given his approval, yes, and Conor was genuinely inspired, sure, but if the two-day workshop was an experiment undertaken to answer the question *Will this show work?,* it yielded inconclusive results at the end.

CONOR MCPHERSON   Matthew said, "Oh, it's good to make *some* progress." It's all progress, that was his attitude.

SHIRLEY HENDERSON   By the end of the two days I felt we had done the best we could in that short space of time.

MATTHEW WARCHUS   [The reading] was a very mystical, almost religious experience.

Did Dylan's "born-again" music sit well beside Conor's "ne'er-do-wells . . . foraging about their deadbeat lives?"

MATTHEW WARCHUS   I just thought, *this is weirdly religious, this whole thing. It's strange.*

It's a critical moment for any show's development. Do the producers, in this case Tristan and Charlie at Runaway Entertainment and Matthew at The

Old Vic, continue investing money and resources into a project that might fail?

TRISTAN BAKER   I knew there was so much good stuff there . . .

Does the writer, in this case Conor McPherson with his lauded track record, continue investing time and effort into a piece that might fail?

CONOR MCPHERSON   I hadn't quite realized that there was a way that it could work.

MATTHEW WARCHUS   It was a sort of mesmerizing, brilliant reading.

What should they do now? If anything?

MATTHEW WARCHUS   Dylan of course has got that [religious] dimension in some of his music, and Conor has that dimension. Conor certainly carries that with him in his work.

Matthew Warchus, having noted that *Hard Tale of Winter* with its unusual construction and inextricable religiosity was "just trying to be what it is," and having sensed the deep, maybe "mystical" connection between Conor McPherson and Bob Dylan, had an idea, a plan for how to press on, a plan that reaffirmed his faith in Conor as a creative artist, a plan that not only aligned with the new-work mission of the Old Vic Theatre, but one that also accounted, in a strictly practical sense, for the various and complex calendars of the artists—Matthew was committed to directing a project of his own— and of the institution itself.

CONOR MCPHERSON   Matthew said to me, "I think you should direct this."

Now, not only had Conor never written a musical, he'd never directed one.

CONOR MCPHERSON   I said, "Oh, I've never done anything like that before."

Matthew was unfazed by this fact.

MATTHEW WARCHUS   Conor always directs the first production of his plays. And I've seen all of those productions and I knew he was a great director.

The two-day workshop revealed an important clue to Matthew about Conor, the playwright with the guitar.

MATTHEW WARCHUS   I hadn't realized how musical Conor was.

The answer was right there in Conor's arms the whole time.

MATTHEW WARCHUS   That was a very reassuring thing for me.

Eureka. Like the reveal at the end of the murder mystery: *It's Conor. It's been Conor all along. He's the director.*
What did Conor think about Matthew's revelation?

CONOR MCPHERSON   I had directed my plays, but never a musical. And Matthew said to me, "Oh, it's just the same as directing a two-hander play, except there's just a lot more decisions."

MATTHEW WARCHUS   I said, "You could direct this, couldn't you? Would you want to?"

CONOR MCPHERSON   I thought, *okay, Matthew is very, very wise.* Matthew is a guy who has a real deep understanding of theater and a great love of theater. And I think he just knew in some way that I'd figure it out.

MATTHEW WARCHUS   And Conor said, "Yeah, well I would be interested in doing that."

Hard Tale of Winter wasn't a bio-musical, it didn't have many Dylan hits, the songs functioned nothing like songs in a "musical," and now the playwright would be directing though he'd never directed a musical before.
    The odds were stacking up against this *working.*
    And what about Tristan Baker? The producer who had the rights to Dylan's catalog, the producer who brought both Conor and Matthew to the production in the first place? What did he have to say about this significant change of plan?

TRISTAN BAKER   We would never normally allow the writer to direct, because that's often a recipe for disaster. But Conor said, "I think I can have a go at this." I'd fallen in love with Conor at that point. I'd absolutely fallen in love with him as a man, as a writer. And I thought, "Well, this is such a singular piece, why don't we just give it a go?"

"Give it a go" meant another workshop produced by the Old Vic, longer than two days this time, with Conor directing his own script now titled *Girl from the North Country*, and a commitment from Matthew Warchus to produce the show the following season.

CONOR MCPHERSON   So we moved along anyway to where the next step was a ten-day workshop, with me directing. And a big part of the process was that Simon Hale had arrived by that time.

SIMON HALE   I remember exactly where I was standing when the phone went off. And it's one of those moments where, wait, it changed my life. It really did.

Enter the Designers

A writer gives a play its words, but who gives it its look? A composer gives a musical its songs, but who gives the songs their *sound*?

TRISTAN BAKER   My husband, Matt [Cole], had just choreographed *Side Show* at Southwark Playhouse. And Simon had done the orchestrations. And Matt said, "You have to use Simon on everything that you do. He's a genius." So I listened to his stuff. I discovered, oh, he's the keyboard player for Seal for ten years, he does all of Sam Smith's arrangements, he's won a Grammy, he did Spring Awakening, all the Duncan Sheik stuff. He does everything. I didn't know any of this. He'd not done a lot of theater by that point, actually. It was all pop.

Tristan's enthusiasm about Simon's resume is charming, but slightly overblown.

SIMON HALE   I played keyboards In Seal's first band for the UK and Europe tour in 1990–1. We also performed at the Grammys in 1991 ... I've done all the string arrangements for Sam Smith's albums going back to *In the Lonely Hour*. I also orchestrated "The Writing's on the Wall" from the James Bond film *Spectre* and wrote the choir arrangement for "Gloria" from Sam's latest album.

Simon Hale habitually nods when he speaks, like he's always saying *yes*. It's the most affirming thing you can imagine. The answer to everything: *yes!* He does have two Grammy nominations, and theater fans know his orchestration work from many shows including the original Broadway cast recording of Duncan Sheik and Steven Sater's *Spring Awakening*.

TRISTAN BAKER   And so I said to Georgia [Gatti, producer at the Old Vic], not having worked with Simon, but I trust my husband implicitly, "Well, you have to use Simon Hale."

GEORGIA GATTI   Conor was actually the reason I got into theater.

Georgia Gatti has thoughtful, teary eyes, as if every play she's ever watched is still caught in them. She's the best kind of theatrical producer— a fan.

GEORGIA GATTI   I don't think I've ever admitted that to him. But seeing *The Weir* when I was a kid was the moment I went, *that's what I want to do, I want to be part of that.* So he's been my favorite playwright forever.

The Weir is Conor's play from 1997 that features a handful of characters telling stories to each other in a village bar in Ireland. I remember feeling hypnotized by the play when I saw it in New York in 1999, and like there was a ghost standing just behind me the entire time almost touching the back of my neck. Conor does that with his plays, brushes against the supernatural, opens up the other side, but just there, in your periphery.

The night after I saw *The Weir*, I saw another Broadway show, something considerably lighter: *Dame Edna: The Royal Tour.* Dame Edna was the Australian drag character created by Barry Humphries who largely improvised each performance, talk-show style, ridiculing pop culture, celebrities, and most-often her audience members whom she would drag onstage to humiliate. I really loved Dame Edna. The night I saw her, she said she was taking in all the current Broadway shows while she was in the city and that she had just seen Conor McPherson's *The Weir.* Then she paused, scrunched up her lips and said, "More like the *Weird.*"

Which made me love Conor's play even more.

SIMON HALE   Georgia [Gatti] said, "We're doing this piece and it's Bob Dylan and it's a musical." And my first thought was, *well that's a slightly weird combination. I don't quite understand what that's going to be.* I'm not sure I still do! But anyway, she said, "Can you come into the office and chat and meet Conor." So I met Conor for the first time.

CONOR MCPHERSON   And me and Simon met at the Old Vic, we had a great chat and spoke about what we might try and do. And we got in there and sort of really started to nail it.

SIMON HALE   We sat down, talked about music, talked about the play, and Dylan, listened to loads of stuff on YouTube. And that was it. We didn't know each other beforehand. And we just started talking and then just got in and then went into rehearsals.

CONOR MCPHERSON   I felt much freer then at that point to basically pick up a guitar and to really kind of slice into it in a way that was organic and to get inside the songs and all of that kind of stuff.

SIMON HALE   Conor's a great musician and he's just so organic. He would sometimes just turn up with a song. One morning he said, "There's this song 'Jokerman,' I reckon we could use it somewhere." I thought, *Okay. I've never heard the song before.* So he got his phone, put a microphone up to it, played "Jokerman" through whatever crappy PA was in the rehearsal room and . . . right, well, I said, "Let's just work out what this might be."

TRISTAN BAKER And I remember [Georgia] phoning and saying they'd brought Lucy to the project, Lucy Hind, because they'd [already] done something with her.

LUCY HIND   I got so lucky. I had just done a one-woman show with an actress, a Beckett show at the Old Vic.

Lucy Hind is much younger than I am, and though she's often laughing, she registers as a wise, elder statesman. She leans forward when she talks, as if embodying the bridge between herself and you along which passes the thought she's offering.

LUCY HIND I don't know why they didn't just go to all the big choreographers in town at the time, but I wonder whether it's because maybe Conor was directing, and he didn't know what he wanted or he wanted someone different.

As a choreographer, or "movement director" as she would have it, Lucy's approach for *Girl from the North Country*, was rooted in the natural, everyday grace of non-dancers.
As a non-dancer myself: *phew*.

LUCY HIND   But the Old Vic said, "Well, we'll put you in touch with Conor." And we had one brilliant phone conversation. That was it. Maybe twenty minutes long.

CONOR MCPHERSON That was really cool too, because [the conversation] became about finding the language in the beautiful notion that everybody back then knew how to dance in a formal way. Lucy was saying that everybody [in the 1930s] would've known some basic dances, because to go to your local dance hall, you would need to know how to foxtrot, or to do other kinds of dance steps. And those steps would be in their bodies. And a natural part of who they were and how they expressed themselves.

Much of Lucy's approach would be teaching the cultural movement of the time period to the actors: the way Americans would have walked in the 1930s, the dances they would have known, the ways individuals would have modified those dances if they were older or injured or *not good dancers*. The formality between strangers, the comfort within families.
Yet another departure from the traditional "musical," where typically every character, despite their age or abilities, would suddenly be sharp and flexible once the dance number starts.

LUCY HIND   Conor had not seen any of my work. He'd never heard of me.

Conor trusts his instincts to an almost alarming degree.

LUCY HIND   We just connected. I said that I wasn't a traditional choreographer, but I was more a movement director.

Most directors new to musicals would stack their team with time-tested musical theater veterans.

LUCY HIND   I didn't have any show reels. I didn't have any work he'd seen of mine. We just had a chat about making work and the type of work we were going to make.

But Conor saw in Lucy a kindred artist. As Matthew Warchus noted, this new musical ". . . was just trying to be what it is." Conor trusted that idea and hired Lucy.

LUCY HIND   He said, "We should just do this."

While the creative team was set, casting remained a question. Shirley Henderson was still hung up on the first workshop.

SHIRLEY HENDERSON   Jessica [Ronane], the casting director, said, "We would like you to do the play." I wanted to find the courage to say yes. I had the feeling *I want to do this and I don't quite know what it is yet*. I liked the feeling of all that but I was still a little scared.

That feeling—*I don't quite know what this is yet*—wasn't ever going to abate. If Shirley wanted to continue with the show, she would have to embrace it.

SHIRLEY HENDERSON   So I went away and thought about it and just by luck they said they were having another workshop and so they gave me a little more time to think about it.

She said yes. And while Conor himself still "didn't know" what the show was exactly . . .

LUCY HIND   He didn't have the answers to say to me, "There's a tap number, there's a jazz hand number." He was like, "I don't know what it is."

. . . he was sure that he was onto *something*.

CONOR MCPHERSON   I would say that was a time in my life where— just one of those times where you just feel you're really at your most inspired.

SHIRLEY HENDERSON   I don't know if I have ever done a big theater workshop like that before . . . They had a band come in towards the end of the week.

CONOR MCPHERSON   And really, I would be at home the night before listening to some Bob Dylan and I'd come in to work the next day and say, "We're going to do 'License to Kill.'"

SHIRLEY HENDERSON   And the songs—it all started to take some shape.

CONOR MCPHERSON   And everyone's like, "What's 'License to Kill?'" And I'd play it through the PA speakers and say, "*This* is 'License to Kill,' let's do it." And they're like, "Okay, can we have time to figure it out?" I'd say, "No, we're just going to do it now!" And we would just do it!

SHIRLEY HENDERSON   That was magical watching that happen.

When an artist says they were feeling "inspired," it suggests to me that they're saying they were *open* . . .

CONOR MCPHERSON   I felt very free.

. . . open to ideas from within and without, open to *chance*. Chance played a major role in the show's development during this ten-day workshop and Conor was open to it, inspired by it; the cast was game to run with it, and in one particular incident involving Shirley Henderson, fearless to embrace it.

SHIRLEY HENDERSON   One of the other actors in the workshop who happened to be sitting next to me was allocated the song "Forever Young" on the first day. The next day he had to go for an appointment so he wasn't at rehearsal when we got to the part where he was to sing "Forever Young." Conor looked at me and the empty seat next to me and said "Shirley. You sing it today."

Shirley had never sung "Forever Young," never rehearsed it, why would she have, it wasn't her song. She could have demurred, she could have punted, she could have flat-out declined. But the spirit in the room was *chance*.

SHIRLEY HENDERSON   And so I did.

Embracing chance and leaving room for indeterminacy led to kismetic moments like this. I think of that charmed, backstage "handshake" between Conor and Dylan that set this fated production in motion.

SHIRLEY HENDERSON   And somehow it just stuck.

As the composer John Cage said, "Ideas are one thing and what happens another."

SHIRLEY HENDERSON   Almost as if what seat you sat in determined what song you sang ... Or maybe Conor had it all in his head all along.

This question comes up a lot when people look back at working with Conor: what was predetermined and what came about organically? Does Conor grasp at sudden inspiration outside of himself, or do his ideas emerge from those deep inner wells? I call it the "glass-of-milk question," which we'll discuss at length in a later chapter. Both Sheila Atim and Kimber Sprawl, the actresses who played Marianne Laine in the British and American companies, respectively, held in their hand a glass of milk the entire time they sang "Tight Connection to My Heart" in act one, and both remember organically arriving at that choice on their own, but how could that be? Was it predetermined? By whom? Conor? Fate? Conor doesn't remember asking either actress to hold the glass of milk.

LUCY HIND   I turned up and watched some of the workshop, they didn't really want any movement that week, so I went and watched the run-through and I thought, "Oh my God, this is *special*."

GEORGIA GATTI   One of my strongest memories from that workshop ... it was ... in a kind of scrappy rehearsal room in Southeast London ... people sitting around battered old tables and ... Conor sitting around with his guitar kind of strumming away and figuring things out. But I remember coming in to watch the sharing and Jack Shalloo who played Elias was standing on ... there was part of the rehearsal room where there was a ladder just going up the side ... that was just *there*. And they were doing a bit of "Duquesne Whistle" and we didn't have any set or anything, so he just stood at the top of this ladder, my God, and belted out the start of that song.[22] And I thought: that's it! I think we all started to realize just what we had. We were starting to hear how the music was interacting with Conor's play. And so that was incredibly exciting.

At the end of this second workshop, and as Matthew Warchus had predicted, *Girl from the North Country* was showing signs of "working."

MATTHEW WARCHUS   I remember seeing Conor with a guitar on his lap playing along during the songs in the rehearsal room. Now I've seen lots of different things and different ways of directing over the years, but

---

[22] "Listen!"

I've never seen the director playing along and singing along with the guitar. And that symbolized for me the kind of fusion between the text and the music—not only were Conor McPherson and Bob Dylan holding hands in this piece, but they were fusing into one voice in this sort of miraculous way.

Matthew Warchus, "a guy who has a real deep understanding of theater and a great love of theater," had made the right call in asking Conor to direct.

Shirley Henderson was convinced. Tristan Baker, too.

Conor was inspired, Lucy Hind and Simon Hale, too.

The only thing left to do was press on.

III. The result

Rehearsals for the premiere production of *Girl from the North Country* began at the Old Vic in the summer of 2017. Ciarán Hinds, the Northern Irish actor, was cast as Nick Laine, opposite Shirley Henderson.[23]

> CIARÁN HINDS   People who've known me would've run a mile from even thinking that I should be involved in a project like this because I don't sing. Okay? *Famously.*

Though a McPherson veteran, having previously acted in the premiere productions of *Seafarer* and *The Night Alive,* Hinds was new to musical theater and he doubted his skill in the genre.

> GEORGIA GATTI   We weren't really looking for singers at that point. It was very much actors who brought something with them vocally.

Ciarán wasn't immediately convinced he was the right choice for the part.

> CIARÁN HINDS   There are so many talented people out there. There really are brilliant people . . .

I asked Ciarán to meet me at Home House, a club in London's Marylebone neighborhood. There's an old-London energy there that I love, creaky wood floors and secret corners. I was set up near some French windows in a kind of elegant garret when Ciarán walked in and introduced himself. He has the

---

[23]Coincidentally, Ciarán is also in the film *Life During Wartime* with Shirley Henderson.

intimidating presence of a world-leader, a large face, x-ray eyes, but when he speaks it's nearly always in admiration of other people.

CIARÁN HINDS   Did anybody ever tell you about the first time Sheila Atim sang?

He asked like he hoped that no one had told me so he could have the pleasure of doing so. I said, "No, no one told me."
He took a deep breath.

CIARÁN HINDS   Sheila Atim . . .

He began telling me about Sheila and the big surprise that awaited everyone in the rehearsal room.

SHEILA ATIM   I obviously knew of Bob Dylan.

Sheila Atim, the powerhouse Ugandan-British multi-hyphenate (actress-singer-writer), was cast as Marianne, the Laines' adopted daughter. She would go on to win an Olivier award for Best Actress in a Supporting Role in a Musical for her performance.

SHEILA ATIM   I've always actually quite liked Bob Dylan's voice and his vibe.

Sheila brims over with creative thought. It's infectious, reminding me of a philosophy student from when I was in college who sat in the front row and who I always wished would take over the seminar from the professor because she knew more than he did.

SHEILA ATIM   Once I started to dig into [Dylan's] back catalog a bit more, I liked how you could really hear the different phases and periods of his life and his artistry. They tend to be my favorite artists—you can chart a journey from album to album. And that feels like real true artistry, responding to both the times and to yourself and what you are actually feeling inside yourself.

CIARÁN HINDS   I'd only met [Sheila] at the first day of rehearsal, cause she hadn't been in the workshop.

First days of new projects can be overwhelming. There's so much to do, where to start?

GEORGIA GATTI   The script was still very alive and still evolving.

LUCY HIND I turned up on day one with not a single step choreographed!

CIARÁN HINDS We spent a lot of rehearsal just trying to get the geography, us all trying to get our bearings.

I can almost sense day-one from Ciarán's perspective. Here's an actor who doesn't sing, and he's at his first day of rehearsals for a musical. Terrifying. He's meeting his castmates, some for the first time, like Sheila, and he's feeling both inspired and out of his depth.
How do I do this? Where do I begin?
Someone has to get things started. Some choices have to be made.

LUCY HIND The microphones were a good starting place for us because we started making rules.

Thank you, Lucy.
Creatives talk about "rules" a lot. What they mean by *rule* is *consistency* in the world-of-the-play. An example of this is Thornton Wilder's short play *The Long Christmas Dinner*, in which generations of a family are introduced over a single Christmas dinner that keeps leaping magically forward in time. A "rule" of that play is that whenever an actor exits stage right it means that they have died. The audience isn't told that outright, but through consistency and repetition it becomes clear. And since theater is an artform of suggestion, the audience accepts this "rule"; it's therefore incumbent upon the production not to break that rule.
In *Girl from the North Country*, one "rule" decided upon early on was that actors would sing their songs into old-fashioned microphones on stands. Conor's original concept was that the play would be performed as a "radio play," making microphones a necessity.

LUCY HIND We thought, *okay, this is going to help us understand the language of this musical.* Because the songs are not *about* the musical, so how do we let them sit in the story? So, great, they always sing into microphones. That's how we allow the songs to sit alongside the play and not feel confusing. If there's a microphone, that creates a slightly heightened world.

Dylan's songs were not meant to be extensions of Conor's scenes. They were breaks from the scenes. Having actors stand at microphones helped to delineate visually.

CONOR MCPHERSON As we were figuring it out, I remember Matthew [Warchus] visiting us and watching for a while. We were still finding our way and trying to figure out the visual language. Also it was the height of summer when we were rehearsing. It was a real big heat, so poor Matthew had to watch people in yellow t-shirts and shorts and sneakers trudging around, sweating. It was entirely the wrong atmosphere for a show set in the darkness of winter.

Conor's take on scene-to-song was an approach to "musical theater" that was just as unusual for the actors who had musical theater experience as it was for those who didn't.

SHEILA ATIM   It was one of the most diverse companies I've ever been in. I've never been in a cast that spans that breadth of ages, races, all of all the different identities ... and so with that brings genuinely lots of different people from different walks of life, from different ways of getting into the industry at different times, different types of actors with different processes and different approaches.

But Conor was inspired, and that was inspiring to others.

SHIRLEY HENDERSON   I loved Conor's way of letting us just jump in there and not censoring us too early. In my case he probably thought some of what I was doing was not the correct way to be Elizabeth but he didn't say that straight away. He let me and everyone else go so far to find out how far we could go with our thoughts and ideas.

SHEILA ATIM   How that extends to the work is that there were no wrong answers. There were no bad offers.

As an actor, part of your job is to make bold choices for your character based on the clues in the text. Everything from how your character speaks to how they walk, how they stand, how they regard others, how they listen or dance or cry. What they believe, how they gesture, whether or not they're lying, what triggers them based on past experiences, what mood they're in from scene to scene. The list of possibilities is endless, and a good actor doesn't expect a director to provide the answers, she brings into the rehearsal room strong "offers," as Sheila calls them.

SHEILA ATIM   There was no bad offer. Everything was met with openness and curiosity and respect and generosity.

Not every "offer" is correct, or even good, but in a safe rehearsal room there is no judgment. A bad offer may lead to a good choice.

SHIRLEY HENDERSON   For Elizabeth,[24] sometimes I went too far. Sometimes in the end you have to know when it's going into crazy land

---

[24]Shirley played the character Elizabeth Laine, wife of Nick Laine, played by Ciarán Hinds, and mother of Marianne, played by Sheila Atim and Gene Laine, played by Sam Reid.

and now you have to make it real and pull it back a bit, Conor was brilliant at guiding me through that. He is not on top of you all the time but just whispers the right thing in your ear.

CONOR MCPHERSON   What's good to do is to try and let the actors do as much as they can for as long as they can without needing you if they can. The thing is—every actor is different, so I don't want to be too prescriptive. You have to see who everyone is as a performer first. And they are all different and have varying strengths at their core. This one is funny. This one is moving. This one is frightening. And I want to make the space to allow them to be as strong as they can be. Some people want you to be prescriptive and give them lots of notes . . . And then at the other end of the spectrum you have performers who are more "*Just leave me alone. Let me figure it out.*" So I watch and wait and—for me—the first four weeks of rehearsal is like recording music. You are getting the tracks recorded. Getting the performances recorded in the performers' bodies. Then, in week four or five, you start to mix the record. Just like with a music mix where you might say—"More bass, less guitar," with ensemble acting it's "More comedy here, less acting there, no need for those pauses . . . just push that part on . . . louder, quieter . . . come in together here . . . this part is a solo moment . . . etc." But you can't do that unless you have already seen what everyone can play and you have those tracks in the can. So basically, I direct by responding to what the actors are already doing—what they bring as themselves—and I try to integrate their natural instincts into the script as much as I can. I honestly want actors to be in their comfort zone. Which is not to say I don't push them if I feel they have untapped resources.

Ciarán's character Nick Laine, it turns out, didn't sing in *Girl from the North Country*, so if he had fear around that as a non-singer, it vanished, and the show leaned into his strengths as an actor.

Unexpectedly, he was thriving. But at our interview, he didn't want to talk about himself, he still wanted to tell me about Sheila's big moment.

CIARÁN HINDS   And then, I dunno, week four, week five, Conor said, "Okay, we'll try and push through the first act, and Sheila, would you sing the song this time?"

In all the excitement of making choices, working on the scenes, creating characters, etc., no one had heard Sheila sing her act one solo, "Tight Connection to My Heart."

SHEILA ATIM   It was important for a piece like this, working with an icon's music, someone like Bob Dylan who is kind of notoriously mysterious and ethereal himself.

Sheila and Conor, along with arranger Simon Hale, had been wrestling with the song in separate music rehearsals, working to translate Dylan's sound to the sound of *Girl from the North Country*. Like they were working on a secret experiment, vital to the show's success, but not yet ready to be shared.

SHEILA ATIM   Just to remove some of those stakes was important. I think that's part of the reason why [Conor] didn't make [*Girl from the North Country*] a play about [Dylan's] life. Aside from that being something that's already been done and something that didn't interest him. But it definitely helped us not feel like, *oh my God, it's Bob Dylan's music* . . . it was just *music*.

Finally the day came when it was time to share the results of the experiment with the rest of the cast.

SHIRLEY HENDERSON   . . . and it was Sheila's turn to sing.

And this is what Ciarán will never forget. Nor would Shirley, who also brought it up.

CIARÁN HINDS   So we start doing the play, act one, and we're maybe twenty minutes in. And Sheila starts to sing. She starts to sing and . . . everything just stopped.

SHIRLEY HENDERSON   And we were just . . .

Shirley gasps, remembering.

SHIRLEY HENDERSON   . . . she took our breath away.

Sheila sang the rendition of "Tight Connection to My Heart," that she and Simon and Conor had been working up in private, with its wrenching chorus, "Has anybody seen my love? Has anybody seen my love? Has anybody seen my love? I don't know, has anybody seen my love?"

CIARÁN HINDS   It was extraordinary. Everything stopped, it was just silence. And words can't describe it, but what happened was *time did stop* and she finished and almost nobody was breathing. After a pause of about, I don't know, ten, fifteen seconds, Conor said, "Are you going to do it like that?"

Ciarán laughs so hard at this that it's like he's captured in his own laugh the laughter of the entire rehearsal room of actors reacting to Conor's joke.

CIARÁN HINDS   One of the most beautiful things that ever happened! In a way that just released everybody.

Sheila's in-rehearsal debut of "Tight Connection to My Heart" had more of an effect than just pleasure. It changed the rules.

LUCY HIND   And then "Tight Connection to My Heart" happened where Sheila just got up and sang in the middle of a scene.

This is the glass-of-milk song. Sheila, as Marianne Laine, stood perfectly still, holding a glass of milk, *not* singing into an old-fashioned microphone.

LUCY HIND   And we said, "Well that's that rule gone! There goes that rule, there goes that rule!"

MATTHEW WARCHUS   Sheila singing "Tight Connection." I think it might be the best bit of musical theater that I've ever seen.

The moment was undeniable. But it broke the "rule" that songs must be sung into microphones, revealing to Conor and Lucy and the other designers that there were deeper layers in the world of *Girl from the North Country* than they understood. Consistent with their approach up to this moment, they trusted chance and pushed ahead into the unknown.

MATTHEW WARCHUS   Certainly ["Tight Connection"] is up there with the greatest things I've ever seen. And I've seen some amazing things on stage and in musicals, some wonderful things . . . turbocharged performances full of spectacle and all kinds of means of impacting the audience, the combination of lyrics, music, staging, dance, the orchestra playing. I mean, these are amazing forces with which to confront and affect an audience. But the stillness of this moment, Sheila standing there with a glass of milk in her hand and singing this stunning song in an amazing arrangement . . . it's unforgettable. Her voice is . . . I don't really know how to describe her voice to justice, but it's a phenomenal instrument, very pure and raw and musically formidable.

There is a video online of Sheila Atim singing "Tight Connection to My Heart" at the Olivier Awards ceremony in 2018. If you watch it, and you should, I suspect you will experience what Ciarán and Lucy and Shirley and Matthew did. Time *does* stop. Live performance doesn't always translate to video well, but here it does. It gets right to the core of what "works" about *Girl from the North Country.* Dylan as hymnist. McPherson as humanist. Atim as "Mary," stuck somewhere between.

SHEILA ATIM   I'd never got cast as a character like her, a character who isn't fully set in their voice yet. I so often get cast as characters that are the opposite. Mrs. Neilsen actually being a kind of example.

Mrs. Neilsen is the boarder having the secret love-affair with Nick Laine. She's strong-willed, certain of her abilities, and able to ask for what she wants and deserves.

SHEILA ATIM   In fact, in the audition they asked me to prepare Marianne, then they asked me to prepare Mrs. Nielsen. Then when I turned up, I did Mrs. Nielsen first, because we all thought in the room, I'm more like Mrs. Nielsen. And I nearly didn't do Marianne.

Auditions are intimidating because actors don't have any power beyond their own performance. When I audition, I find myself trying to balance confidence with affability. I'm Midwestern, so I overdo the affability.

SHEILA ATIM   They said, "Should we just leave it there [with Mrs. Neilsen]?"

If I had been in Sheila's shoes at that audition, I would have sheepishly agreed to "leave it there," having shown them just the one character even though I felt good about the other character I'd prepared and wanted them to see it. Luckily, Sheila spoke up for herself.

SHEILA ATIM   I said, "I mean, I've prepped Marianne if you want. And I'm here, I may as well do it." I was exiting the door. It nearly didn't happen. And that was a big lesson for me in learning to put aside any preconceptions that I may have about myself in this industry and as a performer, then as an actor and a writer and all those things. And just kind of be brave and take those restrictions off myself.

Sheila's bravery paid off for everyone.
   Her self-reflection could be applied to the production itself. ". . . put aside any preconceptions . . . be brave . . . take those restrictions off . . ."
   That's exactly what was happening in the rehearsal room.
   And it was working.
   But one tricky question cropped up: how to sell it?

No Tickets

As the first preview approached and with it the inevitable uncertainty about how the audience would respond, a bigger concern revealed itself: getting an audience there in the first place.

TRISTAN BAKER   We'd placed [the show] at the Old Vic because . . . I just thought that would be a great place to open.

Sure, but the Old Vic has 1,000 seats to fill at each performance.

TRISTAN BAKER   [*Girl from the North Country*] was one of the lowest advances they'd ever had. They hadn't sold any tickets.

CONOR MCPHERSON   We were doing our tech[25] and getting ready for our first preview, and Matthew Warchus wandered into the theater, he says to me, "How's it going?" And I said, "Oh yeah, I dunno. We're doing it." And then I said, deflecting everything, I said, "How are things with you?" He said, "Oh, yeah, fine." "You know," he said, "we haven't sold any tickets for this." And I said, "Oh, God . . . and this is a really long run." It was like sixteen weeks or something. And I said, "That's going to be awful!"

MATTHEW WARCHUS   *Girl from the North Country* didn't have a great advance. That's true.

LUCY HIND   Someone mentioned to me that it was the worst selling show in Old Vic history ever before we opened. I think it was selling at 13 percent or something before previews.

MATTHEW WARCHUS   I think people were just waiting to find out what it was. It wasn't clear what it was.

LUCY HIND   They didn't know how to sell it. Of course they didn't.

What is it? A play? A musical? Audiences didn't know. No one did. This would be a persistent issue, even after multiple transfers of the show.

GEORGIA GATTI   I guess we still didn't really know what it was we were selling from a producing perspective and the endless conversations we had with our marketing department about *do we or don't we call it a musical*? And what's our image going to be and how are we telling people what this was? It was quite nerve-wracking because we didn't know, other than we knew it was good, we still didn't quite know what we were going to be selling to people or how we were going to tell people they needed to see it.

Audiences showed up to the first previews, and while that much was a relief, there were still dismal ticket sales for the actual run of the show.
Matthew Warchus wasn't worried.

CIARÁN HINDS   I remember after the first or second preview we were just coming out and Matthew [Warchus] was walking back[stage], and he hadn't interfered with us at all. It was his theater . . . and he'd obviously been watching . . . and he just stopped and said, "I think you're going to be surprised at what's happening out there."

---

[25]"Tech rehearsal," which focuses on lights, sound, costumes, and props, the "technical" elements.

CONOR MCPHERSON And this is one of my indelible memories about the whole process—[Matthew] said, "Well, there are things in this show I don't think people will have ever seen before." He speaks just very plainly, he just said, "There are things in this that people have never seen before. And when people come to the previews, they'll go out and tell other people." And he said, "And then it will sell out." I wasn't sure precisely what those things were that he was talking about that no-one had seen before. But I trusted his experience of musicals and theater—and what could I do? I just got back to work.

LUCY HIND I couldn't tell you if it was any good or not. When your head's in it . . . all of us as creatives will sit in previews and think, "Terrible, terrible, terrible. I want to die."

SHIRLEY HENDERSON [The audience] sometimes clapped at the end of songs. And Conor wanted us to drive through this. He didn't want the clapping to stop the show. But sometimes you can't keep going. People just do what they do. Especially after Sheila and her amazing voice. They loved Sheila's song.

Early audiences for any show can be tricky. They give you pure response, which is exactly what you've been lacking in the rehearsal room. If you wonder if a joke is funny, the audience will let you know by laughing or not laughing. They give you information that you need. The challenge is then *what to do* with the information. Feed the audience more of what it likes, or withhold, leaving them wanting more? If one is not careful, the audience can take control of the show, they can become a beast that needs to be fed but is never full. *Do they like it or do they not*, while helpful, can become a self-defeating metric.

Did the preview audiences like *Girl from the North Country* or did they not?

LUCY HIND I didn't feel either way. What I could see in front of me was the work that needed to be done to make it more what it needed to be. Rather than "That group of people over there didn't like it, so we have to figure out how to make them happy."

CONOR MCPHERSON At the first preview, I was there watching what we had done for the first time, thinking to myself, *What is going on? Oh my God.* We got to the interval, and I quickly got up from my seat and sort of scarpered backstage. Because I just, I've been in theaters before where you're stuck behind people leaving the theater and you've got to hear what they're saying—and sometimes you don't want to hear it!

LUCY HIND I hadn't even been interested whether they liked it or not. And that was also a revelation, the first time ever. I didn't care what people thought.

CONOR MCPHERSON   I didn't want to be there. So I ran out. I got backstage, there was a little kitchen upstairs at the Old Vic. And I went up there, there was nobody there. And I went in to make a cup of tea or something, and there was a tannoy,[26] and I could hear the sound coming from the auditorium; the audience buzzing about in the interval. And it sounded like a hive of bees, that kind of excited chatter—and I thought, *oh, that is real energy . . . Okay. Okay.* So I went back down, still full of fear that half the seats might be empty.

LUCY HIND   We didn't know what it was. Nobody knew what it was.

CONOR MCPHERSON   But everybody came back . . . And then we did the second half. And in those days we didn't have "Pressing On" at the end of the show. So [the show] ended after "Forever Young." With the doctor saying, "I closed my eyes . . ." And Shirley was doing Elizabeth's last speech, and she did the whole thing—the "baby giraffe in the zoo . . ." and all that. And then I was thinking, *Okay, the audience are going to start getting restless and shifting around here.* But they were just really still and really held, really held. And then Dr. Walker did his last thing, ". . . I looked out on the water. Then I closed my eyes . . ." the lights came down. And then it was just that kind of silence from the darkness. Nothing. Just nothing. And then [*makes a sound like a bomb going off*] I was sitting upstairs in the circle and I looked over the balcony as the lights came up, I just saw everybody just getting up to their feet and I thought, *Oh my God. I Dunno. I dunno how, I don't know what's going on, but this is it. This is what they wanted. Who knew?*

LUCY HIND   And then it opens . . .

MATTHEW WARCHUS   As soon as it started previewing when people saw it, word of mouth was excellent. And it started to shift the tickets. So it sold a lot of tickets quite quickly and ended up doing really well. It sold a lot of tickets quickly, but late.

GEORGIA GATTI   It performed incredibly well at the box office . . . one of the bestselling shows in the season.

CONOR MCPHERSON   Within the next couple of days, we were having a good time doing [the show]. And then the Old Vic were saying that it was the fastest selling show they ever had. And it was sold out. Everything Matthew said was true. He knew, it was so strange.

TRISTAN BAKER   We were all—we just sort of hugged each other.

---

[26]A speaker, so actors and crew backstage can hear what's happening in the theater. This is essential for actors to hear their cues to enter. One can also hear the audience reactions through this speaker.

CONOR MCPHERSON   But then what happened was on the opening night, the reviews were fantastic . . . five-star reviews everywhere . . .

MICHAEL BILLINGTON (review,[27] *The Guardian*)

"A superb cast use Bob's back catalogue to glorious effect in Conor McPherson's astonishing cross-section of hope and stoic suffering in Depression-era Minnesota . . . it is the constant dialogue between the drama and the songs that makes this show exceptional."

CONOR MCPHERSON   . . . except for one: the *New York Times*.

BEN BRANTLEY (review)

"As for Mr. McPherson, one of the greatest dramatists working, he, too, seems to be traveling through the dark without a compass."

CONOR MCPHERSON   Ben Brantley was in London, and he saw [the show] as an American.

BEN BRANTLEY (review)

"It sounds a lot better set to music. And I have the feeling that Mr. McPherson, in writing his dialogue, may have been overly infected by Mr. Dylan's lyrics, which are far more credible sung than spoken."

According to the *New York Times, Girl from the North Country* didn't *work.*

TRISTAN BAKER   I read the review as Brantley *wanting* to love it.

CONOR MCPHERSON   And what [Brantley] saw was British and Irish actors doing this thing which, for him, was a very American story with American music and it just felt problematic for him.

A *New York Times* review can truly determine a show's fate. The playwright Adam Bock and I once wrote a musical adaptation of Shirley Jackson's gothic novel *We Have Always Lived in the Castle.* Yale Repertory Theater in New Haven, Connecticut produced the premiere, and of course Adam and I had hopes that the show would eventually make it to Broadway. We knew in rehearsals that we hadn't quite gotten everything right—*maybe the show doesn't need a chorus?,* we wondered, *maybe we should rewrite the second act?,* our director Anne Kauffman asked—but we figured we would see this production through, we can't fire the chorus because we think the show may be better without one, that would be unfair. So we made only small changes and saved the big rethink for the next production.

---

[27]Five-star review, the highest *The Guardian* gives.

But there would be no next production because the *New York Times* reviewed the show. Negatively. Very negatively.

They weren't wrong to review the show, and they weren't wrong in their critique. All is fair, I suppose. But that single review did scare away every potential second home for the show. And thoughts of Broadway evaporated immediately.

It's a blood sport, this business.

For *Girl from the North Country*, the *New York Times* review was not negative, just not entirely positive. Was that enough to dash hopes of a transfer to the West End?

GEORGIA GATTI   Everyone was talking about [a transfer] and the pressure was on Tris[tan] and their team to then find a West End Theater in that window of time when you've still got all the cast together. It's intense because you kind of have this moment—*this is the moment* and it isn't going to last forever, so you've got to kind of *go now*.

TRISTAN BAKER   The Old Vic and I decided to [transfer the show to the West End] . . .

GEORGIA GATTI   Amazingly, Tris made it work for a limited season.

TRISTAN BAKER   . . . thanks to Cameron Mackintosh,[28] who said, "Let's put it into the Noël Coward."[29] So he moved into the Noël Coward with the original cast.

Girl from the North Country ran at the Noël Coward Theatre in The West End for a limited run of twelve weeks from December 29, 2017, to March 24, 2018.

GEORGIA GATTI   And in my view, [it] should have run much longer.

The production was nominated for five Olivier Awards, winning two for the performances by Shirley Henderson and Sheila Atim.

Forty-two High A Flats

I knew none of the above history when Tuesday, April 17, 2018 rolled around and it was time to perform the reading after only one day of

---

[28]Cameron Mackintosh is one of the theater world's most successful producers, having produced monster hits like *Cats*, *The Phantom of the Opera*, and *Les Misérables* among many others.
[29]The Noël Coward, formerly the New Theatre which opened in 1903, was the home of the original run of *Oliver!* in 1960.

rehearsal. All I knew was that Oskar Eustis and Mandy Hackett, the artistic-director team from the Public Theater, along with some other unknown-to-me-but-powerful-looking types were sitting in the audience to watch the performance. Conor gave a brief, friendly speech, about how we'd only just rehearsed for one day and how wonderful we all were (wishful thinking), and then turned the room over to Or Matias, our musical director.

Or looked at *me*, raised his eyebrows as if to say, "Well, are you ready?" And I, assuming I was speaking for the entire cast, nodded, like, "Yep, we're all ready," and Or played a G major chord on the piano and cued me to sing the solo, opening lines of the show, which I had forgotten I had been assigned.[30] So the reading began with me going "Oh, shit, right I'm singing this part."

I sang:

Sign on the window says, "Lonely."
Sign on the door says, "No company allowed."
Sign on the street says, "You don't own me."
Sign on the porch says, "Three's a crowd."[31]

And then the whole cast joined in the communal, tone-setting chorus of "oohs" that sound like a processional into a humble sanctuary, and we were suddenly doing the play, the musical, which twenty-four hours earlier had seemed like an impossibility.

OR MATIAS   It was just this incredible experience, it felt like we all went on a rollercoaster. It went up, it went down, we got off, everybody was like, *everybody okay, everybody cool?*

Marc Kudisch and I, as father and son, had immediate chemistry in the performance. We just clicked. Papa and son. When my big solo, "Duquesne Whistle," finally came deep in act two, I was no longer scared of the forty-two A flats because the play and the music and Marc Kudisch had so completely drawn me in, that I stopped thinking about what people thought of me. This wasn't about me.

I stood up, as directed by Conor, into the heavy silence that lands hard when Mrs. Burke realizes that her son is dead, and with that first, loud a cappella "Listen!" which Simon Hale scored to be the heralding blast of a divine trumpet, I sang Elias's poor heart out.

---

[30]The opening verse from "Sign on the Window," from Dylan's *New Morning*, 1970, is actually sung by a male ensemble member, but the reading cast only consisted of principal roles, so between us, we covered the ensemble solos.
[31]"Sign on the Window," Bob Dylan, from *New Morning*, 1970.

Listen to the Duquesne Whistle blowin'
Blowin' like it's gonna sweep my world away . . .[32]

This was something special, I felt it at that very moment. I knew this would change my life.

MANDY HACKETT   I will never forget the reading in that little room in East Village. Oh my God. I mean, I will just never forget it.

Jeannette Bayardelle, Sydney James Harcourt, Samantha Ware, David Pittu, Marc Kudisch, and I would all be cast for the production at the Public Theater later that year.

JEANNETTE BAYARDELLE   Oh my goodness. We did that.

Yes, we did.

JEANNETTE BAYARDELLE   We are amazing.

And Jeannette and I fall apart laughing like we would so many more times in the years to come.

---

[32]From "Duquesne Whistle," Bob Dylan, from *Tempest,* 2012.

2

Lafayette

A Hard Tale of Winter

I remember being sixteen years old and driving with my family the flat, 400 miles from our small western Nebraska town to the eastern state capital for the high school boys' state championship basketball tournament. Back home, my dad drove freight trains for the Burlington Northern railroad, and every year he'd take a few days off so we could go to "state," whether or not our school had made it past "regionals" to participate in the games; we had no stake in the outcome, it was just a fun trip to Lincoln where we shared a big house with two other families from our town with whom we were friendly.

I had just discovered musicals thanks to PBS television's airing of *Into the Woods*. The internet was not yet a thing, so I couldn't just find more musicals online, and the nearest city where a Broadway touring production might stop was Denver, Colorado, which is to say, nowhere close by. So my antennae were up for any signal coming from anywhere at all about my new obsession.

In the spring of that year, while my parents and brothers watched the high school boys state championship basketball tournament whittle away at its brackets, my antennae picked up on something actually interesting, actually important happening at the nearby Lied Center for Performing Arts: the national tour of *Les Misérables*.

I got a cheap ticket and sat so far back in the balcony that all I could really see clearly was the enormous wimple on the French nun keeping watch as Fantine lay dying.

Les Misérables was still running on Broadway when I moved to New York City in 1999, and I auditioned for it many, many times. Each time, I got a callback. Each time, I sang the big Enjolras aria that ends on one high Ab. And each time, I felt great about it. I'd call my parents (collect) back in Nebraska from some crusty old payphone near the audition studio and tell them that it was happening. That this was the moment. That I just knew it. That I'd call them back with the good news as soon as I heard from casting.

But I heard nothing.

Each time, nothing.

That's the horrible truth about auditioning: you hear nothing. You're in the room with the casting director, the associate director, the music director, you sing your heart out, you go in for a call back, they're happy to see you, they smile, you smile, they remember your name, you laugh with them, you act out emotional scenes from the script, you sing from the score, you let your hopes rise up as high as your highest notes, which you're nailing, higher and higher, why not, because *this time* it's going to happen. And then . . . nothing. You leave the room, you leave the building, you're back on the street, and the whole thing, the high and the hope of it all, just fades away and no one ever says anything to you about it ever again. *Les Misérables* (*The Miserable*) continues on without you. Everything does.

And you feel so stupid. You never should have told anyone how excited you were, least of all your parents, because now you have to tell them you were wrong. Again. But that everything is fine, don't worry. You hang up the phone, humiliated, and walk all the way home because what the hell else is there to do?

Being a part of New York theater, beyond even just *Les Misérables*, was all I wanted. And failing was crushing me.

I was writing a lot of songs, at least, mostly as I trudged around town feeling sorry for myself, and performing them around town when I could, even getting some Broadway names to sing them in concert.

I recently said to a friend of mine that my songs back then in the early 2000s were ". . . usually about God or a house burning down, I don't know why, I had no first-hand experience of either."

There is a chapter in *The Brothers Karamazov* by Dostoevsky about a monk, Brother Zosima, and I decided I should turn that chapter into a quiet and profound minimalist opera. That'll do it. Philip Himberg, head of the Sundance Institute Theatre Program, selected me as one of a few writers to go on a two-week writing retreat in Ucross, Wyoming. Among the other writers there were Adam Guettel, Rajiv Joseph, and Kate Moira Ryan. This was 2009. It was February. I remember because my husband (then boyfriend) sent me flowers on Valentine's Day and I thought *only Mark Subias could figure out how to get fresh flowers to a remote and snowy ranch in Wyoming in the middle of winter.*

Alone in my cabin, snow piled up outside the window, only a few hours' drive from my small hometown across the Nebraska border, with just a piano and Dostoevsky, I felt like New York had tossed me away, all the way back to where I came from.

Siberia.

The cry of freight trains in the distance, a sound buried deep in my bones since childhood, at once both far away and home.

I did not write a quiet and profound minimalist Dostoevsky opera in those two weeks, but I did write three small songs from the perspective of Brother Zosima, who, in grieving his brother's slow, awful death, finds God.

PRAISING GOD

It's hard to describe God
And Wyoming
And my brother who died when I was very young

I learned to read
From a book of Bible stories
And I loved this book
I loved these stories
That I would read to my brother

Do you know the story of Job?
He never faltered
Even when the Devil took everything from him
He, he, he,
He praised God.

Well, that was my brother
Just like Job
Even as the Devil took everything from him
He, he, he,
He praised
God.
God.
God.

Writing these songs helped me face something important: I was never going to be in *Les Miz*.

Maybe that was okay.

It didn't surprise me, then, that after returning to New York in March, 2009, and after many more years to come of trying, struggling against the great monolith, after more than a decade more of believing that even though all I heard was a repeated "no," I was going to find my place, the slow train all the way from Dostoevsky's Nebraska was going to arrive, that when it did, when I finally heard "yes," when I finally made it to "Broadway," it would be via the cold, hard, God-seeking tale of winter called *Girl from the North Country*.

That's the show I seemed fated for.

Eternal

My character Elias enters the action several scenes into *Girl from the North Country*.

Immediately preceding my entrance is a late-night scene in which two strangers show up to the Laines' boarding house, one of them is maybe a preacher, maybe a Bible-salesman, and the other, cryptically, "has an appointment." There's desperation in their arrival. And it's pouring rain. In the stage-left wing at every performance, my castmate Mare Winningham and I sat on a little bench and listened to this scene with its cold rain sound effect as we waited to enter the scene, mirror-images of the silhouetted figures hovering at the stage-right exit near the end of the play.

The late-night scene turns violent, and the maybe-preacher-maybe-Bible-salesman launches into Dylan's "Slow Train," singing, "Sometimes, I feel so low-down and disgusting."

The newly arrived stranger, Joe Scott, takes over, and this is the moment when you can feel the show click into a higher gear. Luba Mason's spare, sharp groove at the drum kit, Simon Hale's whip-like arrangement strap the audience to their seats and Austin Scott's rock-idol performance bolts the doors.

We're in this thing now, and we're in it together.

There's a slow train comin' up around the bend . . .[1]

You couldn't help but groove with it. And we did, all of us dancing backstage. Onstage, Kimber and Jeannette overtake the mic downstage center, stirring up furies with their "License to Kill" takeover:

> Now they take him, and they teach him
> And they groom him for life
> And they set him on a path
> Where he's bound to get ill
> Then they bury him with stars
> Sell his body like they do used cars . . .[2]

And the ensemble, all of us, blowing in like the agitated sky and storming all around the stage.

> There's a slow train coming!
> A slow train coming!
> There's a slow train coming!
> A slow train coming!

The song slams to an end, and the lights bump straight up into dialogue leaving no room for applause.

This is where I enter.

Luba Mason, amped up from her drumming, smiles at me, takes my hand which slips us into character, mother and son, she gives me a little here-we-

---

[1] "Slow Train," Dylan, from *Slow Train Coming*, 1979
[2] "License to Kill" Dylan, from *Infidels*, 1983.

go shake, and Marc Kudisch, my papa, leads us onstage with his boisterous "Good morning, good morning."

We Burkes clamor our way into a busy breakfast scene, the first scene in which the audience gets to see just about every character in the boarding house in the same room at the same time.

Several characters are just meeting in the scene, so there are a lot of introductions:

MR. BURKE: Good morning, good morning.

MARIANNE: Good morning.

MR. BURKE: Morning Marianne.

MARIANNE: Good morning Elias. The usual?

MRS. BURKE: Yes, the usual.

MR. BURKE: Morning Doc.

DR. WALKER: Folks.

MR. BURKE: Good morning sir.

SCOTT: Good morning.

MR. BURKE: Frank Burke, this is my wife Laura, my son, Elias.

SCOTT: Joe Scott. Pleased to meet you.

MR. BURKE: Mrs. Neilsen.

SCOTT: Ma'am.

MR. BURKE: Dr. Walker.

SCOTT: Sir.

ELIAS: Mommy my scarecrow (*searching for a word*) ah, ah, ah, ah . . . My scarecrow, ah, ah, ah, my scarecrow wears a hat.

ELIZABETH: What the fuck is wrong with him?[3]

And so on. It's a hard scene to get right, because it seems like not a lot is happening, just strangers eating oatmeal and drinking coffee together while talking over and bumping into each other, all politely. But through the politeness there is a lot of information smuggled in about the characters and the general American mood in 1934. Jobs are scarce, money scarcer. The country is in a deep crisis and no one knows when, if, or how we will ever come out of it. Everyone is vulnerable, and everyone needs to eat.

---

[3]McPherson, Conor, *Girl from the North Country*, Nick Hern Books, p. 38. The text quoted is from the Broadway script, which is slightly amended from the published version.

From Robert S. McElvaine's book *The Great Depression*:

As the days without finding a job became weeks, the weeks months, and the months years, it came to be more difficult even to look for work. ". . . You can get pretty discouraged and your soles can get pretty thin after you've been job hunting a couple of months," a Minnesota Depression victim pointed out. First you came to accept the idea of taking a job of lower quality than you thought you deserved. Then you began to wonder just what you did deserve. It came finally, for some, to be a matter of begging: "For God's sake, Mister, when are you going to give us work?" "How," asked the daughter of a long-unemployed man, "can you go up and apply for a job without crying?"[4]

Despite the dire situation the characters found themselves in, performing the breakfast scene in our Broadway run was thrilling. The cast all knew their parts so well by then that the swirling, giddy chatter clipped right along while multiple layers of physical storytelling and mystery-building played out underneath. Marianne Laine, the adopted daughter of the house with a just-visible baby bump serves coffee and oatmeal as usual, but she's just slightly off her game because of a surprising frisson between herself and the new lodger, Joe Scott. Elizabeth Laine, her adoptive mother, in the throes of dementia, playfully interacts with Doctor Walker, who's stopped by to supply her with drugs, while Elizabeth's husband, Nick, makes his weary, eternal, loops as the flailing inn-keeper. Joe Scott, full of secrets, tries to keep himself to himself, unsuccessfully. The Burkes burst in with big, loud Southern entitlement and play out their family dynamic—Frank a businessman without a business thanks to the stock market crash, tries to strike some deals, and Laura, her roots showing, her expensive dress a little tattered, and her impatience with Frank at a breaking point, has her hands full with Elias, their tall, strong adult son with the mind of a young child. Mrs. Neilsen, caught in an unsatisfying love affair with Nick Laine, bides her time until her inheritance comes through and she can start her own business. And Reverend Marlowe, desperate to make himself seem decent, sizes up every potential opportunity he can exploit.

There's a lot to take in, but before the audience can grab ahold of it all, it erupts in a violent outburst between Frank and Laura Burke and is gone. An instrumental, melancholic "Ballad of a Thin Man"[5] takes over, and the play presses on.

I'm going to keep returning to the breakfast scene. That and the Thanksgiving scene from act two. Both revolve around food and fellowship, and both were a part of my recurring and sustained religious experience.

At that breakfast table in 1934 Duluth, Minnesota (Bob Dylan's birthplace), I, as Elias, could not participate in the conversation the way the

[4]McElvaine, Robert S. *The Great Depression: America, 1929–1941*, Times Books, 1984.
[5]From Dylan's *Highway 61 Revisited*, 1965.

others did. If you caught it above, the interaction between myself, my mother and Elizabeth Laine says a lot you need to know about my character. Here it is again:

> ELIAS: Mommy my scarecrow (*searching for a word*) ah, ah, ah, ah . . . My scarecrow, ah, ah, ah, my scarecrow wears a hat.
>
> ELIZABETH: What the fuck is wrong with him?

This is a laugh line, oddly. Not at Elias's expense, but at Elizabeth's uncouth behavior. A great amount of tension (and comedy) in the play comes from Elizabeth's surprising and often cruel language. Another quick example, in a scene between Elizabeth and the Reverend, whom she has easily identified as a "louse":

> ELIZABETH: You get a wash this morning?
>
> MARLOWE: Well of course.
>
> ELIZABETH: You might need to go another rinse. It don't smell so sweet down here in the down wind.

She's mean. But she asks a fair, if harsh, question about Elias. What exactly is "wrong" with him?[6] Conor's script—his entire canon of work, really—is littered with asked-but-unanswered questions. In *Girl from the North Country*, he tells us nothing about Elias's diagnosis. Nor Elizabeth's. We know only through their dialogue, like in the scarecrow scene above, or other passing comments, like in Doctor Walker's opening monologue,

> This is Nick Laine. That's his wife there, Elizabeth. Nick inherited this house from his granddaddy, but he never had no head for business. First he lost the stables and stud, then all the stocks. Managed to remortgage the house long enough for Elizabeth to turn it into decent boarding rooms.
> But she hasn't been so good lately. Nick's tryna take care of everything. Trying real hard. Like a man tryna to run through a wall tries real hard. But the bank has only given him two months grace.[7]

or the occasional stage-direction,

> *ELIZABETH is nearby, staying wrapped up inside herself.*

that Elizabeth and Elias are different from the others in a significant way. That there is something "wrong," to use Elizabeth's word.

---

[6]For the record, nothing is "wrong" with Elias. The term "neurodivergent" did not exist in 1934.
[7]McPherson, Conor, *Girl from the North Country*, Nick Hern Books, pp. 13–14.

Interpreting this between-the-lines diagnosis of a character is fraught for an actor due to the ableist pitfalls. One can play the symptoms instead of the person, which results in reductive and offensive stereotypes. In one of the most profound afternoons of my life, the cast, crew, music director Marco Paguia, and front-of-house staff all gathered onstage, sat in an enormous circle, and discussed Elias, his way of existing in the world, and theater's general state of inclusion and representation of varying abilities onstage. There is a deeper discussion of this circle later in the book, but what it ultimately illuminated for me was that each one of us as a human being knows only what we know. We each have the unique gift of our perspective, and the unique limit of our experience. Not one of us alive sets about "playing" our "diagnosis," whatever it may be; we just live as best we can, using what we know and looking to others for what we cannot know.

Of course I can't speak for the character of Elizabeth Laine, or her stunning portrayal by Mare Winningham, but I can say about Elias that though his ability to express it was narrow, his perception of the world was wide.

Elias showed me the other side. He had access to God.

In the most practical sense, I acknowledge that my religious experience in *Girl from the North Country* could be chalked up to my active imagination playing a game with my mind, incorporating the fictional experience of a character whom I was attempting to embody.

I was just "acting."

But consider: There I was, in a play full of ghosts and Biblical imagery (Marianne's mysterious pregnancy and her suitors both named Joseph), in a haunted theater,[8] playing a character named Elias (a variant of the Biblical name Elijah[9]), who dies and sings a song *from beyond the grave*, the gospel-tinged eleven o'clock number written by the famously devout Christian convert Bob Dylan.

I was set up.

But I didn't fight it. There was something mystical trying to grab hold of me up there and I let it.

"There was a presence in the room . . ."

"It was a physical thing. I felt it. I felt it all over me. I felt my whole body tremble."

"It's pretty scary to think about . . . I'm not preaching . . . It's spiritual—it's not complicated."[10]

---

[8]The Belasco Theatre is said to be haunted by its namesake, David Belasco. Though some claim the ghost is female. Of course, the real question is: are ghosts even real? Yes.

[9]According to Behindthename.com, from a reference by the New York Public library website, the name means "My God is Yahweh."

[10]Heylin, Clinton, *Trouble In Mind*, Route, 2017.

These are quotes from Bob Dylan (assembled by the great Dylan historian Clinton Heylin in his book *Trouble In Mind*); answers to various reporters' questions about the religious experience he had that led him to convert to Christianity, record three consecutive albums of songs essentially praising God,[11] and to tour the country preaching the Christian gospel from the stage to an audience expecting to hear protest songs like "The Times They Are A-Changin'." A controversial period in a controversial career that I didn't know about until preparing to write this book, nearly a year after we closed *Girl* on Broadway. In looking back, that mysterious "presence in the room" that Dylan felt and that I felt to a lesser extent, seems written-in to the script and, vis-a-vis my experience, pre-ordained.

I remind you here of something Conor said about the genesis of *Girl from the North Country*:

CONOR MCPHERSON   A huge thing for me was coming across [Dylan's] Christian era. That knocked me for six. I loved that.

Like Dylan, I, too, felt *a presence in the room*. During breakfast on Broadway, when all of the boarding-house chaos swirled around me, I/Elias would stare into the stage-left wing—the opposite wing we stared into when we died— transfixed by what I/he saw there. During any performance of any given play, there are actors that the audience can't see standing in the wings, watching the action onstage because they are about to enter into it. Stage-light leaks into the unlighted backstage area, and the effect is a kind of eternal-twilight, so in my/ Elias's wide perception, the shadowy figures in that twilight looked not like people, but like other-worldly *witnesses*, waiting for their time to pass through.

"I think that this world is just a passing-through place and that the dead have eyes and that even the unborn can see, and I don't care who knows it."[12]

Of course, the figures watching from the wings were just my castmates. Hard-working, union-card carrying, human actors, showing up to work every day through the most difficult time our industry has gone through. Waiting, ironically, to enter into scenes set during the most difficult time America had gone through. The veil between Depression-era America and Pandemic-era America would eventually become terribly thin.

But before all of that, we started out innocently enough at the Public Theater, knowing nothing of the difficult and tragic path ahead. Had any of us ever used the word "pandemic" in casual conversation at this point? I

---

[11] The three "Christian Era" albums, which some refer to as a trilogy: *Slow Train Coming*, 1979; *Saved*, 1980; *Shot of Love*, 1981.
[12] Dylan, from the notes in his *Biograph* compilation, but accessed here from Clinton Heylin in *Trouble In Mind*.

hadn't. It was summer, 2018. The city was bursting with life in the way only New York City can. I rode my bicycle to rehearsal, many of us did, and I was just getting to know my castmates. The whole thing had a summer camp feel about it. Smiling, hugging, singing, filling up our new personalized water bottles, a first-day-of-rehearsal gift from the Public. All smiles and nerves. Theater people, whom I would soon see as something more angelic.

Why the Public?

Oskar Eustis, the artistic director of the Public Theater and a life-long devotee of Bob Dylan, did an actual spit-take and nearly choked to death on his herbal tea when I asked him in his office on Lafayette Street:

TODD   What did you make of Dylan's Christian era?

OSKAR (*spit-take, coughing*)

TODD   Sorry, you need some water?

OSKAR (*coughing, but laughing*)

TODD (*laughing*)   Oh, no. I think I might have killed Oskar Eustis. Do you want me to get you some water?

OSKAR   I think I'm going to be okay.

After recovering, Oskar answered the question with wide eyes:

OSKAR   Well, I'll say this, it was *noticeable*!

Oskar has been at the helm of the Public Theater since 2005, but my experience with the institution precedes that. It's the home of one of my earliest New York City audition "no" stories. It was 2003 and at that time George C. Wolfe[13] was the Artistic Director. Mr. Wolfe was directing a musical based on the life of the artist Keith Haring called *Radiant Baby*, and the role of "Keith Haring" was down to me and one other actor, Daniel Reichard. The Public called both me and Daniel in for what I can only call an actor-smackdown. Daniel and I sat in the hallway outside one of the five theaters at the Public—I think it might have been the Shiva, the small black-box theater on the first floor, but I don't really remember. Daniel would go in to work with Mr. Wolfe (and composer Debra Barsha) on the material, and I would sit waiting just outside the door, where I could hear Daniel sing

---

[13]George C. Wolfe directed the original Broadway productions of many shows including *Angels in America, Jelly's Last Jam.*

and re-sing the songs. And then I would go in and sing and re-sing while Daniel would sit and wait and listen to me. And we went back and forth like this for maybe three or four thousand rounds.

Daniel got the job, he was great in the show, and he went on to star in the original company of *Jersey Boys*. Whenever we see each other we kinda smile at each other and acknowledge that bizarre day.

So, as ridiculous as it seems given my extensive Joe's Pub experience, my Keith Haring audition, and my three original musicals under the Public Works banner, as irresponsibly belated as it may have been by this point, I asked Oskar Eustis anyway, "What is the Public Theater?"

OSKAR EUSTIS   The Public Theater is a theater devoted to the idea that the culture belongs to everyone. That's a core principle. The idea that culture should not be the exclusive property of any given class or tribe or ethnicity or wealth, that it should be something that we are able to hold in common as people.

Every summer on the Delacorte Stage in New York City's Central Park, The Public produces starry productions of Shakespeare's plays which are free for anyone to attend.

OSKAR EUSTIS   The greatest writer of the English language is everybody's property, not just people who can afford tickets to the new work we do on our stage; our stages are devoted to telling everybody's stories, not just the stories of the privileged and noble and aristocrats.

So what made the Public the right home for *Girl from the North Country*?

OSKAR EUSTIS   Well, let me talk about it in two ways. The first is that the idea that there was going to be a musical from Bob Dylan's music, frankly, you had me at that sentence. Dylan is the biggest artistic influence in my life. I won't go into all of the lengthy, boring, Dylan-obsessive stories that tens of millions of American men of my age can tell. But I was born in Minnesota and ran away to New York City and just admired him enormously.

Mandy Hackett is the Associate Artistic Director at the Public.

MANDY HACKETT   The idea of this piece utterly captivated me and Oskar right off the bat.

TRISTAN BAKER   [Oskar] had come to a workshop [in London] because he loved Bob Dylan.

OSKAR EUSTIS   . . . So the Dylan part got me, but then the second part was Conor himself . . . I was incredibly intrigued by the idea of Conor doing this . . . There's nothing commercial about that choice, it's not like,

"Let's make a ton of money off the Dylan catalog." That's something else. And then when I saw what Conor had done in writing it, I was kind of blown away and mystified at the same time.

TRISTAN BAKER   And Oskar loved *Conor*. So he'd been to a couple of the London workshops . . . I don't think I'd invited him . . . maybe it was Georgia [Gatti] or Matthew [Warchus] said *come to a workshop if you're in town* or something like that.

However it happened that Oskar found himself invited to London to eye, as a potential American producing partner, the Old Vic workshop, and however excited he was at the thought of shepherding the play to New York City, the playwright, Conor McPherson, found himself unsure of how *Girl from the North Country* would even fare with Americans.

CONOR MCPHERSON   I knew then that no matter how good those reviews were in London, this particular production was going to have a very hard time [in New York] . . . because we knew what [Brantley] thought.

And we know the power of a *New York Times* review. Brantley's review hadn't negatively affected the London run, sure, but this was New York they were talking about, and New Yorkers read reviews in the *New York Times*. But Oskar wasn't worried.

OSKAR EUSTIS   This is where I'd say that the connection to the Public's mission becomes deep, because what Conor was trying to do was find a way to dramatize what Dylan's project has been throughout his entire life: to try to write an iconic American folk music that is actually not from any specific period, but rather describes some underlying American themes of survival and oppression and resilience and struggle that are mythic. He's been writing the American myth in his songbook, and weirdly, he's gotten closer and closer to it as he's gotten older, which is just astonishing. And Conor was matching that with his script.

CONOR MCPHERSON   I think a lot of Irish people think they are American. Our culture we get growing up is "American." People of my generation all have relatives living in America. They come and visit us when we're kids and we're like, "Who are these Americans?" You know what I mean? "The Americans are here."

The transfer to America was as close to a fait accompli as it could be, even before the opening night at the Old Vic . . .

TRISTAN BAKER   [Oskar] said, "I want to do it. I have to do it." He said, "You don't need me. If you get great reviews, I still want to do it. And if you don't get great reviews, I still want to do it."

... so while the potential reception of the material was a big unknown, the certainty of the move was not.

OSKAR EUSTIS   I was there opening night at The Old Vic, because by that point, we had become the American partners.

MANDY HACKETT   I went over to London [to see the production] ...

CONOR MCPHERSON   So we all have that connection to America. And a feeling of, I guess a kind of mythical understanding of it.

MANDY HACKETT   ... I came home completely raving about it. We were like, we want to do it, we want to do it, we want to do it.

CONOR MCPHERSON   But having said that, that's very presumptuous. I'm not American, and I probably don't understand America, but we have at least a feeling for it, which is not the same.

At this point in its production history, and though the musical is set in America, has only American characters, and features the music by one of America's most beloved songwriters, *Girl from the North Country* had no Americans on the creative team.

OSKAR EUSTIS   So suddenly you had a musical that was using all Dylan's songs from all different time periods, but was set before Dylan was born in the America that Dylan sprang from the upper Midwest Depression, that working class, northern Minnesota place that he sprang from.

What would Americans make of it?

OSKAR EUSTIS   Conor was like Dylan, tapping into that on a mythic level, and that was ... very *confusing.*

Was it *America*?

OSKAR EUSTIS   It took me a long time to understand this piece deeply ...

Did that matter?

OSKAR EUSTIS   ... but it was also thrilling, and that's why it felt right for the Public.

Was this the right decision?

CONOR MCPHERSON   I suppose part of me thought, well, Bob Dylan sent me.

Before the cast could begin rehearsals at the Public Theater in America, one major question had to be answered: *Who will the American cast even be?*

Transfer

Hit productions from London regularly make the trip across the Atlantic from London's West End to New York's Broadway, and often they arrive with at least most of the original London principal cast, *Prima Facie* and *Harry Potter and the Cursed Child* being recent examples. Jodie Comer won an Olivier Award in London and a Tony Award in New York for her performance in *Prima Facie*. More often, the productions themselves travel but they are recast with American actors, think Tom Stoppard's *Leopoldstadt*, which won both Olivier and Tony awards with both the London and American casts, respectively.

Both systems work: bringing over the London cast and recasting with Americans. How is the choice made? Who makes it?

I asked David Binder, an independent producer who for three years was the artistic director of BAM, the Brooklyn Academy of Music, and, with tremendous success, transferred Ivo Van Hove's production of *Network* from London's National Theatre to Broadway, about the debate of whether or not to bring the original cast of a hit show over for the American transfer.

DAVID BINDER   I think that's always a thing because you look at the success of the show in that original city, whether that's New York going to London or London going to New York, and you ask how that can be emulated.

David brought *Network*'s star, Bryan Cranston (already an American), over from the London production for the Broadway run of the play, but recast the remaining roles with American actors.

In the name of authenticity, should American actors play American roles in American productions?

Tristan Baker, producer of the West End production of *Girl from the North Country*, wrestled with this dilemma.

TRISTAN BAKER   I remembered a number of times that things had come from the UK to America and had not worked because it wasn't right. *American Psycho, Enron...* you can't take "America" to America ...

OSKAR EUSTIS   The London production [of *Girl from the North Country*] didn't feel authentically American to me.

The idea of recasting the show with Americans cropped up.

TRISTAN BAKER   So that was a really fucking hard decision because I had this incredible company from the Old Vic to the Noël Coward and proof—proof!—that they were amazing.

OSKAR EUSTIS   It's not a question of accurate or inaccurate, it's a question of the audience [who think] "I'm an American. Dylan, the Depression, Duluth, those are *mine*."

Unsurprisingly, the decision most often comes down to money.

CONOR MCPHERSON   It wasn't even anybody's decision. There was no offer to us saying, *we are paying you millions of dollars to bring over all of this [original] cast*. It just wasn't on the table. So it wasn't like I was saying, "Hey guys, what a pity, but I don't like this production . . ." It's not like that.

Commercial runs, typically open-ended in terms of how long they will play, have different financial needs than not-for-profit runs.

DAVID BINDER   . . . having come out of the BAM world where of course you would bring over the entire show like *Cyrano* [Jamie Lloyd's production starring James McAvoy] because the show is playing for a much more limited season than if you are going to Broadway where you're hoping to do a much longer run.

Aside from the question of cultural authenticity, there were financial realities to be considered. Relocating twenty actors overseas to New York City and housing them for even a limited run would have been prohibitively expensive.

DAVID BINDER   It's the cost. Because you have to pay all the costs that you would pay in New York plus you have to pay the housing, plus you have to pay the per diems . . . it's just the myriad of things when you're bringing someone from one city to another that are inherent.

CONOR MCPHERSON   Just a fact of life.

OSKAR EUSTIS   . . . It worked for his people in the British production just as it [would work] for our people in the American production.

TRISTAN BAKER   I decided to tell the [London] company that this [New York] workshop was going ahead, because they would've found out at some point.

CONOR MCPHERSON   In terms of a future life for the show in America, the only offers we had to do it [were] to start Off-Broadway. Start all over again with an American cast. That was all that was on the table. So that's what we started to look at doing, unfortunately for the original cast.

But how did the original London cast feel about American actors doing a reading of the musical that they were still performing nightly on the West End to standing ovations?

SHEILA ATIM   When a show is going to be taken beyond yourself, I think the way that's handled is very important to be considered. I don't actually think that the *taking-it-further* is a problem because from the moment you step on stage and open the show up to a paying audience, it's not yours anymore. And I'm not saying that from a righteous place because don't get me wrong, as an actor and as a human being, of course ego is there wanting to clutch onto a thing, but in the ideological sense, I don't think it's yours anymore because people are already experiencing it and taking what they want from it.

SHIRLEY HENDERSON   I think we were probably all a bit sad because ... it was a show like no other for most of us or maybe all of us.

SHEILA ATIM   We are artists, and particularly with projects like this it does impact us emotionally, and it becomes a part of us, of our story in a very deeply personal way. And the way those transfers are handled is incredibly important to be able to pass on the show with love, actually, which I found my way of doing.

SHIRLEY HENDERSON   There were always little hints that we might go [to Broadway]. But it never happened, and I think it was hard to begin with to let the show go.

SHEILA ATIM   I've never held any ill feeling or resentment towards the fact that the show continued without me or that other people stepped into those shoes. But yes, sensitivity around how that's handled is instrumental.

SHIRLEY HENDERSON   But ultimately I feel happy with what we did. I mean we did it once. I didn't know we were going to do it twice. Two runs in the West End and then we won some awards for it. That just took our breath away. So unexpected for us, for Sheila and myself. So in a way you have to think *well that's it. How lucky were we to be a part of it.* This is our part of the journey with this and you have to accept it. But yes, we were all a little sad.

And so the decision was made: the show would be entirely recast with American actors for the American production.

TRISTAN BAKER   We did that first reading [at the Public] and instantly it was like, *well, this just lives.* I mean, it was so different. It was not better or worse, just so different. Because it was America and everybody knew and was grounded in it.

SHIRLEY HENDERSON   But it's okay. It's life and things have to be handed on. And I wanted it to go on and have a next life and I was so happy for Conor. I said to him "Go and do it. Go on the journey."

The Americans

CHRIS HIGHLAND (email)

Todd! Left word for you . . . but hopefully you are somewhere fabulous starting your weekend and hopefully this news will make it even better. Offer for the off-broadway production of GIRL FROM THE NORTH COUNTRY at the Public this summer/fall! Congratulations! We can talk more about it next week but know that their goal and plan is to transfer to Broadway following the Public run and they called to make sure you were professionally clear in 2019 before making the official. Patrick Catullo has come on as the enhancing producer in NY alongside the team from the Old Vic and the Public. Look forward to speaking further. Details below and script once again attached. Wooo!

The phrase ". . . their goal and plan is to transfer to Broadway following the Public run . . ." obviously hit me hard. I was twenty-two years old when I arrived in New York City, ready for Broadway to snatch me up, and I got the email above when I was forty-two years old.

Slow train coming.

Though six of us were cast from the reading at Gibney Studios (Jeannette Bayardelle, Sydney James Harcourt, David Pittu, Marc Kudisch, Samantha Ware, and myself), the remaining actors joined from the traditional casting process.

Including Luba Mason, who made her Broadway debut in 1987.

LUBA MASON   At the callback [audition][14] for *Girl from the North Country*, after I'd done the scenes and I'd sung the songs, Conor said, "So, do you play any instruments?"

Luba knows that actors should say *yes*, they can do *anything*. I once said "Yes" at an audition when I was asked if I could tap dance. "Very well, in fact." I couldn't tap dance. Not very well, not at all. And the casting director found out, as did the director, at the exact same time that we all found out together, all of the actors, when we had to dance one by one in front of each other, which I hadn't anticipated.

LUBA MASON   I said, "Yeah, I play piano." And I said, "Some guitar and some clarinet." And he says, "Well for this character, we would like

---

[14]Actors go through multiple rounds of auditions. There's an initial round where the casting directors see many auditioners for a role; they then select a smaller pool to move forward to "callbacks," which is the round where the creatives (playwright, director, musical director, choreographer) are in the room. Callbacks can be one round or extend to several, each winnowing down choices. Sometimes, as in my Keith Haring story earlier in this chapter, they end with a two-actor smackdown to the death.

her to be playing the drums. How do you feel about that? Do you think you can handle it?" And I said, "Sure, that's fine."

Luba had never played the drums a day in her life.

> LUBA MASON   You're in your fucking callback! You say whatever you have to say to get the job.

She would be cast as Laura Burke, the formerly wealthy Southern wife of Frank Burke (Marc Kudisch) and mother of my character, Elias. Because she said "yes" to playing the drums, she would need to figure out how to do that.
Good luck, Luba.
Caitlin Houlahan, whom I had just seen in Sara Bareilles's wonderful *Waitress* on Broadway, would be cast as Kate Draper, the young woman who has to make a difficult life choice.

> CAITLIN HOULAHAN   I got the callback to come in the next day to be in front of Conor and Marco [music director]. I don't think Lucy [choreographer] was there. And I don't think that Simon [orchestrator] was there. I was really taken by Conor. I think I felt a little starstruck in a way, as I do with anyone who's from Ireland. I get really excited and I remember doing the scene and doing the song, and Conor asked me how to pronounce my "Christian name," and I had no idea what he was talking about! And I was like, "Oh, oh, my *confirmation name?*" I didn't know what "Christian name" meant. So embarrassing.

Colton Ryan, who would stay with the show through opening on Broadway, but not return after the pandemic, was cast as Gene Laine, son of Nick and Elizabeth and brother of Marianne.

> COLTON RYAN   I just read once for I think Jordan and Heidi [casting directors], and then the next time read for Conor, paired up [with potential "Kate" actresses] twice. One was with Caitlin.

> CAITLIN HOULAHAN   I was sitting in the hallway and I thought to myself, *I wonder if Colton auditioned for this show.* And then two seconds later, he rounded the corner!

> COLTON RYAN   And I was like, "Hi! I was just thinking about you!" Because we had gone to college together.

> CAITLIN HOULAHAN   Colton and I went to school together. And I thought, *oh, he must have gotten the role. He's doing the chemistry reads.*

A "chemistry read" is what it sounds like. The casting directors (with the director) will pair actors together in various combinations to see if they have "chemistry," which doesn't necessarily mean "sexual chemistry," it can mean simply "do they naturally create dramatic tension with each other."

COLTON RYAN Those things are so silly, chemistry reads or screen tests and all that stuff. So to have someone comfortable with you, like Caitlin was me, like I was with her, I think they were kind of freaked by it.

CAITLIN HOULAHAN We sang together, and we acted out almost exactly what we ended up doing on stage.

COLTON RYAN I remember Conor getting up and kind of staging it with us. He wanted the whole scene . . .

CAITLIN HOULAHAN He said, Colton, you stand down here, Caitlin up here, and at this part come down . . .

COLTON RYAN . . . we did the whole thing continuously, a one-take sort of, really scene-into-the-song; Conor wanted to see the whole thing played out.

The scene between Gene and Kate is devastating. It's the only time you see these two characters together, but it has enough information between the lines to tell their whole story.

COLTON RYAN It's written perfectly. I loved it. It's the perfect scene. Take it in context. Take it out of context. It just—it's true, it says nothing and says everything.

Here is part of the scene:

GENE: Kate . . .

KATE: I hope it's alright—calling by like this.

GENE: No! Hey . . . Come in.

KATE: I can't stay.

GENE: Hey, that's alright. You want some breakfast?

KATE: No, thank you I'm fine.

GENE: Cup of coffee?

KATE: I can't. I have a ticket for the nine o'clock Greyhound—to Boston.

GENE: (*Steps into the rain, holding a newspaper over his head*) You going to Boston?

KATE: I got a job. Teaching. For a family. It's kind of a governess.

GENE: Great.

KATE: Three girls.

GENE: Wow. That's terrif . . .

KATE: Jed Simons has asked me to marry him Gene. I've said yes.

Short Pause

GENE: Wo . . . Wow that's . . . That's great.[15]

It's perfectly Midwestern. Deep heartbreak delivered politely and never spoken directly. Caitlin and Colton had chemistry.

CAITLIN HOULAHAN   We walked out of the audition, and then two other actors walked in, a female and a male. And we knew, *okay, it's either going to be us or them*!

Taking the reins of Elizabeth Laine from Shirley Henderson would be Mare Winningham, the great Oscar-nominated film and Emmy-winning television actress whom I'd admired for years and had luckily gotten to know personally through our mutual friends, married-couple Sam Gold and Amy Herzog, both powerhouse theatrical innovators.[16] Impossible as it seems given her film and television success since the 1980s (my husband and I could happily watch her in *St. Elmo's Fire* every night), Mare made her Broadway debut in Sam's 2013 production of William Inge's *Picnic*.

Rounding out the American cast would be Tom Nelis as Mr. Perry, the old shoe-mender wanting to marry the eighteen-year-old Marianne Laine; Robert Joy as Doctor Walker, the pill-dispensing and possible pill-addicted narrator; Stephen Bogardus as Nick Laine, husband and caretaker of Elizabeth; and Chelsea Lee Williams, Rachel Stern, John Schiappa, and Matthew Frederick Harris as the "ensemble" and on-stage understudies. Marco Paguia was our new music director, pianist, and band leader.

Rehearsals in America with the Americans for an American audience could at last begin.

Day One

COLTON RYAN   I remember how electric the cast felt about each other.

---

[15]McPherson, Conor, *Girl from the North Country*, Nick Hern Books, p. 47.
[16]Sam Gold won a Tony for directing *Fun Home* by Lisa Kron and Jeanine Tesori. Amy Herzog was nominated for a Tony for her translation/adaptation of *A Doll's House* starring Jessica Chastain.

Our first day at the Public was the last day of July in 2018. Just like the characters in the script's breakfast scene, we were thrown together into a new, shared space, each of us having arrived via our various, complex backgrounds, some meeting each other for the first time, sharing a meal,[17] speaking over and bumping into each other.

> CHELSEA LEE WILLIAMS I remember the first day of rehearsal very well, because I got a call the night before that I was going to read "Marianne" at the table-read.

Samantha Ware, who had played Marianne Laine in the reading and was cast in the production at the Public, dropped out of the show in the days before rehearsal started. A harbinger of what was to come for our understudies, Chelsea Lee Williams found herself, with little notice, suddenly "going on" for Marianne.

> CHELSEA LEE WILLIAMS I thought, *I'm not prepared to do this.*

Most rehearsal processes, at least the ones I've been a part of, start with a table-read, which is exactly what it sounds like: the actors sit at a table and read the play aloud.

> CHELSEA LEE WILLIAMS I know for a fact that I was awful in that reading. Oskar was there. So I do remember that day very well. My God.

> MARE WINNINGHAM I was so nervous. The first read-through that we had, I still couldn't believe I had been cast. I was just so excited and then really nervous about it. I wasn't nervous about "Forever Young,"[18] but I was about "Rolling Stone."[19] And during the first read-through, I realized, *oh, I don't really know what's going on . . .*

But before there was time to get lost in "table-work," an exercise some directors use wherein the actors stay seated after the table-read, sometimes for days, to discuss the characters' histories and motivations, Conor immediately got us up on our feet, and threw us right into scene work.

> CONOR MCPHERSON . . . I used to do table-work, but I found that actually, once we stood up after a week of that, everything we had spoken about seemed to disappear very fast. Because the problems that you have

---

[17]Our stage manager, Artie Gaffin, had set up a generous morning spread. The first of many.

[18]"Forever Young," you'll remember, is the final song in the musical until we get to Broadway and add "Pressing On."

[19]"Like a Rolling Stone," the finale of act one, one of Dylan's most famous songs, was ranked #1 by *Rolling Stone* magazine in their 2010 list of "The 500 Greatest Songs of all Time."

as soon as you stand up are entirely different to the problems you have sitting at the table.

We started with the breakfast scene.

> LUBA MASON　I mean, that first time we ran the breakfast scene, it wasn't like we sat down and talked about the scene.

Luba and I, castmates who had just been getting to know each other over bagels and coffee, suddenly found ourselves sitting over imaginary oatmeal at a prop breakfast table, now mother and son.

> LUBA MASON　I thought I was going to have a heart attack . . . I didn't know my lines yet. No one did.

Our fellow actors, scripts in hand, wandered around the space saying all of those "Good Morning"s and having absolutely no idea what to do, where to go.

> LUBA MASON　And I'm so preoccupied with my son [Elias] at this table, just trying to keep him under wraps. And I had to say my line, and I couldn't hear Marc over there talking to Joe, the boxer, but I couldn't pay attention to anything but you!

I didn't know what to do, yet, as my character. So I tried everything, all at once. As my friend David would say, I could have been given the award that day for "Most Acting."

> LUBA MASON　You were doing everything you possibly could think of, Todd: spilling the cup, hitting the plate, throwing the fork. I put the napkin on you, you take it off, I put it back on, you take it off and put it on your head.

Apologies, Luba.

I'd read and reread Conor's script, and noticed that Elias is a kind of foil to his parents' relationship. They love Elias and he is in constant need of their attention. He is a toddler in the body of a six-foot-five-inch adult man. Since I had only two lines of dialogue in the entire script, I decided that Elias's relationship with his parents needed to manifest physically to create that tension.

For the first few weeks of rehearsal, I overdid this.

> LUBA MASON　Conor works very differently, I find, than a lot of directors. He did not tell us where to go. It was kind of like, "Okay,

breakfast scene!" And we all just kind of enter where we do, and go where we think we should go.

The chaos of that day would feel familiar three years later when we were in the throes of the coronavirus Omicron variant, wearing masks in the wings off-stage, getting test results mid-performance, never certain if the actor playing a role in act one would be the same actor playing that role in act two.

LUBA MASON   We didn't even get through the whole [breakfast] scene that day, but kind of just stopped. And I took the biggest breath and I went, *oh my God, is this what I'm going to be doing this entire scene? I guess so.*

Day one ended and we'd survived.

ARTIE (email)
   Dear Fabulous First Day Cast,
   Thank you all for a really wonderful first day! It was so great to see you all in the same room and to begin this journey to Duluth together. (We hope you all packed your suitcases!)

Meet Artie

The work schedule for an actor in rehearsals is Tuesday through Sunday, generally 10 a.m. to 6 p.m. But depending on what the director wants to rehearse, not every actor will be called for the entire day. So every night the stage manager sends an email to the cast with a breakdown of the following day's schedule.
   Our stage manager was Artie Gaffin.

ARTIE (email)
   Dear one-of-a-kind wonders,
   We know you're a company of lovers rather than fighters . . . so we are bringing in a fight director to make you feel safe during all of the fight moments!
   Please note that we are having a bit of a later start tomorrow! Staggered calls begin at 11am and lunch will be from 1:30–2:30pm.
   Have a great night and once again, thanks for a terrific day.
   Love,
   Mohammed Ali, Mike Tyson, Miesha Tate, Gina Carano, Ronda Rousey
   (aka: our famous fighter alter-egos!)

Artie's evening emails always felt like a sweet little mint on my pillow. Sweet. Comforting.

> ARTIE (email)
> Dear all-
> In the immortal words of *"Les Misérables"* (which we hope you all aren't), one day more . . . until our day off! But we're excited to see you all tomorrow first. Please note we have a 10:30 start time tomorrow, so everyone can enjoy sleeping a little bit later. Have a great night and stay dry!
> Love,
> Jean Valjean, Marius, Cosette, Fantine, and Eponine
> (Your NOT miserable stage managers!)

Waking up and heading to rehearsal was easy, largely thanks to Artie. You knew the feeling in the room would be just as friendly as his emails.[20]

Even on the difficult days. Like the one Luba Mason had early on in our process.

> LUBA MASON   The second rehearsal, Conor said, "So great, everybody can go home, but Luba, we want you to stay." So my heart started beating underneath and then everybody left and Conor says, "Okay, we're going to jam." I've had two drum lessons. And I thought, *okay, I'm going to get fired*. Second rehearsal. Second rehearsal! I'm going to get fired. They want to see what I can do.

As an actor, it's easy to feel like you are auditioning for the job even when you've already got the job.

> LUBA MASON   Marco [Paguia] pulled the piano over to the drum kit. Simon sat down next to me on the floor by the drum, by my seat. Conor pulled out his guitar and they had me sit at the drums and Conor just started strumming some song, I don't know. And he says, "Okay, give me a four."

Knowing Conor, Marco, and Simon, I'm certain this was a friendly jam session, but knowing how it feels being an actor who has said, "Yes, I have that particular skill" when you don't have that particular skill and you're now being asked to demonstrate that particular skill, I'm also certain this was a moment of pure panic for Luba.

> LUBA MASON   I was like, "What do you mean? What do you want me to do?" And they said, "Well, just the snare and the bass." And I just

---

[20]It wasn't a rehearsal "room," we actually rehearsed in The Martinson, one of the five theaters that comprise the Public Theater.

started doing that. And then Marco would come in with some chords and Conor would start playing. And then Simon would go, "Okay, Luba, now the hi-hat." So I add the hi-hat on two and four. And I just started doing that. Thank God I was wearing a cotton blousy shirt; I was sweating profusely under this shirt. 'Cause I was waiting for them at any moment to go, "Oh, she just can't do it. I think we got the wrong girl."

In a room not made so friendly by a stage manager like Artie Gaffin, this would be a moment where cruelty could enter. When an actor is struggling. I filmed a series of beer commercials in 2004 and the set-up was that I was a member of a band looking for a new lead guitarist; each commercial in the series was a different lead guitarist "audition." It was charming. We filmed in the middle of winter at an abandoned warehouse in Brooklyn that had broken windows and no heat. Our costumes were ripped t-shirts and jeans, and because it was so cold, you could see our breath, which the director obviously didn't want. A trick to solve that is to put ice in your mouth, which we did.

It was difficult and uncomfortable and freezing cold and still so much fun pretending to be a rock band. We were having a ball, me and my fellow actors. But cruelty crept in. The director mocked the actors and made us feel small if ever we struggled. I will never forget the time he asked me to laugh on cue, which is a difficult thing to do, try it. On my first attempt, the camera inches from my face, I failed pretty abysmally and instead of saying "Let's do that again," or "You can do better than that," this director made a disgusted face, rolled his eyes, seethed, "Never mind," and pulled the camera away to move on to something else.

Artie would never have allowed that. Luba was nervous and tense, but the room was safe, so she kept at it.

LUBA MASON   I just kept going. And whatever they threw at me, I was just doing it. We did it for fifteen minutes. And then I got a call from my agent the next day. he said, "Conor is thrilled with you. He's thrilled with you. He's so pleased that you're adapting to the drums." And I just went, *whoa, whoa*. Passed the test.

It's a stressful process, making a musical. Playful, sure. But stressful. Every actor carries his or her own level of anxiety—*Am I doing a good job? Is this song in the right key for me? Does the director hate what I'm doing? Am I going to be fired?*
Artie made it easier. Mostly through food.

LUBA MASON   More food than we wanted! More sugar than we've ever seen in our lives. Every day. Every day. He got specific, he figured out what each person liked. I said, "Artie, I can't eat this donut and this cookie and this candy bar!"

The "stage manager" is the overall organizer of the rehearsal room (and later, the performances). They're the camp counselor. The teacher on the field trip. The supervisor at the factory. Actors report to the stage manager, who communicates the schedule, calls the breaks, tracks the union-allowed hours of work, mediates conflicts. It's such a massive job that it takes an entire team including an assistant stage manager and a crew of production assistants to do it.

JEFF BRANCATO (Assistant Stage Manager)   It's hard to give a job description . . . Our job is to help.

Artie with his mussed gray hair and untucked button-down shirt with maybe a sweater over it was the opposite of cruel.

CONOR MCPHERSON   We were doing our auditions for the Public Theater production, and I remember Artie arrived to meet me at the end of a day of auditions, he was late. He'd been stuck in traffic. He'd sort of run up the street. I think it might have been rainy. He was all wet.

JEANNETTE BAYARDELLE   Artie was a godsend! [The rehearsal room] was just peaceful. Peaceful and respectful. And I think that's what, as artists, that's what we want. We want a certain level of peace because things could get chaotic.

CONOR MCPHERSON   And he came in and he was so committed, he wanted to come and meet and talk. And everybody at the Public had just been singing his praises so much and just talking about what a love [he was]. And I just immediately warmed to him. He was so not like your normal stage manager. He sort of was so unassuming and sort of gentle and quietly spoken, very kind and warm.

JEANNETTE BAYARDELLE   You're in this pressure cooker, and at any time anybody can snap or pop.

ROBERT JOY   And then the brunch appears!

Artie would show up hours before the cast to set up a full breakfast.

CONOR MCPHERSON   I don't know how he was doing it, but constantly laying out big buffets of food, which must have taken hours to organize and buy and prepare and lay out!

ROBERT JOY   And then he adds the complication of egg-creams, that only he really has the magic to mix. So, he finds himself going from person to person . . . to put the special chocolate syrup in and mix it with the plastic fork in a plastic cup. Just the perfect thing. And I'd never understood egg-creams until Artie mixed me one. And I thought, oh, this is what it is when they say food that's made with love tastes better. Well, that egg-cream was an extraordinarily loving egg-cream.

Always that sweet, funny email to the cast at the end of the day.

ARTIE (email)
   Dear wonderful company,
   Another great day. You all continue to impress all of us. Have a great night, and here is tomorrow's schedule.
   Also, congrats to Matthew who is getting married on Saturday! We wish you and your future wife the best of luck. And please feel better, Robert! We missed you today!

CONOR MCPHERSON But Artie also had this wonderful kind of steely side to him actually.

COLTON RYAN We were going to do an act one run and I'd always run five minutes late. But this day in particular, I was just so behind, caught in traffic. Fifteen minutes.

Artie would allow occasional lateness, but not a recurring pattern.

COLTON RYAN And I run up to rehearsal, fifteen minutes late, and I mean . . . there's literally the bagel spread out for our first act run through. And [Artie] says, "Cast, go to places and hold one sec."

CONOR MCPHERSON Artie would be very clear-sighted and he would tell you to watch out for trouble brewing.

COLTON RYAN And without physically grabbing me, just grabbed me and read me the riot act about the importance of being here. It wasn't some grand lecture about the idea of being on time or anything. It was just quite literally, "I'm disappointed in you."

CONOR MCPHERSON Artie was always right.

COLTON RYAN And I'd never seen that side of this man. So it broke me. And the next day, of course I show up five minutes early and I still think about this all the time, that he had a candy bar and he came up to me and just with a handshake, just put it in my hand and said, "I knew you could do it."

CONOR MCPHERSON You could see that he ran a tight ship, for all the generosity. He also had really good boundaries. He didn't tolerate any kind of lax attitudes, so he had very high standards.

COLTON RYAN I think about that all the time because I never was good with authority growing up. Shocker. So many times authority figures, they always reinforced negatively with me. They didn't understand me. And so for that reason, they didn't have patience or time to want to. And that man saw the good in every person, X-ray vision.

Artie would die on September 13, 2019, just months before we started rehearsals for Broadway.

A heart attack.

It still feels impossible that that is true.

Girl from the North Country was going to be his final Broadway show as a stage manager, he'd said. His plan was to retire afterward.

How could we have known we would lose him?

JEFF BRANCATO   After Artie and Conor met for the first time, Artie said they had the nicest conversation. That Conor was so easy-going and so mild-mannered. Artie was losing his hearing a little bit, and he especially struggled with accents. He told me, "I was so nervous to meet Conor because I'm so bad with accents." But it's almost like it was meant to be. Conor's accent was easy for Artie to understand. It just seemed like it was so perfect. And I think Conor offered him the job there.

The last time I saw Artie was at a performance of the musical *Rock of Ages* at New World Stages—Jeannette Bayardelle was starring, and I just happened to go to see the show the same night that Artie went. I hugged him and rabbited on about how excited I was to be making my Broadway debut. He said he was excited, too; for me, for the show, for himself, for Broadway.

He never left us, Artie, even after he'd gone. His ghost is in the play and always was and always will be. I still have all of his emails to the cast, which I offer here, interspersed; the memory of our time at the Public Theater, when Artie was still alive and the very *example* of a giving person, is haunted by his benevolence.

Would It Work Again?

LUCY HIND   That was my biggest fear. Did *Girl from the North Country* only work because of the [British] actors? Did it only work because it was new? How on earth were we going to recreate it?

I tried not to think about it in rehearsal, but it was unavoidable at times, especially when I was feeling lost: another actor already created this part. The original Elias in the London production was Jack Shalloo. A wonderful actor and singer. When I struggled in rehearsal, I would try not to ask myself *What did Jack do here?* because the question often led to *I bet he was better.* We all knew that the London production had been a hit. Sold out. People had won awards.

LUCY HIND   I certainly had a failing of confidence, what if I don't remember what I did? What if it only worked because of that formula?

Even the creatives like our choreographer Lucy Hind couldn't shake *what had been*.

LUCY HIND   I think everybody felt that a little bit . . .

Could we recapture *what had been*? Was that even our job? Or were we making something new again?

COLTON RYAN   It felt like maybe [the show had] industry excitement, murmurs—just the elevation of [being at] the Public. Which had its own kind of like, "Well didn't this already play very commercially in the West end? Isn't it kind of a strange move to go off-Broadway?"

There's a common shape to any rehearsal process: You start out on an excited high.

LUCY HIND   . . . but as soon as we got in the room and after one day of rehearsals, I thought, *Oh, the magic's here.*

And then as you dig into the work you begin to feel lost. What felt so exciting only weeks before now feels uncertain, incorrect. Maybe even *bad*.

COLTON RYAN   I loved it because the whole thing just felt subversive. It was like, we have multiple Tony nominees in here and yet it's somehow still a gamble.

JOHN SCHIAPPA   When we were down at the Public, I felt that Conor was finding and discovering new things, 'cause he was working with an American cast and American sensibilities . . . Musically, the whole thing felt like a session at a pub. Everybody's playing an instrument and singing and I mean, you layer on American sensibilities, what we know about the depression . . .

One "American sensibility," as far as actors go, is over-emotional acting. In college I played Miss Prism in a gender-blind production of *The Importance of Being Earnest*, one of the great English comedies by Oscar Wilde. After a particularly terrible run-through, the head of the acting department pointed her long finger at me and said, "And *you!* You gave that monologue about the baby in the handbag as if this were *MEDEA!* This is a *comedy!*"

ROBERT JOY   A couple of times I let myself explore [emotional moments] in rehearsal. And at the end of the play, especially when basically [Doctor Walker] is going to walk off and kill himself … Conor looked at me in the note session afterwards and said "God, it was like, you were going to break down crying or something!" Then I said, "Yeah," and he said, "Don't do that." He didn't really like emotional displays.

It's a hard moment in the process to get through. The scenes aren't clicking. You're second-guessing your choices. The beats aren't landing. Why did you say you could play the drums or sing forty-two high A flats? You over-act to compensate.

MARE WINNINGHAM   I loved those note sessions where he would just say, "I don't know what you guys are doing, are you having a moment? I don't want any moments. As characters, you don't know how you're going to get through the night. You don't have time to cry or whine or be sentimental."

This is the moment in the process that is the hardest to navigate.

MARE WINNINGHAM   "Try and get through the day. Try and get through the night. If you have to wonder about anything, wonder about how you're going to make it. But do not give me any of this reflection. I do not want you reflecting."

You have to keep moving through the discomfort.

MARE WINNINGHAM   I just loved those [notes] for everyone. I think it made everyone leaner, meaner.

This would become a theme of rehearsals. Conor offered up the metaphor of a bank. He'd say, "It's like we all have a shared bank account, and that account is this show. Every time you have an emotional moment in the show, you're withdrawing from that account, and every time you push through and don't allow yourself to indulge in one of those moments, you're putting in a deposit. Right now, you're all withdrawing from our account, and soon we'll have nothing left."
No crying and no long pauses.
Only deposits, no withdrawals.
Easier said than done.

ARTIE (email)
Dear tip top cast,
A tip top day as we learned the tip tops of Acts 1 and 2! We know you may not agree, but we think you already sound performance-ready!

Tomorrow we'll be doing more music, movement, and start some scene work and staging. And most importantly . . . we meet Kimber tomorrow!

KIMBER ELAYNE SPRAWL   I was on tour with *The Lion King* . . .

Conor and the casting department had found our new Marianne Laine in Kimber Elayne Sprawl.

KIMBER ELAYNE SPRAWL   Touring is what you make of it. People usually party a lot. But I had a huge spiritual awakening . . . I was finally starting to ask the universe for what I wanted and what kind of artist that I wanted to be. Because when I initially moved [to New York City], I just auditioned for everything. And I did get lucky, but I was begging people to put me in their shows. I wasn't actually going after things that I wanted to do. So I had a really great spiritual time with myself, really figuring out who Kimber was, not only as a human, as a woman, as a black woman, as a queer woman, but as an actor. And how that would translate once I got back to New York.

The day I met Kimber, my mind was preoccupied with Cincinnati, Ohio. In the few months between the reading of *Girl from the North Country* and rehearsals at the Public, I had gone off to the Ensemble Theater of Cincinnati to play the title role in *Hedwig and the Angry Inch*. Lynn Meyers directed. I've had a relationship with the theater since I attended the nearby conservatory, CCM, of which it turned out Kimber was a fellow alum.[21]

KIMBER ELAYNE SPRAWL   I just wanted to be on Broadway for so long. Then I was on Broadway, and I was just kind of like, *okay, well, what next?* . . . And I left *The Lion King* without a job. I put my notice in and everyone thought I was crazy, "Did you book something?" And I'm like, "No, I'm just leaving. I'm just going back to find what I need to find." And before I left the tour, I was offered my first principal contract to play Jane in *A Bronx Tale*. And I was like, *see, the universe answers you.*

CCM musical theater graduates are all over Broadway.

KIMBER ELAYNE SPRAWL   But before I even start the job, [*A Bronx Tale*] gets their closing notice.

I was in the classical music department, but some notable grads from the musical theater department in my day were Leslie Kritzer, Sara Gettelfinger,

---

[21]The College-Conservatory of Music at the University of Cincinnati. Yes, that mouthful is the name of the school. CCM, for short.

Shoshana Bean, and Karen Olivo. Kimber, continuing the proud tradition of CCM job placement, took the part in *A Bronx Tale* even though the show was closing. The show needed an actress to finish out the run.

On the morning she was to join us, we were all abuzz to meet Kimber—*Oh, she's in* A Bronx Tale. *She's incredible, Conor's very happy with her.*

KIMBER ELAYNE SPRAWL   When I was rehearsing for *A Bronx Tale,* I was getting better auditions because I'm playing this principal on Broadway . . . and *North Country* came in as replacing Samantha [Ware]. And I didn't know [the show]. I knew *Hamilton,* and *Hamilton* felt attainable to me. And I thought, I'm not going to do *North Country.* My agent thought I should read the script.

Artie had scheduled me for a 12:15 p.m. one-on-one music rehearsal with Marco Paguia, our music director, and I decided I was going to tell Marco what I had learned about my voice doing *Hedwig and Angry Inch* in Cincinnati. Hedwig sings a lot of high notes like Elias does but Hedwig's high notes are all G's, and G is one half-step lower than A flat.

KIMBER   I read the script near my house on this beautiful pier near the water where I would often meditate. And it was just a breath of fresh air. I'd never read anything like it before. I never felt anything like it before. And so I dropped everything to audition for it, to just put my heart into this.

"Duquesne Whistle" with its forty-two A flats was making me sweat. Like Luba and her drumming test—I was convinced that this was the day I would be fired. Adrenaline got me through the song at the reading, but now that I was properly working the music into my body, I knew the key was too high for me.

I noticed on the schedule that our new Marianne Laine was arriving that day and that she would be working with Marco right before I would, from 11:30 to 12:15. It did occur to me that my fellow CCM alum Kimber's first day would be my last. Bringing such shame to our alma mater.

So I was all nerve-and-panic when the vocal-rehearsal room door[22] opened and Kimber, wrapping up her session with Marco, stepped out and introduced herself. She has a beatific ease, Kimber, like someone who is already enlightened but who meditates anyway. Meeting her is easy and comfortable. I smiled and pretended that I wasn't about to be fired.

Kimber and I gave each other the secret CCM handshake, and she said she was going to sit just outside the door at the bank of empty chairs there and look over her script until she was needed at rehearsal across the street in the Martinson theater.

---

[22]The Public often used small rehearsal rooms across the street at 440 Lafayette, an NYU building.

She closed the door and I turned to face Marco.

My husband, Mark Subias, is a producer and artist-manager. He once said that a career in show business is "A series of humiliations with some occasional bright spots." As an optimist, he means this as an endorsement. Those bright spots are worth it, he believes.

Cue the series of humiliations.

I squawked and hollered my way through "Duquesne Whistle," knowing that Marco was either going to agree to change the key or give me my walking papers, and that my new castmate, a fellow alum of my beloved CCM, Broadway's Kimber Elayne Sprawl, was sitting just outside the door hearing everything.

"Actor fired and humiliated, Conservatory revokes diploma," read the headline in my head.

But cutting to the non-chase: Marco agreed instantly to lower the key and Kimber never let on that she heard me squawking.

These are good, kind people.

ARTIE (email)

Dear first-week finishers!

Thank you all for a great week one. Can you believe we've almost completed all of Act 1! At this rate, we'll be ready to open in a week and a half! (haha)

Enjoy a much-deserved day off and we'll see you all at 10am on Tuesday!

Like a Rolling Stone

OSKAR EUSTIS   I don't think Conor made some huge change to how he was approaching [the show] with an American cast. I think what happened is the American cast brought the American experience to it.

The "American" question seemed to be answering itself in the affirmative as rehearsals pressed on.

MARC KUDISCH   Conor came up to me during rehearsals at one moment, and he said to me, "So what do you think? Does it feel organic? Does it feel true? Does it feel American?" I looked at him and I said, "Well, yeah, it's American, it's Irish!" And I said to him, "What's more American than Irish?"

But the other question, the bigger question, was ... *What about Bob?* The invisible giant in the room with us?

SIMON HALE   Oskar [Eustis] was giving a speech, and he said, "Dylan's in our DNA." And he's talking as an American. Of course, I'm not an

American. I thought, *God, it's bad enough thinking about the responsibility, now I'm discovering that this guy's in your DNA, and there's me screwing around with it* . . .

It's not just America, but Bob Dylan's America that is at the heart of *Girl from the North Country*. People on the streets were calling us "The Bob Dylan show." Dylan fans were skeptical. Were we going to ruin Bob Dylan?

CONOR MCPHERSON We're not going to *explain* Bob Dylan or situate him in a way where we say *now this* [song] *makes sense*. You know?

"Bob Dylan." In quotes. Icon, self-mythologizer, the greatest songwriter in American history, the most annoying singer you've ever heard, genius, thief, truth-teller, rebel, fabulist, protestor, sell-out, better-acoustic, better-electric, has-been, innovator, past his prime, currently writing his best music; *whatever* he is to you, he's all of those other things as well. There are countless books about him, some *by* him. We all know who Bob Dylan is, and that fact alone says an awful lot about the man.

My friend Pamela used to burn playlists onto CDs for me of random songs she liked by different singers, and the one I always gravitated to was the Bob Dylan song—she always included at least one in every mix.

SIMON HALE As cerebral and brilliant as [Dylan] is, he's always in the moment about what feels right.

MARE WINNINGHAM So much of my musical awakening was [from] Dylan records. I had these older brothers that were very into him, and then a younger brother that . . . he went deep. He knows every record, and he's probably seen him live, I don't know how many times . . . The fact that I met [Dylan] when I have these brothers . . .

Mare and Jeannette, who would both be nominated for Tony awards for their performances in the show, would soon find themselves sitting backstage at the Beacon Theater with Bob Dylan himself.

MARE WINNINGHAM I had told Jeannette about her song "Gypsy,"[23] that my brother said "You know what that's about right? It's when he met Elvis in Vegas." So when we met Dylan, Jeannette said, "I heard that Gypsy was about when you met Elvis," and Dylan went from being this smiling man to—he just got straight-faced and said, "No. I don't know who told you that. People say shit. They say shit all the time. That's just not true." Because of something my brother said! So I told my brother

---

[23]The song "Went to See the Gypsy," Bob Dylan, from the album *New Morning*, 1970.

that, and we laughed at that, and of course he went and got the interview that Dylan did when he talked about meeting Elvis.

This is a classic Dylan encounter, *fact* instantly transforming to *mystery*. Bob Dylan is prismatic, he's multi-, we each have a version of him in our lives. I think of this Frankenstein's-monster invoking lyric from his recent album *Rough and Rowdy Ways*:

> I'll take the *Scarface* Pacino
> And the *Godfather* Brando
> Mix it up in a tank
> And get a robot commando
> If I do it up right
> And put the head on straight
> I'll be saved by the creature that I create[24]

This song, called "My Own Version of You," is a long song, like so many of Dylan's songs are; it holds tension like a lit fuse, slowly burning through verse after verse, a sustained threat. Not like a theater song at all, despite its dramatic imagery. It would never work as a theater song; theater songs have a narrative structure. I've heard them described as little plays.

Dylan's songs are not little plays, they're poetry, even his story-songs. He writes in waves of images that hypnotize the listener. They're meditations on a theme. Prayers. If they were in a hymnal, I would join the choir.

I'm a late-in-life convert. How could it have taken me over forty years to discover that I'm a Bob Dylan fan?

What about everyone else in show?

SCOTT SANDERS (Audio Engineer)   I taught myself guitar when I was fourteen, or whatever, thirteen, I was thirteen in 1969, I guess. So in '69 during that whole thing, I had taught myself guitar. "Blowin' in the Wind" was the first song you taught yourself because it was easy and you knew it.

LUBA MASON   I was not a big Dylan fan other than his hits. I was unfamiliar with a lot of the tunes in the show. So I only listened then to the ones that I knew to get a sense of maybe how his songs are going to be used in song and or how they were orchestrated.

KIMBER ELAYNE SPRAWL   I barely knew his music, to be honest. But now, man, just, I know he's a philosopher. He's that guy. He's so special to me, his lyrics just always undo me.

---

[24] "My Own Version of You," from *Rough and Rowdy Ways*, 2020.

I like to listen to Dylan when I'm alone, it's too private, too personal to share. Like a dream. I can describe a dream to you, but you won't know how it felt. And you won't be interested in how much it meant to me anyway.

But that was our task as a cast: to share Bob Dylan. Not only among ourselves, but for an audience. At a press conference in San Francisco, Dylan once joked that he wasn't a singer or a poet, he was a "song-and-dance man."

We were a roomful of song-and-dancers, how could we become poets?

Our orchestrator Simon Hale showed us the way.

Tom Nelis puts his hand over his heart when he speaks about it.

TOM NELIS That Simon [Hale] said, I'm only going to use instrumentation that was around in the 30s before Dylan's born, so we don't have to worry about folk music and we don't have to worry about rock music because none of it had happened.

CONOR MCPHERSON   Simon was very particular about that.

TOM NELIS   The music predates Dylan and *oh wow*. The sense is this is the music that would've been in his ears as a young man as he went on to write this thing. So it's an incredibly powerful thing that Simon decided to do that—he never had to compete with Dylan or with the *sound of Dylan* or anything.

A great orchestrator can translate textual themes into sound. Two theater examples I immediately think of are from the scores of *Sunday in the Park with George* and *Phantom of the Opera*.

In Stephen Sondheim and James Lapine's *Sunday in the Park with George,* the main character, George Seraut, is an artist inventing a new way of painting—dubbed "pointillism" by contemporaneous critics—in which the painter, George in this case, stabs at his canvas with a brush making tiny perfect dots that, when viewed from afar, blend together in the viewer's eye to form image and color. Michael Starobin orchestrated the score with a keyboard patch that sounds almost like a harpsichord. Though a harpsichord looks similar to and is played the same way as a piano, it cannot sustain pitches the way a piano can. The result is a sharp, pointed, stabbing sound for each note played, rather like the painting style of George Seraut. The music sounds like what we are seeing, making the orchestration itself a kind of aural painting.

The Phantom of the Opera, with music by Andrew Lloyd Webber and lyrics by Charles Hart and Richard Stilgoe, approaches the orchestration in a more literal sense. The Phantom, living beneath the Paris Opera House, spends his time either pestering everyone in the opera house or writing an original opus for his muse, the soprano Christine, at his giant, gothic organ. The organ, even when it is not seen by the audience, is ever-present in the score, thanks to orchestrations by David Cullen and Lloyd

Webber, reminding us of the Phantom's menacing grip on the characters in the story.

Both *Sunday in the Park with George* and *The Phantom of the Opera* have a particular "sound-stamp" thanks to these orchestration choices, lifting the shows from a generic "theater" sound to something singular and instantly recognizable.

How did Simon Hale approach this question for *Girl from the North Country*? The songs' lyrics are anachronistic in the context of the script, what about the *sound* of the songs?

> SIMON HALE I'd had an idea of using a Hammond organ, and so I looked up, historically, they were *kind of* early 30s. It's a great instrument used by Dylan, it's got a real gospel connotation. And I thought, *yes, this is fantastic*. And I said to Conor, "We use a Hammond." "Oh, I love that," he said. And then I woke up one morning, just thinking, *Nick Lane wouldn't have a Hammond in his house*. I mean, he wouldn't have a band in the kitchen either, to be fair. But if we just skip that, he wouldn't have [a Hammond organ].

Simon chose to anchor the sound in the instruments of the time period. More specifically, to the instruments available to the characters.

> CONOR MCPHERSON If the instruments were 1930s, that would help us. I thought, *oh, they had drums, oh, they had double bass*, so we could have bass and drums and the guitar.

Conor wasn't sure it needed to sound like the period.

> CONOR MCPHERSON I was always leaning towards the later sound, but because we were sort of getting away with it. There is something magical about when the music starts and people start singing—it goes outside of time, essentially.

> SIMON HALE It felt anachronistic to me. We needed to be dustier and cruder and more "old" than that.

A Hammond organ, which now seemed incorrect to Simon for the story, still felt correct to him for the sound. Which way to bend?

> SIMON HALE That's where the harmonium came from. This can give us our organ, if you like, in the case of a harmonium, a small one. But it's also a portable thing that a reverend would carry around to congregations, to play hymns.

You'll hear it at the top of "Like a Rolling Stone." An organ-like sound, but humbler. This is church, yes, but church in a tattered suitcase.

SIMON HALE   I remember going into the Old Vic, Conor was having a meeting with [set and costume designer] Rae Smith about the show and was saying that I had a really great idea about the Hammond organ, and how much she would really love it. I had to tell him, "I don't think we should use a Hammond, I think it's the wrong thing to do." And I explained why. He was disappointed, but he said, "I see what you're saying."

The harmonium gives the orchestrations—which would win Simon a Tony Award in 2022—a unique sound-stamp, as the harpsichord-like keyboard did for *Sunday in the Park with George* and the pipe-organ for *The Phantom of the Opera*.
Especially for Mare Winningham's first act solo: "Like a Rolling Stone."

MARE WINNINGHAM   Growing up and having Dylan be such a soundtrack of so many moments, your first make out session, the first time you have . . .

Mare blushes, pauses, and smiles.

MARE WINNINGHAM   *Blood on the Tracks* was of a period of time in my house. We got our musical gifts from my mom, she sang and played piano beautifully, and she liked the music we played, she was into it. But once my brother David was playing a Dylan record, it must have been, oh, whatever record was out . . . And my mom just said, "I don't get it. I just don't get it, it's not singing." . . . the fact that she would end up—that she would end up just so mad for our show, the music, mad for it all . . .

Mare's mother would pass away as we were reopening the show on Broadway for an unprecedented third time, the pandemic having forced two premature closures on us. I remember gathering as a cast in Mare's dressing room to sing "Happy Birthday" over FaceTime to Mare's mom, who, as Mare says above, loved our show and " . . . end(ed) up just so mad for all of it."

MARE WINNINGHAM   Yeah. Full circle.

COLTON RYAN   I remember distinctly halfway through the second week watching [Conor's] soul light up again. And that's when changes started coming in. And we would rehearse that. I remember it was really, it all kind of anchored around Mare's reimagining of "Rolling Stone."

The song "Like a Rolling Stone," arrives at the end of act one, and although different from the majority of the show's songs in that it was a recognizable Dylan hit, it stands as a great example of how the music functions in the show overall.
Shirley Henderson sang the song in the original London production.

SHIRLEY HENDERSON   Before doing the play/musical I didn't know [Dylan's] music was so tender and beautiful and amazing. I didn't know that. I knew some of his songs but I had never listened to them the way I finally listened to them, and I couldn't hear the tunes before the way I hear them now. That sweetness that was brought out, such sweetness in the melody. The melodies are so beautiful but you don't always hear it because of the style of the singing. To have been able to work with this material and discover the beauty of the songs and the stories they tell, I have such huge respect for it. I have come to it a bit late in life and I came with no preconceptions but I have been moved by the brilliance of Bob Dylan.

The dramaturgy of the "Like a Rolling Stone" moment is bizarre. Elizabeth Laine is a hard woman scraping by during the Great Depression and suffering early onset dementia. She's been sitting at her regular perch, an old wicker chair downstage right, and after a tense scene between Mr. Burke, Elias, and the preacher, Reverend Marlowe, she stands, grabs an old-fashioned microphone from somewhere, faces directly upstage, her back to the audience, and sings to no one.

The sixties lingo in the song stands firmly outside the period of the play, to say nothing of the rock beat in the drums, played inexplicably by Mr. Burke (Marc Kudisch), right in the middle of the Laines' kitchen. Some of the lyrics line up with the story, most don't at all. The plot is not pushed forward by what is lyrically revealed in the song. And though it is the climax of the first act, there is a lengthy scene that follows.

There is no gentle on-ramp, but rather a sudden crash into Elizabeth's mind via one of Dylan's—one of the world's—best known songs.

So, how does it feel?

SIMON HALE   Intimidating.

The moment breaks nearly every rule of musical theater writing.

SIMON HALE   Intimidating is a really good word actually, because . . . pre workshop and then rehearsals I was thinking, *What am I going to do? This song is iconic.*

Simon and Conor's goal in setting each of Dylan's songs in the play was not to break every musical theater rule they could. What was their goal? What was their guide? How did they know when they'd gotten it right, when every convention (per the notes given by Oskar Eustis) was telling them they were doing it wrong?

OSKAR EUSTIS   There were all sorts of things that I turned out to be completely wrong about. I kept saying . . . "You've *got* to have the actors singing to each other, not the audience like a concert!" Could I have been more wrong?

What made it feel so right to Simon?

SIMON HALE   Watching [Dylan] talking about himself as an artist, as a writer, and as a performer. Thinking about him as a young man coming to New York, getting up on those stages with the guitar and telling stories. All that was really useful for me. Not actually thinking about *what would Bob do?*—because that's not something for me to contemplate—but *how does he feel about his art? What's his ethic?* And at the end of it, just do what you think is right, do what you feel is the right thing. Because, as an artist, if you're thinking, *what would Bob do?*, well, who knows?

OSKAR EUSTIS   I realized I was applying this old, deeply-rooted sense of theater structure to something that was really pushing new boundaries. And there were just so many times when I gave notes or first responses that as the weeks went on, I went, *oh, no, I was wrong about that, Conor's right about that*, and how thrilling it is for an artistic director and a dramaturg to be patiently taught by the artist how to view his work.

SIMON HALE   So for me, it was just getting over that hump of this huge responsibility and privilege and everything else of working on this catalog, but then going, what do *I* think is the right thing for this point in this play and this piece of art?

MATTHEW WARCHUS   If you go right back to the origins of musicals, book-musicals where you're talking about text and then singing, text and then singing, you're in a very similar situation to a Greek play and also to a religious ceremony like a church service or even pre-church religion where there would be readings and text and little bits of story and then singing and sometimes some dancing and then more. So this is sort of a form, an ancient form of ritual. And that evolved, one part of it evolved into book-musicals and this felt like it was part of an ancient tradition. So I did think [the show] was much more of a ritualistic thing, kind of a bit Greek and kind of reminded me of a church service as well.

CONOR MCPHERSON   Matthew Warchus [had] said to me, "This is a church service." I mean, he got it quicker than I did. He said, "It's a church service with hymns." And I thought, *oh, okay*. And from that point on, I realized, oh, it *is* actually, it is.

SHIRLEY HENDERSON   Originally the musical was meant to be just a play where you walked to the front of the stage to sing a song. It was meant to have the feeling of a radio play.

MATTHEW WARCHUS   The weird thing about hearing Shirley sing ["Like a Rolling Stone"] is that without functioning in any literal way, and perhaps that's the key, it was a sort of abstract poetic overlay between the song and the narrative, rather than trying to literally tailor a narrative around a song or forcing the song to fit the narrative, which would've been hard to do. But it became apparent that in this sort of abstract poetic overlay version, the songs would really amplify the emotion of this story that Conor was writing. And I thought that was a surprise. And it's kind of rare that that happens.

Finding the original staging of the song was as tricky as finding the arrangement. The scene ends and the song starts. They are not connected by transitional material.

SHIRLEY HENDERSON   Every time we got to a song the question was "How are we physically going to get a microphone on the stage, how are we going to do this without it being clumsy?" There were a lot of ideas. "Try just walking on with it." "Try that it's already there before we even get to the song."

MATTHEW WARCHUS   It was very revealing how a song, in a drama, a song in a story, a song is a vehicle for feelings, emotions, ideas, and preexisting songs sometimes aren't good vehicles for those things. They weren't built to be a vehicle within a narrative. And so when you have a jukebox musical, sometimes it's kind of hard for the songs to further the narrative or to character development. They weren't designed to do it.

SHIRLEY HENDERSON   I don't think that was all fully worked out by the time we started performing it . . . "Shall we do it fast? Shall we do it slow?" We did it slow. We tried it really slow. And some people loved it and some were like "Oh let's see it fast." So we tried it fast and then it went crazy fast where I was reaching out for them—the girls—doing a rock and roll thing and lifting my skirt, just making stuff up. Anything to try to feel like Elizabeth.

MATTHEW WARCHUS   The first time I heard Shirley sing "Rolling Stone" was in the first workshop, and it was completely staggering.

LUCY HIND   Shirley's Elizabeth was, I mean, unreal, unexplainable; Elizabeth was this creature, this kind of feral creature. There was a moment in rehearsals with Shirley where she cut her hand and . . . she kept going and the blood was everywhere. And we were going, "Shirley, Shirley!"

Shirley's performance is wild and fearless. It feels on the edge of something.

MARE WINNINGHAM   I was petrified of "Rolling Stone" because I very much admired how Shirley did it and how powerful her voice was.

CONOR MCPHERSON   Shirley was such a lovely person, very modest, unassuming person. And she'd come to rehearse and she had this black anorak on. She was just kind of very quiet. And yet, when she would do her work, just this dervish exploded and it was incredible. It was like Patti Smith, it was punky.

MARE WINNINGHAM   I even said to Conor, "I hope this isn't a letdown" or whatever. And he kind of wiped that away and just said, "We're trying to find the right way for each person to sing these songs. We're not trying to build on another."

CONOR MCPHERSON   With Mare . . . she rooted [the character] in a kind of more recognizable person. You can see the echoes of a real intact life in there somewhere, only now it's fragmented. She's able to give you that in a beautiful way . . .

Simon and Conor wanted *Mare*'s version of the song, which they knew would be something different from Shirley's, as it should be.

CONOR MCPHERSON   I was saying, "Mare, you're Linda Ronstadt. You're, you're Joni Mitchell. You're not Patti Smith."

MARE WINNINGHAM   That was liberating, but it still left me feeling like, *but what were we going to do with this?*

It's a tall order: sing Bob Dylan's most famous song but make it your own.

MARE WINNINGHAM   We rehearsed "Rolling Stone" a lot . . . I went from the paranoia of, "Oh man, we have to do it every day because they don't know what to do with me, and it's not working!" to, "No, this is how they work. This is how, don't be an idiot. They want to switch it up."

It would take a lot of experimentation.

MARE WINNINGHAM   The original arrangement didn't fit my voice well.

Marco Paguia, our musical director and pianist, was the only creative in the room who hadn't been involved in the London production, so Shirley's performance wasn't in his mind. He saw and heard only Mare.

MARCO PAGUIA   I always feel like if you're going to try to force somebody, force another actor into the performance of somebody else, just get that other person.

MARE WINNINGHAM   I started to bring in all my favorite records that I thought—like the Linda Ronstadt records—that I thought would be a good voice-possibility for a version of the song. Some Emmy Lou . . . I have a folky voice.

MARCO PAGUIA   My gig was to facilitate where it wanted to go . . . Mare is a completely different singer, and she knew that.

CONOR MCPHERSON   So I was like going, "If there's a bluegrass version of this," or "if there's a country version of this, if there's a folk version . . ." So that was what we were trying to find.

MARCO PAGUIA   The music had to feel good.

We could all sense, as a cast, the significance of this song in the show and the necessity of getting it right. Although *Girl from the North Country* is an ensemble piece, Mare was really the heart of it. The "lead."

What often happens in a rehearsal room is that "the lead" actor sets the tone. If that person is cold and demanding or unpredictable or unkind, the rehearsal room becomes cold and demanding or unpredictable or unkind. Which poisons the process.

Mare is warm and generous. Open, thoughtful, and *kind*. Which set a tone of patience and generosity.

CHELSEA LEE WILLIAMS   We started working on "Rolling Stone" and . . . wow, Mare is *singing*. Who knew?

Oh, those who know, know. Mare has been recording solo albums since the nineties, and she famously sang in the 1995 film *Georgia*, for which she was nominated for an Oscar.

MARE WINNINGHAM   "Rolling Stone" intimidated me. I mean, it's the greatest rock song ever written.

It took us weeks to find the arrangement of "Like a Rolling Stone." For the rest of us, our solos were set, arrangement-wise. Maybe a key change here or there. But with Mare's big song, Simon and Conor worked tirelessly to find an all-new arrangement to fit Mare's style, a style different in almost every respect to Shirley's.

RACHEL STERN   I loved working all together to find the greatest thing and the fact that Simon was so open to it and Conor was like, "Whatever makes you feel like a fucking rockstar, we are going to do it." Change the key. Change the harmonies. Let's change the whole mood.

At some point in rehearsal every day, we would gather—the cast, Marco, Conor, Simon, Lucy, and Mare—to continue our search for "Like a Rolling Stone." Maybe a new groove, or a new order of verses, new harmony parts for the ensemble or all of the above.

RACHEL STERN   And I remember Mare, God bless her. She was like, "I feel so bad." And we were like, "No, it's amazing. We're doing something great here!"

These sessions were a masterclass by Mare in diligence and craft.

COLTON RYAN   I mean Mare's just such a singular artist, she's the nicest punk there ever was.

JEANNETTE BAYARDELLE   It's almost like the Bible, how they say the Bible is the living word, and everybody has their own interpretation.

Mare's humble determination was inspiring.

COLTON RYAN   There was this insistence, this really polite insistence on every single person just not relenting in their excitement towards the piece. That's what it felt like to me. It was like you've collected all these really eclectic players who all very uniquely do things . . .

During these "Rolling Stone" work sessions, Simon would take over the piano from Marco, and Conor would walk among us with his acoustic guitar in his arms. Suddenly the room felt like a songwriting session; we were the band awaiting instruction, and Conor and Simon were Lennon and McCartney.

ROBERT JOY   When Conor would get that look on his face! During a break he'd go over to Marco and say, "What if we did this?" "Yeah, let's play this." And he'd, he'd talk to Simon, and he'd take out his guitar and say, "Oh, yes! No, maybe not!" Or "Maybe so!" And then things would take shape in his head.

CHELSEA LEE WILLIAMS   And then all the different variations that we did of "Rolling Stone." Probably thirty different versions.

We had a four-week rehearsal process, more than enough time to put a musical together. As we neared the end of those four weeks and prepared to leave the rehearsal room for a week of tech rehearsal on stage, almost every element of the show save one was ready for the next step. "Like a Rolling Stone" was proving tricky. It's *the* moment in act one, and we couldn't find it, though everyone was determined to get it right.

LUCY HIND   ["Like a Rolling Stone"] is probably the most different [than the London production]. I think it definitely stemmed from Mare not being Shirley and then having to find it, which again, Mare had to go on her own journey.

A surprising key unlocked something for Mare.

LUCY HIND   She didn't want to wear a flimsy dress.

It wasn't just the arrangement of the song that felt off to Mare, it was her clothes. Actors often wear rehearsal-room versions of the costumes they will eventually wear in performance. It's a useful tool. Years earlier in London, Shirley Henderson zeroed in on her clothes as well.

SHIRLEY HENDERSON To me the colors were important. I wanted her to wear lipstick. Splashes of bright color. And her underwear. Something that catches the eye so that it's not all doom and gloom. There is a woman underneath all this and she will never be what she was but you might still like her.

MARE WINNINGHAM I was fighting with the dress . . .

As much as acting can be an inside-out process (exploring the mind of the character), so too can it be an *outside-in* process (exploring the physical state of the character).

MARE WINNINGHAM . . . this dress, what am I doing . . . ?

What you wear affects *how you feel*, how you move. You can try it yourself. Go to work in flip-flops. Or moon boots and a ball gown.

MARE WINNINGHAM I had a pair of culotte pants that I would wear to rehearsal. And Conor said, "I like Mare in that, when she wears those pants, can we just put her in pants?"

Eureka.

MARE WINNINGHAM And I remember feeling, *Oh wow, thank God!* It changed everything.

LUCY HIND Then Mare came in with this image of Bob Dylan's hat with all the flowers and the makeup that Bob Dylan wears . . . and then we looked at the folkiness of that and Mare's own folkiness. Her style and her nature.

What finally made it click, surprisingly: the costume. Outside-in.
Shirley had had a similar epiphany.

SHIRLEY HENDERSON I don't know what you did in [the New York] show, but I wore pale pink satin shorts, ankle boots, bare legs and a silk camisole with my bra underneath. I felt free in that. To me the underside is as important as whatever we find on top and that we can move and we can dance.

MARE WINNINGHAM It felt immediately right and helpful.

The day finally came when Mare, in her pants and her hat and her voice, found her "Like a Rolling Stone."

MARE WINNINGHAM   I remember Sydney [Harcourt] was outside the [rehearsal room] door because you couldn't come in while people were working, and he'd gone to the restroom and was outside. And I was singing the new ending, and for the first time I found something full-voiced, and Sydney came in and gave me a compliment. And it made me feel really good.

Mare's arrival with the song inspired Simon and Conor to make one final adjustment.

RACHEL STERN   I remember that one day of really figuring out those "Ahhs."

MARE WINNINGHAM   For me, it was all, when Simon showed up with that breakdown in the middle . . .

If you listen to the Original Broadway Cast Recording you'll hear it at minute 2:50.

SIMON HALE   I mean, talking about the added vocals in the latest version [of "Like a Rolling Stone"] with Mare, I would say that that's a little image there of Simon Hale feeling more comfortable about it, about himself.

At the climax of the song, the beat falls away as Mare holds the last syllable of the refrain, "Like a Rolling Stone," and the ensemble sings an a cappella choral "ahh" that feels like something taking flight. Over the next sixteen measures, the band members enter one by one back into the groove as the choral "ahh" unfolds and develops like a chorale from a Bach Mass, while Mare, still on the vowel of the word "stone" rips and tears an improvised melody that is somewhere between keening and praising.

I get full body goosebumps when I hear it. There's Mare Winningham, standing in her full, unique power as Elizabeth Laine, in pants, the struggle of finding this moment adding kaleidoscopic depth to her vocals, and then here comes Simon Hale, meeting her head-on with a complex choral arrangement even he never saw coming.

SIMON HALE   As a musician, that [choral part] is definitely me thinking *I can do something now I didn't believe I could do before.* And I've, I've never said that to anyone else before actually.

It's hard to believe, but before *Girl from the North Country,* Simon Hale had never written vocal arrangements. Orchestral, yes. String, yes. Band, yes. Vocal, no. He discovered that part of himself during this process.

SIMON HALE   I know that suddenly I felt different.

We all did that day.

Has Anybody Seen My Love?

Here's the glass-of-milk question.

Besides "Like a Rolling Stone," the other big solo in act one is "Tight Connection to My Heart (Has Anybody Seen My Love)," sung by Marianne Laine, adopted daughter of Elizabeth and Nick Laine.

SHEILA ATIM   My reading of the script when I auditioned wasn't that Marianne was an adopted daughter. She was a daughter.

Sheila Atim played Marianne in the original London production, and Kimber Elayne Sprawl played Marianne in New York.

SHEILA ATIM   So my understanding, or at least my assumption, was that people of many identities were being seen for that role, including white actors as well. So actually for me, from my perspective, in terms of things that changed [in the script after the workshop] that are really notable to me, was the addition of some discussion around race, which appears in the play.

Marianne Laine is a young Black woman living as the adopted daughter in an all-white, midwestern family in early twentieth-century America.

OSKAR EUSTIS   It was my initial feeling [when the show was in rehearsals in London] that having a Black Marianne was not something you could naturalistically justify in Duluth in the early 1930s. I was from Minnesota. I just knew that this idea of a Black girl being raised by a white family would be so utterly anomalous that there was no demographic historical truth to it. But Conor A.) insisted that she was Black and B.) insisted that he put in a story to explain . . .

SHEILA ATIM   I think Conor handled it really deftly. Because there's enough of it to shine a light on that as a situation without having it being on the nose and unsubtle. I'd sort of go to him with a thought or an idea and he'd kind of just go away and then come back and then the script was different.

OSKAR EUSTIS   And I'm glad Conor won that one, it turned out to be a brilliant choice.

In the first scene of *Girl from the North Country*, the shoe-mender Mr. Perry, who, according to Mrs. Neilsen ". . . must be seventy years old if he's a day," arrives at the Laine's boarding house with a small bunch of flowers. Mr. Perry has been invited there by Nick Laine so that he might propose marriage to Marianne, who is nineteen years old. When offered a drink, Mr. Perry requests a glass of milk, which he holds in his free hand, the other hand being occupied with the sad little bouquet. Here is how Nick describes adopting Marianne:

> *MRS. NEILSEN comes back with a glass of milk.*
>
> MR. PERRY: Oh, thank you.
>
> ELIZABETH: You're welcome.
>
> NICK: You know how Marianne came to be our . . . how she came to live here, right?
>
> MR. PERRY: I heard something . . .
>
> NICK: This couple checked out. Left a bag in the room and you know what was inside?
>
> ELIZABETH: Marianne!
>
> NICK: Marianne! She was only a baby. Tiny little thing. I mean we tried to find the parents, but . . .
>
> ELIZABETH: Nick stuck her in an orphanage while I was sleepin' didn't ya?
>
> NICK: Well, I . . .
>
> ELIZABETH: Stuck her in a home. Twenty little kids in cots in one room. No glass in the window, no-one taking care of 'em. I went straight down there—took her back out. I had to.
>
> NICK: There was glass in the windows.
>
> ELIZABETH: He'd already lost one baby girl.
>
> NICK: Ah, it seemed the best thing was to let her stay and work here right? No-one ever came back. I mean. She works here.
>
> MR. PERRY: You're good people.
>
> NICK: She works here. So . . . [25]

Nick is trying to find escape routes for his children, because he knows the house is collapsing around them, literally and metaphorically; the pipes are bursting and the bank is repossessing. Not only does he wish desperately to marry Marianne off to Mr. Perry, a hail-Mary lest she be left homeless, he presses his son Gene, an aspiring writer, to take a job, *any* job, on the railroad.

---

[25]McPherson, Conor, *Girl from the North Country*, Nick Hern Books, pp. 23–4.

GENE: Yeah, what is it? Punching tickets?

NICK: What do you care? You know what other guys'd do just to get in the door? Just to sweep the damn platform? I ain't gonna tell you the favors I had to pull. Had to sweet talk an old girlfriend.[26]

Neither Gene nor Marianne wants the life that Dad is pushing so hard for, and it is the source of their conflict.

Complicating the matter for Marianne is the fact that she is pregnant. And though she will be one of the only characters to have a "happy" ending at the play's conclusion, when we first meet her, we know that Marianne Laine is nineteen years old, adopted, Black in a *very* white world hostile to Blackness, pregnant, and talking with an old man to whom her father, she now learns, has all but promised her in marriage.

It's a lot for any young person to handle. I asked both Kimber and Sheila how they approached the character.

KIMBER ELAYNE SPRAWL   I don't know, how did I begin thinking about Marianne? I think that in some way that I began to—I think I just discovered our likeness. She just reminded me of myself.

SHEILA ATIM   Every character is fighting for something and they're fighting very hard. I think that's why the backdrop of the Great Depression is perfect, because stakes are high immediately . . . I mean, for me, that moment with Mr. Perry—a young woman at nineteen being married off to a guy in that circumstance and of that age is crazy in any case. And then for me, the racial undertones of it just became even more alarmingly stark.

Tom Nelis, who is fit, trim, agile and striking—he played Captain Ahab in Dave Malloy's *Moby Dick*—played the ailing shoe-mender, Mr. Perry.

TOM NELIS   One of the things I didn't know is what was Conor borrowing from what he'd already seen and what was he letting me find?

Some elements of the show went through major transformations in the American rehearsal process, "Like a Rolling Stone," as we've seen. But one element . . .

TOM NELIS   So when he said "Hold that glass of milk," I thought, *oh, this is fabulous.*

. . . small and seemingly insignificant, a simple glass of milk, arose organically in rehearsal for both productions, London and American, as if it were an unbreakable strand of the show's very DNA.

---

[26]McPherson, Conor, *Girl from the North Country*, Nick Hern Books, p. 45.

TOM NELIS   I also said at the same time, *I wonder if this* [glass of milk] *was already in the show.*

Mr. Perry, alone with a visibly uncomfortable Marianne, doesn't so much propose marriage to her, but more of an arrangement that includes marriage.

SHEILA ATIM   And really the thing that really helped me in that song was the glass of milk that was instrumental.

Marianne says *no* to the proposal, in so many polite Midwestern words, and Mr. Perry, upon leaving, insists that she "sleep on it." Instead of offering her the flowers he's holding in one hand, he gets confused and offers her the glass of milk he's holding in the other. But he doesn't notice he's made this mistake as he shuffles off self-satisfied, still clutching his small bouquet.

TOM NELIS   That's Mr. Perry. Flowers that are dying throughout the course of the show, but he never manages to give them away. And that's the character in a way, never really manages to unburden his heart or whatever, his sorrow from having lost his own wife. And so I assume that that has always been part of the show. A very powerful thing.

And there is Marianne. Stuck holding this confused old man's strange offering and facing a complex predicament. Just then music enters; the band plays the stark introduction to "Tight Connection to My Heart (Has Anybody Seen My Love)."

SHEILA ATIM   It always felt sticky because before singing the song, I'd have to put down the glass of milk. So I always had it where he gave it to me, and I just sort of sat there with it. And then I put it down and it felt weird.

It's the iconic image of the character: Marianne Laine, just beyond girlhood herself and with child, holding sustenance in her hand, as if outside of herself. The imagery of Mary, the Mother of Christ from the Bible, creeps in here . . .

SHEILA ATIM   I've never really thought about it before, but there was something about putting the glass down that felt like I was "preparing" for the song. And I think the big key to success around this show is that the songs, relatively speaking, don't feel "prepared." They kind of happen, they fall out of these moments.

. . . There's no room for Marianne in the inn . . .

SHEILA ATIM   I remember once we were asking kind about the logistics of something in some scene, and Conor said, "Guys, there's a drum kit in the kitchen." And we were all like, "Oh yeah, fair enough." He said, "Don't worry about it, guys."

. . . When she's asked who the father of the child is, her answer is essentially "the wind" . . .

SHEILA ATIM   Throwing away that kind of marriage to logic, hard logic, and allowing ourselves to really build that world—in the way that I think magical realism works, if you want to call it that—can be difficult to do because it's not full blown fantasy, it's just a flavor of something that's a little bit out of the ordinary.

. . . And because this is a musical, she sings about all of this, but because it's Dylan, it's cryptic and poetic.

SHEILA ATIM   And where do you draw the line, how does that rule work? It's challenging. So you just have to kind of surrender and trust in that.

> I'll go along with the charade
> Until I can think my way out
> I know it was all a big joke
> Whatever it was about
> Someday maybe I'll remember to forget . . .

> Has anybody seen my love?[27]

SHEILA ATIM   And I just remember one time singing the song I asked Conor, "Can I just keep the glass of milk in my hand in the song? Is that weird?"

KIMBER ELAYNE SPRAWL   I did listen to Sheila sing the song. And I thought she was beautiful. I was just enamored with her, but I knew that I couldn't be her. You know what I mean?

SHEILA ATIM   And he said, "No, try it." And then I did. And then it was just perfect.

A similar conversation to Mare's with "Like a Rolling Stone." How can Kimber make "Tight Connection" *Kimber's* version and not just a copy of Sheila's version? And how did Sheila even make it *her* own to begin with?

SHEILA ATIM   At the time, ["Tight Connection"] was just another song in the piece that had to be learned, it had to be orchestrated. And we

---

[27]"Tight Connection to My Heart (Has Anybody Seen My Love)" Bob Dylan, from *Empire Burlesque*, 1985.

were working with Bob Dylan's music, which is often very speak-singy, and the melody is sometimes barely there. And that was definitely the case with "Tight Connection." If you listen to the original, he kind of speaks it pretty much.

The song, from Dylan's *Empire Burlesque*, has a distinct 80s sound, production-wise. It's a mid-tempo dance, rife with flashy guitar solos between verses, and, to Sheila's point, has no discernible "melody" in the verse. Dylan's idiosyncratic sing-speak is in full-force.

In *Girl from the North Country*, "Tight Connection" is perhaps the most transformed song, arrangement-wise; Marianne's quiet, unadorned and mournful version a stark contrast to the original Dylan recording.

SHEILA ATIM   The day that we came to look at it as a song, Conor played a bit of guitar and he was like, "I'm thinking kind of *this*."

SIMON HALE   I mean Sheila . . . what she did in creating Marianne's vocal part in the verses in particular is down to her and her brilliance.

SHEILA ATIM   We were figuring out all of the songs, we just kind of did a sing through at first where we are all just going wherever the melody takes us. And then they would say, "Okay, well yeah, go home and do what you want."

SIMON HALE   That song is a bit of a mystery, how it kind of happened actually. Sheila had a great deal to do with it . . . we just got in there and just made it what it was.

SHEILA ATIM   Simon Hale did such a brilliant job of accommodating people's voices, orchestrating around that, and then encouraging that even further. So there was a real symbiotic relationship. And it's, people always say, "How did the song 'Tight Connection' come about?" and it's a very hard thing to pinpoint, because in my head, suddenly it was just a song. There was a day when it wasn't a song, and then there was a day when it was a song.

It seemed to all that the arrangement came through Sheila fully formed, almost as if that's how it had always been.

And so did the glass of milk.

KIMBER ELAYNE SPRAWL   There was a time I didn't have the milk, when I did the scene. I would set it down and sing the song. And then one day, maybe a month into rehearsal, I had just forgotten I was holding it, and I ended up doing the whole song with the cup in my hand. And I was like, *oh man, I forgot to put the cup down*. I think I remembered halfway through the song, but it was too late because I was far away from the table, and I didn't want to backtrack. And Conor was like, "No, leave it. I like it."

Both Kimber and Sheila arrived independently at holding onto that glass of milk. It's even in the clip of Sheila singing the song at the Olivier Awards.

SHEILA ATIM   I remember asking my stage manager, our company manager for the Oliviers, "Can I? I need that glass of milk!" So she made sure I had it. I just don't even know if the song works if I don't have . . . will I be able to sing it if I don't have it? Is it going to be like Samson's hair?

Because the moment arose organically in rehearsal, Kimber assumed the idea was hers.

KIMBER ELAYNE SPRAWL   And then I went back to see the video, and I was like *she does have a cup.*

But maybe it was Kimber's idea. As it had been Sheila's idea before.
This is the glass-of-milk question. Which feels bigger than a should-she-or-shouldn't-she hold a small prop in a play. It feels somehow like the ur-question of humanity. What is predetermined?

CONOR MCPHERSON   I want it to be the actor's idea as much as possible.

What is fated?

CONOR MCPHERSON   Because when people are close to what their own thought process is, then there's really not a lot of acting needed.

Do we have free-will?

CONOR MCPHERSON   They're kind of already in that place. It's instinctive and they're not reaching hard.

Is it possible for Marianne Laine to sing that song without a glass of milk in her hand?

KIMBER ELAYNE SPRAWL   Everything was kind of mysterious and just worked in that way.

Is every decision really just an inevitability?

CONOR MCPHERSON   I think the audience can just feel how real that is.

Are we all just waiting for that slow train coming?

Harmonica/violence

It wasn't only Luba Mason who had to learn a new instrument. Marc Kudisch also had to learn the drums, and I had to learn the harmonica. We Burkes made a lot of noise.

Marc is a skilled musician. He learned to play the bass guitar for *Fucking A*, picked it up right away, easy, and the same was true with the drums. When Elias dies in *Girl from the North Country* and sings "Duquesne Whistle," his father, Mr. Burke (Marc), is at the drums, driving the rhythm of the song like a train conductor. Like Luba, Marc was able to *act* while playing the drums, and in this instance, his acting was several contradicting layers deep: joy at making music with his son, devastation at his son's death, horror, relief, guilt, shame, pride. All while laying down a groove.

> MARC KUDISCH   I felt I was responsible for the beats, the rhythm, the pace, the song has to have a solid backbone. But the joy of playing—your joy became my joy on the drum in some ways. I just wanted to make sure that the rhythm, that the tempo was never behind. What I just felt was that responsibility. That you were being given what you needed in that moment.

In the Thanksgiving scene that leads to the revelation of Elias's death, the specter of unspeakable violence is invoked. We know that Elias has died, but *how* did he die? Mr. Burke was the only one there when it happened, and in his drunken, confused ramblings, which unexpectedly segue into a joyful gospel number by the ghost of his son, Mr. Burke seems to half-confess that Elias's death was his doing, or if not his doing, somehow his fault, or at the very least the result of horrific negligence.

> MRS. BURKE: (*Turning off the wireless*) Francis. Where's Elias?
>
> MR. BURKE: He's sleeping. I told you. We went for a walk is all. Went for one of our long ones. Down for a look at the water.
>
> MRS. BURKE: Where is he, Francis?
>
> MR. BURKE: I told you.
>
> MRS. BURKE: He's not here!
>
> *She goes out again. We hear her calling for ELIAS.*
>
> DR. WALKER: Where is he Frank?
>
> MRS. BURKE: (*off*) Elias!
>
> MR. BURKE: The water was like iron.
>
> MRS. BURKE: (*off*) Elias!

DR. WALKER: Where is he?

MR. BURKE: It was an accident. That's . . .

MRS. BURKE comes back

MRS. BURKE: Where is he?! Where is he?

MR. BURKE: It was an accident. I couldn't stop it.

Silence

NICK: What happened Frank?

MR. BURKE: He's on the shore, Nick. He's asleep.

Silence

MRS. BURKE: . . . What?!

MARLOWE: Oh Mrs. Burke.

MR. BURKE: Where's your God now, Reverend huh?

MARLOWE: He's everywhere.

MR. BURKE: That's right.

MRS. BURKE: Are you kidding me? Are you fucking kidding me?

NICK: Frank. What happened?

MR. BURKE: The water was like iron.

MRS. BURKE: You fuckin' . . . You fuckin' . . . You didn't even . . . (*She goes to Mr. Burke, starts thumping him with her fists.*) You didn't even say nothin' you never said a goddamn thing! You dirty bastard![28]

Marc carried all of that to the drums.

As for me, I took harmonica lessons from a man way out in Red Hook, Brooklyn before rehearsals started at the Public. I hadn't anticipated how complicated the instrument was, I don't know why. Everyone knows how to play the harmonica, you just put your lips together and blow. *Wrong.* There's theory and technique and finesse, and sure, some people, like my friend Ben Mayne, just pick it up and start playing like they've been doing it for several lifetimes. I had to practice.

Elias hides a toy harmonica in his pocket at the table in the breakfast scene, and when Mr. and Mrs. Burke begin arguing with each other so aggressively that all other conversation in the room ceases, Elias puts the toy harmonica to his mouth and makes as much unmusical noise with it as he

---

[28]McPherson, Conor, *Girl from the North Country*, Nick Hern Books, pp. 86–7.

possibly can, like a toddler might by banging silverware on the table. Mr. Burke, in the first bit of violence to erupt within the family, slams his hands down on the table, yanks the toy harmonica away from Elias, and screams, "Jesus Christ, Elias, not at the table!"

The violence turns to love and back to violence again and again with Mr. Burke and Elias.

At the top of act two, the cast enters and instead of launching directly into a scene, we sing Dylan's "What Can I Do for You?" a hymn of gratitude, and "You Ain't Going Nowhere," a song of earthly pleasure. In the middle of "What Can I Do for You?," Elias steps downstage with the harmonica to his mouth, and though he'd just only caterwauled with the instrument up till now, he plays a simple, beautiful tune.

But underneath any beauty lurked violence, always.

Right near the end of our days in the rehearsal room, Marc Kudisch and David Pittu and I were working on "the fishing scene," a pivotal act one scene in which the audience learns that the Burkes are perhaps on the run, fleeing the consequences of a violent act Elias may have committed against a young woman. As Mr. Burke and Elias prepare a fishing rod for an afternoon outing to the great lake, Reverend Marlowe does some fishing of his own, hopeful he can use the Burke's predicament to his advantage:

MARLOWE: Yes it was last spring. There was a terrible story goin' around. About a poor girl's getting attacked up in the woods. Suspicion fell here and there. Some said this, some said that. Someone even said maybe it was a man or child didn't know their own strength. Maybe was a little feeble in his mind. Who can say? You know how it is with rumors. A family by the name of Shepherd. You hear anything about that?

MR. BURKE: No, can't say I have.

MARLOWE: These things can happen so easily. I once officiated at a funeral for an infant whose own mother had crushed him to death with an overly fervent embrace. Can you imagine?

MR. BURKE: That's terrible.

MARLOWE: Life is terrible.

MR. BURKE: It sure can be.

MARLOWE: But you and your wife seem united. And that's the main thing, I guess.

MR. BURKE: What you driving at?

MARLOWE: I ain't out to cause trouble. World's already full of trouble. But like they say there's a man going round with his wife and his grown son saying he lost his business. Maybe that's just what he's saying. Maybe he's been moving round 'cause he's got something to hide.

MR. BURKE: You're in the wrong garden Preacher.

MARLOWE: Maybe. But I got to be where I am. Just like the next man.

MR. BURKE: Train's leaving son. Whoo whoo. Couple up.

MARLOWE: Five hundred dollars should do it. Say five o'clock tomorrow. You meet me here, fine. If not, I'll call by the precinct. Just tell 'em what I know. Look at that! The sun's coming out.

MR. BURKE grabs MARLOWE. ELIAS starts sighing repeatedly. His high-pitched sighing is almost a cry.

MR. BURKE: Now you listen to me you son of a bitch. You want to threaten people, you want to get your due, I'll give it to you. You so much as say a god damn word about me to anyone I'll cut your fucking throat. You keep your lies to yourself. I don't know a damn thing what you're talking about.

MARLOWE extricates himself.

MARLOWE: WhooWee. Then what you getting so riled up about? Huh? Good day. I'm famished. Five o'clock tomorrow. May your catch be bountiful Elias.

MARLOWE puts on his hat and leaves. MR. BURKE angrily takes the fishing rod from ELIAS.

MR. BURKE: Elias what are you doing? Gimme that! Look! You took 'em all off! Goddamn . . .

ELIAS sits quietly for a moment, then his face contorts and he silently cries. MR. BURKE sees him.

MR. BURKE: Hey that's alright. Daddy didn't mean to shout. That's alright.

He holds ELIAS. ELIZABETH just watches, then switches on the wireless. A harmonium begins to play "Like a Rolling Stone."[29]

This is how we rehearsed it, because this is what the script said. Marc would shout at me "Elias what are you doing? Gimme that!," etc., and I would contort my face and silently cry as per the stage direction.

But it didn't feel right. And so much of what Marc and I were doing everywhere else in the play *did*. The choice I'd made to be constantly hanging on Marc, grabbing at him, tugging on his arm, or nearly choking him with hugs, created the tension we'd hoped for. But this moment of crying just fell flat, it wasn't "working."

---

[29]McPherson, Conor, *Girl from the North Country*, Nick Hern Books, pp. 54–5.

At this particular rehearsal, we got to the part where Mr. Burke explodes at Elias with "Elias what are you doing? Gimme that!" and before I could silently cry, Conor said: Why don't you just pick up your father and slam him on the table?

"Excuse me?" I said.

I didn't know how to "just pick up [my] father and slam him on the table."

Conor said, "You're a giant, just overpower him."

It was one of those precipice-moments in life: you feel yourself suddenly standing on a dangerous ledge. Yes, obviously, this was the correct choice, I am a giant, 6'6" tall, so pick Marc up and slam him on the table. Yes. I just didn't know how to do that. I got scared. This was more than grabbing my father's hand too tightly, or squeezing his neck too hard, this was big violence.

"Okay," I said. "Great. I . . . I'll just need some time to figure out how to do that . . ."

But we were out of time. At least in the Martinson Theater. Rehearsals were at an end. That was it. It was time to move to the theater.

Shit. Just as I was feeling *ready*. Ready with my character choices, ready with my song, my harmonica, my entire *track*.

There's a line in the Laurie Anderson song "The End of the World," from her album *The Ugly One with the Jewels* about how prepared her grandmother was to die when her time came, how *excited* she was in fact to be at the end of life because she would finally get to meet Jesus. She had been preparing all of her life and was in no way afraid. But right at the last moment of life she ". . . panicked because she couldn't decide whether or not to wear a hat."[30]

That was me. Just when I thought I was ready to pass over from rehearsal to the stage, I panicked. Like Laurie Anderson's grandmother, I "went into the future in a panic."[31]

But with Kimber's glass-of-milk moment in hand.

And "Like a Rolling Stone" tailor-perfect on Mare.

And Luba and Marc's drumming snug in their pockets.

Lines (mostly) learned, harmonies tight, and choices made, we were ready to press on.

I would just have to go into the future in a panic because the end was here. Time to go.

Artie laid out one final feast in the room; a goodbye and a greeting to what was and what was to come.

---

[30]"The End of the World," Laurie Anderson, from *The Ugly One with the Jewels*, 1995.
[31]Ibid.

3

Downtown

The Stairwell

New York City in September of 2018 was unusually hot, which I didn't mind. 57th Street in Manhattan, where I live with my husband, is a twenty-five minute nearly straight-shot bike ride to the Public Theater; you zip down 9th Avenue which becomes Hudson Street after you cross 14th, then you lean into an easy drift left onto Bleecker Street where you can then rip through Greenwich Village ringing your bell at delivery trucks, taxis and distracted pedestrians all the way. You cross 7th Avenue, then 6th, then press on through NYU-land, which straddles the West and East sides with its ever-expanding real estate. Pedal eastward faster to really get the westside behind you, pick up some speed and just when you pass Mercer Street Books & Records on your right, squeeze your brakes because you've finally made it to Broadway.

Well, kinda.

It is the same Broadway as the light-bright one forty blocks north in midtown, yes, but this is *down*town Broadway. And you can't take *down*town Broadway *up*town to Times Square because the traffic flows one way the other way, and since you don't want to battle oncoming city buses, taxis, and a flood of one-way Manhattanite drivers, you'll have to press on for now to the next avenue over, Lafayette. Lafayette is where you make your first and only hard turn to the left, look up, and there's the Public Theater, two blocks away, its giant banners flying.

This was my daily ride. I'd lock up outside the Public next to Luba Mason's cruiser or Stephen Bogardus's hybrid or Tom Nelis's classic—so many of us in the cast rode our bikes to work. Then, drenched from that heat, I would bound through the heavy glass door, smack face first into the shock of air-conditioning, and glide through the Public's lobby to the secret actor entrance, a door that opened on a stairwell to the underground backstage/dressing room area of the Newman Theater.

This stairwell had a fantastic echo, and for some reason I almost always found myself in it alone whenever I arrived for a performance. Leaving after a performance each night was a different story; this same stairwell would be crowded with cast members heading up to see friends in the lobby or famous people coming down to say hello to actors they knew in the cast, usually Mare. Val Kilmer came to the show twice, and I passed him each time, post show, on this stairwell; him coming down to see his friend Mare Winningham, me going up to unlock my bike and make the reverse trip home.

ARTIE (email)
    Dear all,
    Thanks for a really terrific first preview. It isn't a secret that the audience loved you all and the show, proving what great taste these first previewers have!

Sleep. Wake up, do it all again: Zip down 9th Avenue! The ride was fast, hot, loud, and chaotic, lots of bell-ringing and horn-honking; I usually had one ear-bud in so I could listen to music. It was a calorie-burning commute, sweaty and a pleasure. 14th Street, drift left. Bright. Crowded West Village. Distracted pedestrians. Hot pavement. NYU, Mercer. Broadway. *Down*town. Lafayette. The hard-left turn. Look up, there's the Public. Lock up, shock of air-conditioning, lobby, slip through the secret door into the cool, echoey stairwell. Down one flight, down another, all alone, a closed door at both ends, a perfect echo chamber, my body still vibrating from the streets outside.

I was in my best-ever form, vocally and physically. The new key of "Duquesne Whistle" had settled nicely, those forty-two high G's were *fun* to sing, and just to prove it to myself, I'd belt out one long high G all the way down the stairwell. And the echo! Like the sound effect of a science fiction transportation device. A few giddy bounds down from Manhattan streets to a different world altogether.

The greenroom down there was dark and shabby but comfortable, reminiscent of a dormitory common-space. Half of the cast was in one dressing room, the other half in the other, a long mirror in each along the wall with a chair for every actor and just enough space for make-up and a few personal items.

Cozy.

A greenroom is a kind of waiting room, a *purgatory*. You could sit on the couch, you could take a shower if you needed (as I definitely needed), you could have a coffee or a conversation or you could meditate, stretch, write, read, text. Ultimately: you could *wait*. Wait to hear Artie, over the intercom, saying "places."

At last, we were out of the rehearsal room and ready to take the stage for preview performances. With costumes and lights, the band, microphones, scenery. All of it.

A paying audience waiting to see what we'd made.

Were we ready?

The Audience

JEFF BRANCATO   I remember the first preview: the show is lit in a very dark sort of way, very intimate. And Jeannette went upstage to pour milk and she came offstage and said, "I just poured milk all over the floor because I couldn't even see the pitcher."

Not everything went perfectly at first . . .

JEFF BRANCATO   And we said, "Okay, note taken."

. . . but this is what previews are for, figuring out what's wrong and fixing it. So Jeannette got a little more light upstage the next night.

I worked with a stage-combat expert on picking up Marc Kudisch and slamming him on the table. You learn violence by breaking it down into tiny movements: touch the arm, lock eyes, grab the collar, move together stage-left step, step, step, hands on neck, hop, slam, move neck and hands together up then down, left and then right, choke, choke, roll-eyes, gasp, every micro movement stitched together and then eventually sped up to look naturalistic and dangerous.

What distinguishes the "preview period" of a show from the "run" of a show is that during the preview period, the show is still technically in rehearsal.

ARTIE (email)
   Dear super second-night-previewers,
   Congrats on another show in the hole . . . too soon? #ripleonora[1]
   We think you're all terrific and can't wait to see you at rehearsal tomorrow at 12:30. Thank you again for your patience and focus throughout these long days. How lucky are we to get to continue developing this wonderful show?
   As always let us know if you have any questions or need anything!

   Love,
   Artie, Jeff, Kaelyn, Sam, and Cheyney

   PS- Tomorrow is primary day! Don't forget to vote!

The audience for a preview performance sees the full show, complete with all technical elements, musicians, cast, etc. But the director, producers, designers are all in the audience watching as well, taking notes, so that they

---

[1]A bit of gallows humor. Leonora is a character from Nick Laine's past, his sister who died tragically when they both were young. Nick was meant to be minding her and she fell into a taconite hole.

can gather together for a post-show meeting to discuss what issues should be addressed the next day.

For me, beyond my foray into physical violence, the first preview marked my initial encounter with Elias's death. And that exit to God.

My bike-ride home that night was unsafe. I was so rattled by what I had experienced onstage that I couldn't concentrate on the road. Elias dies. I die. And I exit the play, as if I'm exiting life; Elias transcends to the world beyond the play, and the world beyond the play is *this* world. My world. Once he's through that door, Elias becomes *me*.

It reminds me now of a night I had during the pandemic, which I ended up turning into a song for Amber Gray called, "I Don't Know About You."[2] I was sleeping, dreaming, and in my dream a voice told me to "transcend." I told the voice that I didn't know how to transcend and the voice said, "Oh, it's easy. You just close your eyes and say, 'My name is Maine.'" My husband and I were living in Maine at the time in a house we'd bought in 2019 just months before the world shut down. To "transcend," according to the voice, I essentially had to say aloud that I *am* the place where I am. So I did what the voice said; in the dream, I closed my eyes and I said, "My name is Maine," and I felt myself *transcend* from the dream to my real-world bed in Maine, where I opened my eyes and gasped. The voice was right. I transcended.

I couldn't sleep after that.

Transcending from Elias's death to my life was what I was thinking about riding my bike home, a surefire way to transcend my way to the Emergency Room if I didn't pay better attention to where I truly was: traffic.

ARTIE (partial email)
    Rehearsal tomorrow in mics, but NO costumes/hair/wigs, from 12:30-4:30pm. We will start with mics and notes in the green room.

Our trouble in previews was *pacing*. We were slow and soggy and the show was overlong. To use Conor's bank metaphor, most of us were taking withdrawals.

MARE WINNINGHAM   All the way to previews [Conor] would tell us, "I can tell whether the show was good or not by the timings. And I know you're going to think that's base or too simple, but it's just true. Because when it starts to spread, I know you're taking moments and doing that thing that I don't want you to do."

Conor tried another metaphor: *Crowd the fucker.* Which meant, don't allow space around lines. Push each other. Crowd each other, psychically.

---

[2]From the Broadway Records release *Artists in Residence,* 2020.

MARE WINNINGHAM   And that really, really worked great for [my character] Elizabeth, especially her anger. And so all of that acting stuff, that acting stuff was going well. I felt like I was really having fun figuring stuff out.

COLTON RYAN   I remember during the first week of previews and [Conor] was like, "Hey guys, this is good. It's good. Last night it was two hours and twenty minutes. Tonight it's going to be two hours." And we were like, "Okay, where are the cuts?" And he said, "There's no cuts."

How do we take twenty minutes off the run-time without lines being cut?

COLTON RYAN   And I remember just thinking, *well, good luck with that.*

I told my friend Sherie Rene Scott once, after seeing her perform her autobiographical Broadway musical *Everyday Rapture,* how great I thought the show was. And she said, "Is it? I've never seen it."

She was making a joke, of course, but she had a point. When you're performing onstage, you can't know how the audience is experiencing you. Sherie was right, you never *see* the show you're in.

We were performing *Girl from the North Country*, but none of us saw it. Conor did, every night. But a note like "Take twenty minutes off of the show" with no lines being cut by the playwright can feel, frankly, *ridiculous*, not to mention impossible. What, are we all just supposed to talk faster?

In a way, yes. To Sherie's point, since we don't see the play ourselves, we have to trust our director.

COLTON RYAN   The most electrifying thing was actually experiencing an experiment like [Conor's note] *working.* At two-hours-and-twenty-minutes, we would get people to stand at the end of the show and they'd be clapping and they'd be nice. And then we would do it in *two hours* and they would leap to their feet screaming, tears, just screaming for it.

We could feel the difference onstage, we knew Conor was right. The show felt better faster. No withdrawals, only deposits.

Some actors struggled with remembering lines, which slowed things down and added to this *spread* that Conor was fighting.

JEANNETTE BAYARDELLE   It is so important that we take care of each other in those moments.

Watching Jeannette Bayardelle balance her own performance and a scene partner who was struggling with lines was a lesson in generosity. These performances were more than just a preview of our show, they were a preview of how we as a cast would function when things got difficult years later.

JEANNETTE BAYARDELLE I knew that my assignment at that moment and in every show was to take care of this person, was to help carry this person through whatever they were dealing with. And I feel like it's really important to be sensitive to stuff like that. Because that could be me in the future. You know what I mean?

Three-and-a-half years later we will close on Broadway for the second time (we will open and close still a *third* time, believe it or not), and Jeannette will apply this same wisdom to the situation. It will be in January, 2022, we will just have gone through the worst months on Broadway; the Omicron variant has knocked out most of the cast, our understudies are covering every possible role they can, the audiences are small and masked and scared. Broadway has "reopened" but seems close to collapsing again due to dismal ticket sales and sick casts. There we will be, the cast of *Girl from the North Country*, at the Belasco Theater, in the beautiful greenroom that the producers have decked out in a costly retro design: long sofas, a bar, records and games, a photo of Bob Dylan on the wall. We will have just finished a performance for a small audience, and Tristan Baker, our lead producer, who's flown in from London just for this meeting, will break the news that we are closing. Closing *again*. All of our heads will drop in absolute defeat. Except for Jeannette's. She will see this moment as something necessary for us to survive. Ever the prophet, she will predict, in a rousing, impromptu speech, that it isn't over, that we will be back.

But in October of 2018, we were just getting started, just learning what our characters felt like on the stage.

LUBA MASON I remember the first time I did my dancing thing . . .

Luba is tall and lean, a dancer, and she created for her character "Laura Burke" a distinctive, noodly way of moving.

LUBA MASON . . . and Conor had our notes session during the day, I remember him coming—this was before rehearsal—he and Lucy were coming at me and I went, *oh fuck, they didn't like the noodle dance. He's going to tell me not to do it.*

Previews are the time for actors to take big swings.

LUBA MASON And he just came up to me, him and Lucy . . . And I said, "What? It's too much. It's too much. I'll cut it. I'll cut it."

Sometimes the big swings miss.

LUBA MASON Conor said, "No, no, this is great for the show! Do it!"

But sometimes they connect.

LUBA MASON That's when I started to inject some *comedy*.

Of course, the big question we *all* had was, "Do they like us?"

ROBERT JOY After we started performing, I realized how powerful the show was.

LUBA MASON The feedback was odd. Some people really loved it.

OSKAR EUSTIS There were, of course, some people who didn't respond to it.

LUBA MASON There were some people who I knew, they were just kind of like, "What is this about?"

OSKAR EUSTIS The vast majority of people were shocked by how much they responded to it. My wife, who was dreading the show, honestly, doesn't respond to Dylan. And when she saw it [at the Public], it became her favorite show that we've done for years, because she suddenly saw why her husband loved Bob Dylan.

Did they like us? Well, *yes*. And a little *no*. The houses were packed and the ovations were standing.

OSKAR EUSTIS Because we're hearing you sing it, because we're hearing all of this incredible cast sing those songs in those orchestrations that really focus on the characters and the humanity of the songs. So Dylan fans loved it. And people who hadn't loved Dylan suddenly loved Dylan.

I would rush up that echoey stairwell after each show, excited to see whatever friend had been in the audience that night.

DAVID PITTU The show gave me the best kind of distraction from what I was going through in my personal life, not to mention the general disease I think we all were suffering at that time known as Trump.

I remember going to a musical adaptation of *Romeo & Juliet* by Matthew Dean Marsh on the day the election was called for Trump, and the audience sat in complete silence before the show began. No one spoke, we were all too crushed.

Not everyone loved our early performances of *Girl*.

LUBA MASON   I had several friends come that right at the beginning of our previews and then never bring it up.

I had a friend do something similar. She emailed me to say that she was coming to the show that evening, and how excited she was. Then when I saw her after in the lobby, she talked about anything and everything except the show I had just performed in and she had just seen.

LUBA   I had a friend who saw the show, and I said, "So what did you think?" She said, "I loved your wig."

But mostly, *yes*. People loved it.

Email from a friend:

> Just saw your show. I AM FLOORED!!!!!
> Brilliant, moving, so inspired.
> Xo

ARTIE (email)
> Dear There's-No-Stopping-How-Great-You-Are Cast,
> You made it through another 2 show day ... with only one more of these to do ... this weekend. Thanks for 2 terrific shows.
> Tomorrow, to celebrate opening, there will be a bagel brunch hosted by Mr. Marc Kudisch and Mr. Arthur Gaffin (You may know him as "Artie"). All we ask is that you bring your appetite. We will be all set up by noon!
>
> Have a great rest of the night.
>
> Love,
> Artie, Jeff, Kaelyn, Sam, and Cheyney

The Judges

In the final week of previews, leading up to the opening night, the show is "frozen." Meaning, no more rehearsals, no more changes. This is it, this is the show. Ta-da.

Now the critics come.

I can't decide which is better, which is worse: In London, shows have a "press night." It's the equivalent of our "opening night" in that friends and family come to one gala-like performance and stay for a party afterwards, but it's also the night that every single reviewer sees the show. The show's critical reception hangs on just that one performance.

In New York, reviewers come over a handful of shows in the days leading up to opening night. For a week of performances, you know they're out there scribbling down their reactions, but you don't know exactly *which* night *which* critic is there. It's a full week of review pressure, but not all of that pressure is on one performance.

Both systems are horrible. Reviews are horrible. Or they're wonderful. They're like the weather. Unpredictable. You could get perfect sunshiny days for your family vacation, or you could get a tornado on your wedding day. You can't guess, and you really can't do anything about it, anyway.

In 2010 two shows that I'd written got absolutely trashed in the *New York Times*, which was hard for me to accept, especially because they were my first shows to be reviewed at that level.

My husband said, "Look at it this way: You got a terrible review in the *New York Times*, you're in great company."

He was right. There's a book I love of bad reviews theater artists have received, compiled by Dame Diana Rigg, called "No Turn Unstoned." Take, for instance, the review of *A Streetcar Named Desire* by Tennessee Williams, considered by most to be a masterwork of modern theater:

J.C. TREWIN (review in the *Observer*)
   Now and then good writing glimmers, but little to explain the Broadway reputation and run.

CONOR MCPHERSON   When the critics came . . .

LUCY HIND   I was standing with my agent downstairs at the Public around that reception area having a drink [on opening night].

The Public threw the opening night party in the lobby of the building. If that sounds unglamorous, it was actually a good time.

LUCY HIND   I looked up to the balcony and someone was calling me, I think it was Tristan. And he said, "Come now." And Sherri, our assistant director, lifted up her phone. She was saying, "Reviews are out."

There comes a moment at an opening-night party when one of two things happens: either the music gets louder and the dancing begins; or, the room goes quiet and people start leaving. It all has to do with the reviews; they start appearing online at around ten o'clock.

CONOR MCPHERSON   . . . when Ben Brantley saw it again . . .

Ben Brantley of the *New York Times* had not been convinced by the London production. He had not thought that the show, which was telling a very American story, was at all *American*.

LUCY HIND   I just remember looking over at people's heads going, *this is the moment. This is the thing.* I went upstairs to The Library, and we'd been gathered; we walked in and it was very quiet.

"The Library" is the name of the bar and restaurant on the second floor of the Public Theater. A quick story about that name: Years ago while on a lunch break from a rehearsal of my musical adaptation of *The Winter's Tale*, I was sitting on the steps outside of the Public Theater, just enjoying the sun. A family of tourists, visiting from Eastern Europe (my guess, listening to them speak) approached me politely and one of the women asked, "Is this a library?" I looked at the posters advertising the Scott Z. Burns play that was running, thought about the bar/restaurant on the second floor, regarded the building itself and said, "Well, there's a play running right now called 'The Library' and the bar on the second floor is called 'The Library' and this building itself used to be a library, but *no*, this is not a library."

She turned to her family and didn't bother translating what I'd said. They walked away.

History is the ultimate judge of art, of course, as with *Streetcar Named Desire*, but on our opening night in 2018, the gavel was in the hands of a few critics.

LUCY HIND   I thought, "Oh no."

But before she could panic, Lucy heard the music get much louder in the lobby; the verdict was in and the critics were nearly unanimous in their praise. Even Ben Brantley changed his mind.

CONOR MCPHERSON   [Brantley] was like, *Oh, okay. I kind of can see it now.* Which was great.

LUCY HIND   And Oskar said, "Congratulations, we're going to Broadway."

BEN BRANTLEY   (review, *New York Times*)
    . . . last year, when I saw "Girl" on its opening night in London, with a British ensemble straining for Americanness, the script often felt labored and imitative.
    With a uniformly excellent American cast that wears its roles like confining and prickly skins, and on a smaller stage, "Girl" feels far more convincingly of a piece.

JEANNETTE BAYARDELLE   I remember when we opened, and we had gotten that love letter from, what's his name? Bill Brantley. Ben . . . What's it? Ben Braley?

Ben Brantley.

JEANNETTE BAYARDELLE   Okay. That name. I remember we got that love letter.

BEN BRANTLEY (review, *New York Times*)   You may find yourself thinking that this is as close as mortals come to heaven on Earth.

JEANNETTE BAYARDELLE   And I remember driving home after the party and I just started crying. Sobbing. Sobbing. And I didn't know what I was sobbing about.

We danced and danced in front of the box-office in the Public's lobby.

Successful opening nights off-Broadway quickly become all about *Broadway*. Everyone wants to move uptown.

LUCY HIND   Someone said, "And this is Aaron [Lustbader]. He'll be taking us to Broadway."

Aaron Lustbader is a general manager with Foresight Theatricals.

AARON LUSTBADER   A general manager always does the budgets for a show. Contract negotiations, understands union agreements, and sets a schedule that should work within them.

He sits very still, Aaron, too still. As if he's moored to something. As if he knows about a coming storm that you don't.

AARON LUSTBADER   On this show, we were also the executive producer, which merges with the general manager in terms of giving some high level strategy, expertise, recommending who key partners would be, such as the advertising agency and the press agent and what have you.

I was in the lobby dancing and having no idea that the powers-that-be were upstairs talking the nuts and bolts of a Broadway transfer.

LUCY HIND   I sat with Conor and with Simon, both Simons, and with Rae[3]. And they told me stories of Broadway. And it was amazing because they'd all done Broadway. And Conor told us about his first Broadway show. We spent the whole night, the rest of the night right there, planning, scheming.

Of course, I'd never forgotten my agent's original email with the line, ". . . their goal and plan is to transfer to Broadway following the Public run . . ." It hovered daily, but rushed to the forefront on opening night when I caught Jeannette Bayardelle's eye. Through a cautious smile she said, "It's a rave."

---

[3] Simon Hale, orchestrator, Simon Baker, sound designer, and Rae Smith, costume/scenic designer.

JEANNETTE BAYARDELLE   Maybe I knew something was coming . . .

Jeannette's prophecies around the coronavirus would become something of an inside joke with the cast. She sounded alarmist, but was always right.

JEANNETTE BAYARDELLE   . . . but that night I saw it as excitement. Because we put so much into it. And to have that [rave review], it was such a great feeling. But at the same time, I just was crying uncontrollably driving home. And I didn't understand why. It was joy, but then there, it was almost like I knew of a load that we would have to carry, which I don't even, because that's what it felt like. We made it to this point, but now we have ways to go to the next point. That's what it felt like.

ARTIE (email)
Dearest opening night cast-
Congrats to you all on an absolutely spectacular and special opening night show. It was so great to be a part of the show tonight, watching you all do this show for those you love and care for who were in the house . . . and the ones who love you the most backstage!
Enjoy your much-deserved day off tomorrow, and we'll see you for a plain-old show call on Wednesday! We have a 7:30 show, so 6:45 fight call, 7:00 half hour!

A nice day off. And then . . .
Zip down 9th Avenue! Tear through the Village! Pass Broadway (with a hopeful glance uptown). Lafayette! Lock up! Lobby! Stairwell! Greenroom! Costume! Places!

DAVID PITTU   I remember getting a sense of the power the show had when we would go out into the lobby after each performance. I mean, there were the people we knew and our friends, yes, who either liked it or didn't like it . . .

New York City is a theater town. Everyone goes.

DAVID PITTU   . . . but then I remember people who were total strangers, along with the more famous strangers like Jessica Lange, who I think came three times . . . her tear stained face, and Michael Moore, who was not someone I expected to see at the Public! And it really hit me that there was something about the show that was, I don't know, like an AA meeting, a place for people who had the same problem—I don't know what to call it, Trump sickness?—to go to mourn the country, you know what I mean? Because it was Dylan music, from the generation who thought the world was ending *back then*—in the sixties and the seventies! And then to have to endure Trump! And we hadn't even gone through the pandemic yet! And you could just feel how much people appreciated it. All that beautiful crazy Dylan music and poetry. It was like church. Better. There was something so uniquely beautiful about it.

KIMBER ELAYNE SPRAWL   I think [the Public] was our hottest time.

RACHEL STERN   It felt, well, it felt *downtown*. You know, that wonderful feeling of downtown theater. There's a freedom . . .

We were always aware, in that fall of 2018, when there was a notable person in the audience, because the show would start late. Artie would announce over the intercom that we were "holding for the house."

On those days, we would start the show ten minutes late. During act one, one of us, usually Rachel Stern, would spot the *somebody*, and by intermission we would all know who the somebody was. "It's Sting." "Paul McCartney's here." "Angela Bassett, fourth row."

CHELSEA LEE WILLIAMS   Sarah Paulson, one of my favorite actresses. I remember her. I took a picture with her. And Bryan Cranston. I remember being so awkward: "Can I have a picture with you, please?"

Sometimes, as with Angela Bassett, Bryan Cranston, Chelsea Clinton and even Justice John Roberts, we got to say hello to the somebody in the greenroom.

Other nights, as with Sting and Paul McCartney, only a lucky few of us got a close-up glimpse. There was a special VIP entrance to the theater that wound the guest through the backstage left wing into the house, avoiding the crowds in the lobby. This was also the VIP's exit, which meant that the actors stage-left at the end of the performance would cross paths with the VIP as they were escorted out.

CHELSEA LEE WILLIAMS   That was the first time I ever experienced that kind of, I mean, we had the rock and roll greats come to the show. Sting!

Jeannette was one of the lucky stage-left actors. She would say things like, "He's the guy from U2, right?"

JEANNETTE BAYARDELLE   I grew up in a Haitian household, okay? A lot of these people, I did not know who they were.

This drove Rachel Stern crazy, both not bumping into rock stars, and Jeannette's unstar-struckness.

RACHEL STERN   I had to exit stage right. So I never got to meet anyone!

I adore Rachel Stern. One of my favorite details of her Broadway career is that she played an egg in Jeanine Tesori's musical adaptation of *Shrek*.

RACHEL STERN Also, I never really looked out into the audience except for in your song, Todd, in "Duquesne Whistle." We would flip around and the light was bright and I remember seeing Bono. And I knew it was Bono because all I saw were these circle, purple glasses—that's Bono! . . . I really wanted to meet him.

CHELSEA LEE WILLIAMS Yeah, icons were showing up, and it was always like, *okay, this person has a security detail.*

DAVID PITTU Oh and Annette Bening. She definitely came to see it more than once. Something about the show sort of melted people. They seemed very approachable in the lobby afterward, less standoff-ish than people usually are after a show, kind of lonely. And Justice John Roberts came and we actually took a photo with him! I was shocked to see him there. An old Dylan fan I guess. I wish I could have had a few minutes with him to talk seriously. Of course this was before Ruth Ginsberg died and the Supreme Court reversed Roe and let's not go there . . .

My husband and I ran into Annette Bening at the Tony Awards in 2019. We were standing near the stage at Radio City Music hall, milling about during a commercial break, and there she was with her husband what's-his-name, Warren Beatty. Mark said hello to them (Mark knows everyone) and I reached out my hand to introduce myself to her as the actor she saw in *Girl from the North County* and she stopped me and said, "I know who you are!"

As was the case with the London production, the rave reviews and the great word of mouth translated to ticket sales.

OSKAR EUSTIS It sold exactly as well as *Hamilton*.[4] The frenzy wasn't quite as much, but when you can't keep a ticket in the house, that's selling out. And that was the same with *Hamilton*.

So. We were a hit.
And Annette Bening knew who I was.

The Stranger in the Hoodie

JEANNETTE BAYARDELLE Okay . . .

Jeannette knows I love this story.

JEANNETTE BAYARDELLE . . . what happened was this . . .

---

[4] We were performing in the same theater where *Hamilton* had premiered, The Newman.

The first question people ask me about *Girl from the North Country* after they've asked (and I've answered), "Did you play Bob Dylan?" ("There was no 'Bob Dylan'") is "Did Bob Dylan come to the show?"

CAITLIN HOULAHAN   From what we were told, the Public always saved Bob Dylan a seat because they never knew if he was going to come to see the show. But he was in town playing at the Beacon Theater, I believe. So we knew that there was a chance.

I love answering "Yes. Yes he did."

COLTON RYAN   I remember when we had super cool people come like Paul McCartney, we would hold for eight minutes or so and then . . . we held that one that night, that last Saturday, whatever, for seventeen minutes. Right? No one said anything. But I knew, I was like, *it's him*. It's got to be.

There are a few key players in the story who made contact with Dylan: Jeannette Bayardelle, Mare Winningham, Mandy Hackett, and Scott Sanders.
    The rest of us were in the building the night he came to the show, but Jeannette and Mare and Mandy and Scott had encounters with the man. And we who didn't gathered around them to hear the tale, like cold hands around a fire desperate to be warmed.
    Several weeks prior to the night *he* came to the show, Jeannette suggested the possibility.

JEANNETTE BAYARDELLE   I did *The Color Purple*[5] with Carol Dennis; Carol and Bob [Dylan] have a daughter, Desi. And I had been in communication with Desi on Facebook. I think it was Facebook. And I'm like, "Girl, you've got to come see this show, girl. You've got to come see your Daddy's show!" And she said, "I'm coming, when I come to New York, I'm going to come." Because she lives in California.

Jeannette gives her friends' names more emphatic vocal italics than she gives any celebrity, including Bob Dylan.

JEANNETTE BAYARDELLE   So then I remember Mare saying that she was going to see Bob Dylan in concert [at the Beacon Theater].

Not only was Dylan's daughter going to be in town, but Dylan himself would be here.

---

[5]Musical adaptation of the Alice Walker novel.

MARE WINNINGHAM I have to give Jeannette props. She's the reason we got to meet Dylan. [My husband] Tony bought me four tickets to see him at the Beacon. He bought me them in August for a Monday night in November, knowing we would be in the middle of the run. . . Jeannette and I sat next to each other [in the dressing room] and she asked if I was going to go [to the Bob Dylan concert at the Beacon]? And I said I was . . . And she said, "Should I?" And I said, "Yes, you should go. You're in the Dylan Musical!"

JEANNETTE BAYARDELLE And I was like, you know what? I'm going to get a ticket. It doesn't make sense—how could we be doing a Bob Dylan show and not go see Bob Dylan? I need to get a ticket. So I got a ticket.

Jeannette decided that she and Mare needed not only to see Dylan in concert, but that they also needed to go backstage and meet the man.

MARE WINNINGHAM She buys a great seat, and later she asks me to find out from Conor if we can go backstage to meet him.

JEANNETTE BAYARDELLE I said to Mare, "We have to get backstage to see Bob Dylan when we go see the show [at the Beacon]."

MARE WINNINGHAM I tell her "we are never gonna go backstage to meet Bob Dylan, it's not gonna happen, it's not like going backstage to meet someone after a play, it's Bob Dylan and he doesn't do that." She made me ask anyway.

JEANNETTE BAYARDELLE [Mare] sent the email to Tris[tan] like, "Hey, Tris, *Jeannette* wants to go backstage . . . ," and I thought, "It's okay, Mare, you can blame me!"

MARE WINNINGHAM I kinda threw her under the bus when I wrote to Conor— "Jeannette wants to know if . . ."

JEANNETTE BAYARDELLE And the initial message that she got back was "Oh, well, it's tight backstage at the Beacon. So, it's a 'no.'"

This was not surprising to anyone as Bob Dylan is famously reclusive.

JEANNETTE BAYARDELLE That Saturday matinee [Dylan's daughter] Desi came. And I saw her in the audience, she sobbed the entire show. The entire show. She came backstage, and I said, "You got to get your dad here! Get your dad here, get your daddy!" And she said, "I'm going to see him tonight and I'm going to tell him to come."

Then on November 28, 2018, the day before Dylan's concert at the Beacon Theater, the impossible happened.

JEANNETTE BAYARDELLE   I get this message, I can't remember who it was from [on the creative team], but it said, "I don't know what you said or what you did, but [Dylan]'s coming to see this show." So I knew when he was coming. I think Mare knew. I don't know who else knew.

MARE WINNINGHAM   I didn't know.

SCOTT SANDERS   There was rumor that he might come. He was in town to do his concert at the Beacon. So the minute his concert got to town, I went down to the local store, and bought a bottle of his booze [Heaven's Gate] and had it there with two glasses sitting on my little table next to my console by the desk there. Cause I knew if he was going to sit there, either I'd see him walk in or they were going to put him back there with me.

MANDY HACKETT   Conor called, I think it was a Saturday, and he said, "Mandy, I'm going to give you the name of Bob's road manager, he needs to come and look at the theater because it looks like Bob's coming tonight to the show."

Associate Artistic Director of the Public Theater, Mandy Hackett, was used to managing a VIP.

MANDY HACKETT   I got [the road manager] on the phone, and I said, "Why don't we meet at the theater at one o'clock or something? I'll show you around." So we get to the theater, and he was very clear that Bob was going to sneak in the second before the show started and that he wanted to sit in the last row on the aisle.

This was going to be trickier than Sting or Bono.

MANDY HACKETT   And then we made a whole plan for intermission: I would be right there to take him and sweep him upstairs to the second floor where the offices are, wait with him, and then bring him back down right before act two went up. And then do the same thing at the end of the show—just whisk him right out. We made this plan that he would be in the car with his guests, and when we called "places," I would text them and he would come in.

And a harder secret to keep.

MANDY HACKETT   And I remember they told me, "You can't tell anyone, literally *any*one that he's coming." And I said, "Well, I have to tell the house manager." "No, he won't come if you tell anyone." And I was like, "I have to tell Oskar, because Oskar is the biggest Bob Dylan fan. Oskar will be at the theater tonight, can Bob Dylan say hello to Oskar?" "You can't tell Oskar that he's coming."

Poor Oskar.

MANDY HACKETT   I thought, *you know what, I have to tell Oskar.*

OSKAR EUSTIS   So Dylan came, and I was told in no uncertain terms that I was not even to approach him.

MANDY HACKETT   And Oskar said, "Well, do you think I can meet him?" I was like, *I don't know.* I said, "If you want to try to just be around when he comes in, you can meet him." We tried to figure it out. I remember sitting on the mezzanine level with Oskar, having this conversation with him. And I felt so badly because I know how much Oskar loved him. So we decided, *Okay, let's just play it by ear. We'll feel it out.*

SCOTT SANDERS   And sure enough . . .

MANDY HACKETT   So sure enough . . .

SCOTT SANDERS   [Dylan] did come.

MANDY HACKETT   . . . we get to "places," I text, they swoop Bob Dylan in.

SCOTT SANDERS   He walks in with two other people, in a hoodie, fully in a hoodie. But all I had to see was his profile.

MANDY HACKETT   He walks in looking like a Jedi master. He had this black cape on with a hood, and he had a few people with him, and they whisked him in.

SCOTT SANDERS   I typed back to the girls [backstage] "Guess who's here." And they typed back to me, "No!" And I said "Yes." And then I said, all right, now I got to do two things: I got to keep one eye on him, and I got to make sure I mix the best show I've ever done.

MANDY HACKETT   And he was sat in the last row house left, on the aisle. And then Oskar and I came and sat on the steps and watched.

CHELSEA LEE WILLIAMS   That was the giveaway: Oskar sitting in the aisle, and I remember him being there like pre-half-hour looking very nervous. And I was like, *This is the leader, who would make him nervous in the room?* I knew, okay, whoever is coming to the show tonight has to be super-important.

During act one, Rachel Stern scanned the audience, but couldn't see Dylan sitting all the way in the back row.

RACHEL STERN   It was around intermission when I forced Artie to tell me. Or maybe it was [assistant stage manager] Jeff Brancato. I stared *someone* in the eye and said, "I need to know who's here tonight."
    "It's Bob Dylan."

Intermission came and the news ricocheted around the greenroom downstairs, while upstairs, Mandy Hackett proceeded with the plan, which I like to imagine as accompanied by bank-heist movie music.

MANDY HACKETT   And then I got into position when act one was ending. And I opened the door and I swept him upstairs. I said to the women that were with him, "There's some water. If you need anything, I'll just be over here waiting to get the call to bring him back down the elevator."

OSKAR EUSTIS   So we set him up in the mezzanine for intermission, right up here, fifteen feet away; he came in with the hoodie, pulled low, I didn't try to talk to him. I'd introduced myself and then I just stayed back.

MANDY HACKETT   So I'm just standing at the front of that hallway that leads you to the bathroom, you know? And I was just minding my own business, checking my texts, waiting to get the call to go down. They're all talking.

OSKAR EUSTIS   I heard his companion going through the program, and I overheard, "Oh, look, she was in 'Law and Order!'" Which, for those in the theater, *everybody's* been in "Law and Order."

Oskar made himself scarce, remembering that he "in no uncertain terms" was to approach Dylan. But no one said what to do if Dylan was the one who did the approaching.

MANDY HACKETT   All of a sudden [Dylan] walks up to me, and I thought he was going to ask where the bathroom was or something. And he did not have the hood on. He looked at me with those blue eyes. And I'm not "a fan." This is where the irony is crazy. But I'm telling you, it was a religious experience, looking into those eyes, it was the depth of soul. I can't explain it. I couldn't believe it. I really was kind of speechless. And he said, "How long does the show run?" And I said, "Oh, I, well, the second act is another hour" or whatever it was. And he said, "No, no. How much longer does it run?" And I said, "Oh, we're running into December," it was another six weeks or whatever it was. He said, "Do you think it's going to be like *Hamilton*?"

Mandy should work this story into a set for a comedy club. Her timing is golden.

MANDY HACKETT   And I said, "Well, people love it. I think it's its own thing." And then he said, "The actors are incredible." No, he didn't say the *actors*. He said the *singers*, "The singers are incredible" and that "You don't get singers like that in the music industry." And then he said something complimentary about Conor, and the whole time I'm sitting there thinking, *I can't believe I'm standing here talking to Bob Dylan.* And then I'm thinking to myself, *where the fuck is Oskar?*

Mandy, it turns out, is a big U2 fan.

> MANDY HACKETT   Bono came to a matinee. Same drill. We brought him upstairs for intermission, but Bono walks in and . . . there was no drama about it. No *whisk him in, whisk him out.* I think they're just very different personalities. Bono was saying "Hi" to everyone, and he was asking me a lot of questions about Conor, and then I walked him to his car and I got a picture with him.

She beams, remembering Bono, while she returns to her Bob Dylan story. There she is, alone with the icon, locked in Dylan's gaze.

> MANDY HACKETT   I remember trying to will it: *Oskar, walk by. Walk by right now.* And I was thinking to myself, *Oskar's going to kill me.*

Mandy's telepathic message didn't reach Oskar, but he would get an audience with B.D. after the show.

> MANDY HACKETT   And then Dylan just kind of moved away. And then two minutes later, we went back downstairs.

Downstairs we got our "places for act two" call from Artie. Everyone knew about Dylan's being in the audience except for me. I don't like to know who's in the audience, friend, celebrity or critic. I get in my head and think about how they are perceiving my every move.

So people knew not to tell me. And they didn't.

Except for you, Rachel Stern.

I'm not mad at you.

Anymore.

We're standing in the hallway backstage, moments away from starting act two. I'm warming up my harmonica, which I do every night, by breathing into it to moisten the reeds, a necessary step before playing. Dry reeds squawk. (This will be an issue when we perform live at the Tony Awards four years later, as part of our number features me playing the harmonica. Due to a bizarre confluence of transportation issues and union rules about props—which the harmonica officially considered, not an instrument—I was told I would have to play a brand new harmonica that would be waiting backstage at Radio City Music Hall, fresh out of the box, with dry reeds, that I would *not* be able to warm up at all before playing on live television.)

Rachel walks up to me and says, "He's here. It's Dylan. He's here."

And right then we get the cue to start act two, which, if you'll remember, features a harmonica solo by me downstage center.

I don't know if you've ever *panicked*.

The next ten minutes were like an *I'm in high school again in my underwear and I didn't study for the exam* anxiety dream; me, onstage, in a spotlight, in front of people, harmonica to my dry mouth, playing a solo on the instrument synonymous with Dylan *for* Dylan himself.

SCOTT SANDERS   Right, harmonica solo. For Dylan. What could be harder?

Scott, at the soundboard, had a similarly anxious evening, live-mixing Dylan's music for Dylan himself.

SCOTT SANDERS   I made sure I didn't lose focus, but I kept watching him as much as I could. I literally just sat there and watched what his reaction was the whole time.

I'm told my harmonica solo went fine, I don't remember. My song, "Duquesne Whistle" at the end of the act? Who knows? I sang it, allegedly. I died as usual, I exited, like I was supposed to, and I bowed at the curtain call, they say.

MANDY HACKETT   At the end of the show, I went to get [Dylan] and I opened the door and he was standing and clapping, and I thought that they would want to sweep him right out. But he just stood there, stood up and clapped through that entire standing ovation.

SCOTT SANDERS   I mean, he stood up right at the end, and he was applauding, and then he was wiping his eyes, and then he was talking to his wardrobe person, and then there's more applause, more applause. Everybody's still standing. His manager grabs him by the elbow and starts pulling him off that riser to get to the exit. And he pushes him away and stands there, he waited for you guys to exit and then he beat feet.

MANDY HACKETT   And then we walked out and he put his arm around me, and he said, "That was incredible. I'll definitely be back."

SCOTT SANDERS   I never got to shake his hand. That's all I wanted was to shake his hand.

CAITLIN HOULAHAN   Oskar was sitting on the stairs and just beaming. And we all knew that he was obsessed with Bob Dylan. He's beaming, and we were pretty sure the rumors [that Dylan had been at that show] were true. So that was an incredible night.

OSKAR EUSTIS   I'm standing right outside in the lobby, and as the curtain call is going on, he slips out and as he slips out, he just glances at me and he stops and he turns back and he runs straight up to me. And I said, "Did you like it?" He said, "I loved it. Come see me backstage." He slid off. And I was in ecstasy.

MANDY HACKETT   And then he was whisked off into the night.

But the visitation wasn't over. If Bob Dylan's seeing our show was act one of a drama called "The Stranger in the Hoodie," then act two was Mare and Jeannette's seeing Bob Dylan's show at the Beacon Theater the next night.

MARE WINNINGHAM   Then it's Monday [November 29th] and I'm on the phone with Conor and I say "We're going to see Dylan tonight [at the Beacon]. It's going to be amazing. Conor says, "Jeff [Rosen, Dylan's manager] just wrote and says that he wants you and Jeannette to come before the show to a side entrance of the Beacon."

Mare is stunned. She believed there was *no way* they were going to be able to meet Dylan, and hadn't they officially heard "it's a no" from Dylan's manager? What changed?

JEANNETTE BAYARDELLE   Mare got an email saying that Bob Dylan, absolutely, after he saw the show, that he *absolutely* wants me and Mare to come and meet him in his dressing room on Monday.

Once again, Bob Dylan was proving unpredictable.

MARE WINNINGHAM   That would never have happened if Jeannette hadn't insisted that I ask. God bless Jeannette. So we go [to the Beacon], it's raining like it is now.

Mare told me this story in her sitting room of the home she shares with her husband in Connecticut. There we were again almost too poetically, the two of us listening to the rain, real this time not a sound effect, just as we used to do backstage every night before *Slow Train Coming*.

MARE WINNINGHAM   And we go in and there's a freight elevator, and one of his people puts us in the freight elevator and says to get to the third floor, and the elevator opens, and there's a woman there, she's his dresser. She was the woman that was [with him at *Girl*] that night because she said, "Oh, it's so nice to meet you all. I was there last night. It's a beautiful show. Bob was very moved. Wait here." So we're standing outside the elevator and she walks, opens a door. I could sort of sense that it was a dressing room. Turns out it's about the size of a closet, super tiny. And she comes back out and she goes, come here. He's ready to meet you. And so we go forward and he's in there and he's in a, he's so small, and he's in a sleeveless t-shirt before he's going to change into a really groovy spangly jacket. He's in a sleeveless t-shirt and pants, and there's a cigarette burning and a guitar on a coffee table, and there's a couch. And he offers us the couch and he goes and gets a chair. And I think I went in for the hug, or maybe Jeannette did, or maybe we all did, but we all hugged and he's super sweet, super sweet.

While she was recounting this story, Mare and I could see her husband, Anthony, working in the pouring rain, digging trenches for the "water and electrics" that would connect to the outdoor stage he was building on their property, right next to a tree they'd planted in memory of Artie.

MARE WINNINGHAM [Dylan] starts talking about how moved he was. he said, "I don't even know what happened. And I walked around afterwards, I didn't go home." And I'm thinking, *he's walking around Greenwich Village.* But he said, "I went into the Starbucks and got some napkins. I saw those crosses at the end, you know those telephone poles? They were coming at me as crosses."

He's referring to the final scenic element of *Girl from the North Country.* As Mare sings "Forever Young," a black curtain slowly rises behind her, revealing a painted image of Duluth—a few crowded homes near a small cemetery, three giant telephone poles standing tall in the foreground. It's just a picture of a town until you notice that the telephone poles look like crosses, and suddenly this mundane small-town image evokes the single most powerful image in the Christian faith, the cross, specifically the three crosses of Jesus Christ's crucifixion scene at Golgotha. For certain people, like Bob Dylan, it's a real wallop.

MARE WINNINGHAM And I said [to Dylan], "Yeah, Conor gave us permission when we had to speak about the play to the press, that we could say it was a nativity piece." And that stopped him. And he's like, "Oh, *yeah.*" And then he said something about David Pittu. He said, "That preacher, that shit was real, that preacher that was real." And then he said something about—Conor just cannot believe it still, he blushes when I remind him of this. [Dylan] was talking about Conor, and he said, "That guy, that guy, man, that guy's going to put Duluth on the map!"

I can't help but note: here's "Bob Dylan" in his mythical realm, *backstage.*

JEANNETTE BAYARDELLE We just had the most lovely conversation with him. He talked about the show, he said, "You guys were amazing." He said he cried, he cried, he cried. I think he had to go across the street to get tissues from Starbucks. He loved the fact that I was in communication with Desi. He talked about her so much, how much she loved her, and how he supported what she was doing. He asked, "So is [*Girl from the North Country*] coming to Broadway?" And Mare was like ... "Is it?! Oh, no doubt. No doubt."

MARE WINNINGHAM   Jeannette said, "What did you think of your songs?" He said, "Those weren't my songs. They were coming at me another way." And then she said, "I got to sing 'True Love.'⁶'" And he is like, "Yeah, 'True Love.' Turns out that's a good song."

JEANNETTE BAYARDELLE   And he said, "Yeah, 'True Love' is a great song." I said, "That's a song I sang." He was like, "I know. That's the song you sang."

Jeannette, ever unfazed by celebrity, found it easy to speak with Dylan.

JEANNETTE BAYARDELLE   It felt like talking to an old friend, I literally wanted to say, "Let's order some pizza. He's not doing the show tonight!" We just talked and it was great.

Mare made us some popcorn while she recounted this night backstage with Dylan. She wishes she'd written it down and then she remembers that she did, in a way, in an email to her brother, the Bob Dylan superfan.

MARE WINNINGHAM   Here it is!

She pulls up the email and reads parts of it to me.

MARE WINNINGHAM (email)
   "He was very Diminutive with a wonderful open face and piercing gaze. We talked for forty minutes. He couldn't find the words for how much the play moved him in so many ways. So he just kept going on as he remembered different things that he loved. And I told him a lot about Conor, and Jeannette was her funny, warm self. We talked about movies versus theater."

She looks from her phone at me, mouth open in surprised remembrance.

MARE WINNINGHAM   That was a big one!

She elaborates, the rain is really pouring down now on Tony outside.

MARE WINNINGHAM   The movies versus theater thing was a really funny part of the conversation because he said, "Ooh, I don't like movies. I like theater." And then he said, "Well, there's one movie I like."

---

⁶"True Love Tends to Forget" from *Street-Legal*, 1978.

I don't know why, but this makes us laugh. It's somehow funny that Bob Dylan likes one movie. *Which one?* Your mind goes on a mad easter-egg hunt.

MARE WINNINGHAM   "And what would that be?" I asked. And he said, "*The Rider.* Have you seen *The Rider?*"

The Rider is a 2017 film by filmmaker Chloé Zhao. It's set in South Dakota, right where my brother Travis used to live, in fact, and features a real-life rodeo rider playing a fictionalized version of himself.

MARE WINNINGHAM   He said, "Yeah, that I like that. That. That's my favorite movie." Made me think about [Dylan] must be so attuned to falsity in that even great acting isn't the same as being caught in the act of being real.

Continuing the email she wrote to her brother:

MARE WINNINGHAM (email)
"About Duluth, he was very animated to share his feeling about his childhood home and the particularities of the place and how much it meant to him to have it explored in the play.

"He spoke reverentially about its spirituality, its depth, and the holiness. He loved the music and felt that he was listening to something other than his songs. Jeannette asked how he disassociated from his own songs, and he said they were coming at him in a new way. He said that the songs were only chunks of a song, and that sometimes they were coupled together in pairs or threes, and that he liked the way that was done.

"He said, for instance, that he doesn't do 'Hurricane' anymore, but that it does have the same chord progression as 'All Along the Watchtower,' so that was a good combo.

"He turned, he looked at me and he said, 'And you had to do "Rolling Stone"'. And I turned beet-red and said, 'I know.' And he said, 'I have to do "Rolling Stone" tonight in front of you guys. I'm kind of nervous now, but we do it in a new way, too. So I'm curious what you think of the songs, how the set comes across to you guys. So write me your thoughts. Send it to Jeff or Jerry. I'm curious what you think.' He was so humble and he still cares about what we think. I wrote him an email last night when I was fresh off the concert so I could remember my thoughts. And I sent it off, mostly a gush fest because it was a great show.

"We stayed with him yapping until seven-twenty. And then I said, 'Shouldn't we let you get ready?' And he said, 'Yeah, I better get ready.' And we hugged him goodbye. And then his wardrobe woman took us to the elevator and she whispered to us. 'I was there last night. It was very special. It was so wonderful. Thank you.'

"Afterward, We went down to the theater and had a glass of Prosecco because it was as close as I could get to Champagne."

Mare stops reading the email for a moment, taking in the enormity of that night.

The next day was a Tuesday, we all gathered for the first show of an eight-show week. In the greenroom, we listened breathlessly to Mare and Jeannette tell the story.

Like every classic Dylan tale, the story grows and changes over time. *Did he mention the song I sang? He must have.*

CAITLIN HOULAHAN   I believe he said something about "I Want You," but I might be making that up.

"I Want You" is the duet Caitlin sang with Colton Ryan.

CAITLIN HOULAHAN   I'm going to believe it.

The New Faces

In 2017 I sat my husband down and I said, "I think this career is not working out for me. I need to figure out what I should do instead."

At that point, I'd lived in New York City for about twenty years, and even though I'd worked some as an actor, written shows that had been produced in New York, LA, San Francisco, Boston, Miami, and more, performed on the Delacorte stage in Central Park, written music for a play on Broadway (a revival of Michael Frayn's *Noises Off!* in 2016), and music-directed and/or arranged music for Broadway singers like Kelli O'Hara, Andrew Rannells, Sherie Rene Scott, and Laura Benanti at venues like Lincoln Center and Carnegie Hall, all of which sounds like a lot of success when it's written out like this, I just couldn't get a hold on a single *career*. I was an actor. I was a composer. I was a musician. I was a writer. But I didn't have a career as any one of these things.

You know how I knew? Each of those professions has a union and I'm a proud member of each: AEA, SAG, Local 802. And every year, as a member of each union, you get a statement in the mail detailing the current state of your pension in that union.

My statements were always (are still always) barely into three digits. I had accrued 290 dollars in pension as an actor over several years. That made it pretty hard to say I had a career in acting.

This is no way to survive.

So the big question facing me, when I confessed to my husband my doubts, was *what could I do instead of this career whatever this career was?*

When you're young, and you decide to become an actor or a writer, someone somewhere will say to you "Only do it if you can't imagine doing anything else." And I used to think they meant that you have to be passionate about the craft to be good at it. Which is true, but I've come to realize what they are *really* saying is that if you choose this career, you will paint yourself into a corner and you won't be able to get yourself out of it should you decide you want to. It'll be too late.

I was forty-one years old when I told my husband Mark that I should think about another career. What could that even be? I'd painted myself into a corner.

I found myself Googling "Job" and "Career" and "Help."

One thing I'd wanted to do as an actor was to revisit the role of Hedwig. I'd done the show in 2001 and again in 2003 both times at the Ensemble Theater of Cincinnati. I was in my twenties at the time and felt instinctively that I would play the part better once I'd had more years and some real heartbreak behind me.

Googling "Help" in my forties felt like perfect timing.

I said to Mark that before I threw in the towel I would reach out to Lynn Meyers at ETC and suggest that we finally do *Hedwig and the Angry Inch* one last time, which we'd always wanted to do. She agreed, we got the gang back together again, designers and musicians, I pulled myself together physically, vocally, and mentally, and we did the show.

But just before I left New York for Cincinnati, I got the call from Heidi and Jordan via my agent to do the reading of *Girl from the North Country*. I am convinced that *Hedwig* saved me. Had I not set that goal for myself, had I not pulled my confidence and vocal technique and stamina together I would not have been prepared to play Elias that day in April.

Girl from the North Country changed my life in many ways. I didn't know it was coming, and I didn't know I needed to work so hard to prepare myself for its arrival.

It's something to remember as I move forward in life: *I didn't know it was coming, and I didn't know I needed to work so hard to prepare myself for its arrival.*

As we neared the end of the three-month run of shows at the Public Theater, two major things happened.

First, we started having conversations about a Broadway transfer, and second, our cast expanded to include off-stage swings and understudies.

Ben Mayne joined the company in November of 2018 to cover me, Colton Ryan, and the two male ensemble tracks, John and Matthew.

ARTIE (email)
    hi all!

Some Exciting news—starting tonight, we will be welcoming a new cast member, who will be a swing and covering Gene/Elias Burke. His name is Ben Mayne. He will be around at half hour today for a fitting (and the men in the 6-person dressing room will find they have a new dressing room station in there). He will also stay to watch the show.

We're very excited to have him join our Duluth family, especially now that we will have a swing to cover ensemble tracks when an understudy goes on.

Love,
Artie and Jeff

Ben has a country smile, like a character in a rom-com that takes place half in New York and half in Montana. He had auditioned for our show when it was originally casting for the Public cast.

BEN MAYNE I made it down to the final couple of people for [the character] Gene and ended up getting let go when Colton eventually got the part. And I was so bummed. I remember calling my agent every day asking her for updates. I ended up going and doing this production of Holiday Inn instead. And then I was down to the finals for *Waitress*. My last audition was this dance call. It was all really difficult for me because I'm a terrible dancer. And I bombed, *bombed* it. And I went out for drinks that night with my friend and got drunk and I was like, "I'm going to fucking quit. Theater is the worst. This is horrible." And then the next morning, Teresa, my agent, she calls me and she goes, "Hey, I got a job offer for you." And I was like, "No fucking way"—I'm really hungover— "I bombed that [dance] audition. I can't believe they called me. That is so weird!" And she said, "No, no, you're going down to the Public, so put your pants on and go take a shower. You got to go down there to rehearse today."

As is often the way when cast in the role of a swing, everything happens suddenly.

BEN MAYNE I threw my pants on, I took a shower and I came down there to watch the show that night. And that was when I met y'all. My head was spinning, but I was so excited. I watched the show and I cried and I cried; I was so overwhelmed. Artie watched my back and took me under his wing. I asked him a thousand questions.

Bob Walton joined a week later, to cover Bob Joy, Tom Nelis, and the male ensemble tracks.

Swings become a very important part of the story of *Girl from the North Country*. It's one of the more difficult jobs as an actor, and those who are good at it are rare creatures. A requirement for a swing is the ability to handle sudden, intense pressure. Ben experienced this pressure right away and later, once we got to Broadway, he would nearly be crushed by it.

BEN MAYNE Everybody [in the cast] had this electric feeling of something special happening. And it was this strange emergency situation. Sydney [Harcourt], who was playing Joe, had been out the previous weekend and Matthew [Harris] was on, and then Matthew was supposed to go on that Friday for Elias.

I had one pre-approved absence in the calendar for a concert with Laura Benanti, something scheduled before I was cast. The plan was for male ensemble actor Matthew Harris to play Elias that night and for Ben to swing on for Matthew's ensemble track.

BEN MAYNE But they were worried that if [Sydney] was going to call out again that Matthew was not going to be able to do both tracks. So when they hired me, whenever it was, that Monday, they said, "You might be needing to go on for Elias on Friday," which was terrifying.

And though I essentially knew the feeling myself, I asked Ben what it feels like as an actor to go from *I'm quitting the business* to *I might be going on Friday for a part I've never rehearsed*?

BEN MAYNE What does that feel like? I mean, it's kind of the reason that we do it. It's like it's just this absolute thrill of, and challenge, I mean, it's this feeling of *I know that I'm good enough to do this, I can do it, and I can face the challenge and I can put in the work.*

But everything went according to plan, Sydney was on, Matthew stepped in for me to play Elias, and our new swing swung on to do Matthew's ensemble part.

There was no need for the new swings to panic.

Yet.

We're Going to Broadway, Right?

The slow train, Broadway, that I'd been waiting on for decades was getting closer. It was just around the bend. I could almost see it.

CAITLIN HOULAHAN All of the girls shared one dressing room, and there were four on one side with mirrors in between three on the other. And Jeannette was on the other side. And she was the queen of . . . she was on the Broadway message boards:[7] "These people are saying this about our show." And so she was really my source of information.

Jeannette's position as the company prophet took root here.

CAITLIN HOULAHAN   We really looked to her for all of this, and we realized we started feeling a little superstitious. So we decided we can't *name* this; we decided to call it the "Kitty."

JEANNETTE BAYARDELLE   And the girls, we had this thing backstage, because Mare told this story about her *really wanting* a cat when she was younger. And I, maybe she can tell you more about that, but she wanted this cat. And when she stopped thinking about it, that's when she ended up getting the cat. So the girls all called our Broadway transfer the "Kitty."

CAITLIN HOULAHAN   Anytime that we talked about potentially going to Broadway, we'd say "Any news on the Kitty?" We had this code so that we wouldn't upset the universe and the energy.

JEANNETTE BAYARDELLE   At some point, Kimber brought us all little kitty mugs. So every time Mandy [Hackett] would have a meeting with us, we all came with our kitty mugs.

Associate Artistic Director of the Public Theater Mandy Hackett called several cast meetings that took place in the Newman Theater. The cast sat in the audience gaping up at Mandy on the stage as if she were the show. We waited for her to reveal our fate. The girls with their kitty mugs. *Are we going to Broadway?* Mandy would say something like, "We just wanted to keep you updated. Our intention is to move this show to Broadway, but we have no concrete plan or information for you yet . . ."

Nothing. No Answer.

I sat with Mandy recently at a restaurant near the Public and asked her about these meetings and asked her why we had those meetings when there was no news.

MANDY HACKETT   I feel like *transparency*, number one. Number two, I feel like if we give you information, even if it's not, "We have a theater," I hope that it, at least for a minute, quiets down the spinning: "What did you hear? What did you hear? We're going, we're not going" There can be so many rumors swirling, so just to be able to say, "If you don't hear it from us, it's not real." And it's tricky for me to decide how often to have those meetings. We don't have a lot to say, but we just don't want to let too much time go by. What's your perspective on it? Were those meetings annoying or were they helpful?

---

[7]Online forums where people discuss industry news and gossip.

I got my hopes up every single time.

MANDY HACKETT   Oh, God. That's good for me to know.

Mandy's transparency was appreciated. I tried to imagine it from her perspective, a room full of disappointed actors staring at you.

MANDY HACKETT (*Sighs, heavily*)   I just love you guys so much. I love our *Girl* company.

Mandy has a hard job. No one wants to be the messenger when it's bad news.

JEANNETTE BAYARDELLE   I'm smart enough to know now that if Mandy walks in the room alone, it's not happening. If she walks in with Oskar, it's happening. If Mandy showed up alone, we just put the teacups down on the floor. This is not it.

CAITLIN HOULAHAN   And I remember most Jeannette speaking about *which theater we would go into*, and we would discuss every theater and that *this one's* [stage is] *too long, this one's too big, we need a small space*, it was all of that. And I honestly know the Broadway theaters so much better now, because we talked about it so often. I just remember the buildup.

TRISTAN BAKER   We knew it was going to go to Broadway. We knew we could get the money.

So, why didn't we just transfer immediately? It's not that easy.

AARON LUSTBADER   There are forty-one Broadway theaters, but when you add up the number that are occupied by either long-running musicals or plays or owned by nonprofit theaters, it becomes a very small pool. And we knew the story we were telling—this is not a story that is going to live well in an eighteen-hundred seat theater. It needed intimacy.

TRISTAN BAKER   We knew it was just about whether we could get a theater. And then the Shuberts loved it. And Dessie [Moynihan] loved it. And they came in.

DESSIE MOYNIHAN   It was a terrific production.

Dessie Moynihan, a VP with the Shuberts, describes the organization as

DESSIE MOYNIHAN   . . . Broadway's largest theater owner. We have seventeen Broadway theaters. We also have six off-Broadway theaters—

New World Stages and Stage 42. We own Telecharge. And we are producers, co-producers and investors. We're very supportive of the shows that are in our theaters. We care very much about them. The Shubert Organization is owned by the Shubert Foundation. It's an unusual arrangement. The Shubert Organization is a profit-making, tax-paying enterprise, but all of the profits go to the Shubert Foundation to be given away to theater and dance companies across the country, as well as arts-related organizations, and educational institutions. If you go to any regional theater and you look at the list of donors, I pretty much guarantee you that the Shubert Foundation will be there. In May of 2023, the Foundation gave away 37.9 million.

Producers like Tristan approach theater owners like the Shuberts in the hopes of finding a Broadway home for their productions.

DESSIE MOYNIHAN   It was clear that [the show] needed a little more development, maybe some casting changes, but when it came to booking one of our theaters, we thought it was a very worthy project.

TRISTAN BAKER   So then we started that process with [the Shubert Organization]. And then it was actually about, the reason we waited so long was that Aaron Lustbader, who's a genius, knew that for us, we didn't want to open in the autumn.

AARON LUSTBADER   There are shows that need to open at specific times. We knew we had and which was proven time and again, was an artistic piece of great merit that was going to be well received by critics and would presume we'd be well received in award season. And there's a string of shows that have opened into award season because even if they don't win the Tony Award for Best Musical, the amount of conversation that surrounds the show and its merits and the media is very worthwhile and helpful with respect to ticket sales and establishing a show. So *Girl from the North Country* was not a show that could open in the fall because of how hard winter is, struggling through that.

TRISTAN BAKER   We were offered a theater for the summer, for a limited run, but we'd passed.

AARON LUSTBADER   And it certainly couldn't open in the summer, which some lighter entertainments can do very successfully.

MANDY HACKETT   We were offered another Broadway theater . . . but we all felt like that theater was just too big. The proportions were not right for our show. It's a beautiful theater, but it sort of removed the intimacy. And that was a really tough moment: do you take the bird in hand?—we all know how hard it is to get a theater—or do you wait to get the theater that is going to be a better fit?

AARON LUSTBADER So it had to open in the spring. So it was a limited window of time. The theater we thought we were going to go into wasn't available.

CAITLIN HOULAHAN I remember [Mandy] saying the intention was, *yes, we're moving to Broadway* and that we don't have a theater, which is a good thing for Broadway. It was a great thing for Broadway at the time that there were so many shows.

AARON LUSTBADER We were very far along in conversations with another theater owner. No promises had been made, but implications were certainly there. And that was not a good match at the end of the day. And then there were simply no theaters available. By the time we learned that the theater we thought we were getting was not available, there was not a way to pivot.

CHELSEA LEE WILLIAMS Every day it would be like, "Okay, we're going to have a meeting before half hour just to discuss a few things, let you know where we're at in the process of getting the, securing a theater." I thought, *oh, it's about to happen. We're going tomorrow. We're going, we're transferring this season.*

I thought the same thing as Chelsea. Christmas was approaching, which didn't help with my anticipation of a miracle. Santa, I only have one thing on my list. But there is no Santa Claus and there is no Broadway fairy-godmother. But there are theater owners. Business people who decide what shows will play in their houses.

CHELSEA LEE WILLIAMS It blew my mind when I realized, *Oh, there's levels to this that I have never even taken into consideration.* You have these physical pieces of real estate ... and, you'll have to get the exact numbers, Todd, but there are, at any given time, like thirty shows that are trying to get on Broadway, or forty shows that have the money, they have the producer, they have cast, they're just like circling. Hoping the theater owner says, "Okay."

Chelsea's right, even with a financed show, great reviews, and a full, available cast, there's still *one more* hurdle for a show hoping to open on Broadway: getting a theater.

CHELSEA LEE WILLIAMS Honestly, it was the first time that I got a glimpse into the idea of real estate in theater. The business of theater. No one talks about that in drama school. But it made me understand the business of Broadway in ways that I never had.

How many shows like ours are trying at any given time to get into a Broadway house?

DESSIE MOYNIHAN   In any given season, there are probably forty shows looking for homes, and those are the ones that are really "real." And then there are the others which are aspirational. The list can grow to fifty. People say, "Well, there are forty-one theaters on Broadway. Why can't I get a theater for my fantastic show?" But you have to remember that there are five nonprofit theater spaces.

A few not-for-profit theater companies (Manhattan Theater Company, Roundabout, Second Stage) have Broadway houses, which, honestly, as an actor, I've always found confusing. The ticket prices are at Broadway levels, the work and the time-commitment of the actors is at the Broadway level, but the pay is not. I've had it explained to me multiple times, why the actors at these theaters are on Broadway but not being paid Broadway salaries, but I still don't understand it.

DESSIE MOYNIHAN   So you take those out and then you count the legacy shows, *Wicked*, *Lion King*, *Chicago*, *Book of Mormon*, *Hamilton*, things like that, which are taking up theaters. And then you have the hits of more recent vintage, and once you start taking those out, and *three theaters are too small and two are too big* for your show, you're getting down to single digits.

Even when a theater-owner takes on a show, there's the question of availability. One show must close and move out for a new one to move in and open.

MANDY HACKETT   We knew the Shuberts loved the show, but they said, "We just don't have a theater. We just don't know." Because they don't know when shows are going to close. I think the thing when you're producing on Broadway is everybody's looking for a theater. And for me, I never like to put any negativity out into the world. So you don't want to . . .

To wander around Broadway cursing shows to close.

MANDY HACKETT   Exactly. Or, "Ooooh, we're looking at the grosses, and that show's not doing as well . . ." I don't like that. It's musical chairs when you're producing, and you all sit in every chair eventually. You know what I mean? And you're going to be the show that's doing everything you possibly can to keep running.

(And we would.)

MANDY HACKETT   You don't want every other show breathing down your neck. And so when I'm in the other position, I'm not trying to breathe down anyone's neck.

KIMBER ELAYNE SPRAWL   Just so many ups and downs! We never knew, but we were just so hopeful. And I think I would show up expecting her to have good news.

Me too. Every time we had those meetings,

KIMBER ELAYNE SPRAWL   It was the same news: "We're working on it. And it's our greatest hope for the show to be on Broadway. We love you guys. We're doing our best." We had a lot of meetings.

A lot of meetings.

CHELSEA LEE WILLIAMS   There was a part of me that was like, *I appreciate the transparency,* but there was another part of me that was like *this rollercoaster ride I did not sign up to be on.*

We eventually just ran out of days to hope for good news. The run was coming to an end. And the message at the cast meetings didn't change: no news.

KIMBER ELAYNE SPRAWL   . . . that last meeting, I'll never forget it. She said, "We didn't get the theater and now we're releasing you guys."

Oof. I remember that.

KIMBER ELAYNE SPRAWL   And it was like a deflated balloon. And I'm like, *well, what does that mean?*

It meant we weren't going to Broadway. Or we were. Later. Maybe. Hopefully.
It meant there was no news.
It meant *nothing.*

ARTIE (email)
    Dear all,
    Is it possible that tomorrow is our last day? It has been a joy watching all of you every performance, giving so much of your talent and energy to our loving audiences. We shall miss you all, but as they say, this isn't a final goodbye but rather a goodbye for now.
    One last thing: There will probably be so much applause at the end of tomorrow evening's show, an extra bow would be appropriate. So, please don't exit right away. If the applause continues, please look to Stephen and he will lead you into "stealing an extra bow."
    Have a great night everyone!

Love,
Artie, Jeff, Kaelyn, Sam, and Kayliane

The feeling was familiar to me, like my early years in New York, calling home to mom and dad saying, "I'm going to be in *Les Miz* on Broadway," and then crashing into the wall of truth: *No you're not.*

This time, I kept it to myself. It probably wasn't going to happen. I'd let myself get too excited, stupid of me. Don't tell anyone that you think you're going to be on Broadway because then you'll just have to tell them you were wrong. Again.

Just tuck it into that same deep pocket of disappointment and be grateful that you had this experience. Maye you're not meant for Broadway. That's okay, it's just a place. Go write a song about God or a house burning down.

Girl from the North Country closed at the Public Theater in December, 2018, right before Christmas. We toasted backstage. We cried. Our summer-camp days were over. I took a cab home with my husband after the last show, I had too many things to carry for my bike. Artie had given us blankets and pillows for our greenroom naps, and I wanted to keep everything, the books and cards and photos and flower vases.

As I lay in bed that night, I thought of the freight trains I heard every night in childhood, the railroad tracks running through my small town. A sound once both far away and near. Always around the bend.

I frequently get restless and blue. Can't sleep. That night after our final meeting with Mandy, where we found out there was no plan to transfer, my insomnia was bad. Mark asked me if I was okay. I said I was. And I was, really. How lucky had I been? *Girl from the North Country* was over, that's okay, it had been thrilling. Foolishly, I'd let my hopes rise.

Eventually I fell asleep. I dreamed I was back in my small hometown again, and it was all snow and broken pianos. The slow train was blasting its horn, signaling its eternally imminent arrival.

Go away, train. I don't believe in you anymore.

On January 1, 2019, Mark and I threw a New Year's Day party, as we always do. There's a lot of singing at our New Year's Day party. Jeannette came that year and performed "I'm Here" from *The Color Purple*; she'd been in the original Broadway production. I accompanied her on the piano, a comfortable place for me to be.

Everyone asked me what I was going to do next, now that *Girl* was closed. "Or is it transferring to Broadway?" I smiled, "Oh, we'll see!" I answered, not breaking my vow to tell no one my hopes, it's just too humiliating.

It was a new year. I was playing the piano for a friend. That's all I could say for sure.

But the slow train *was* coming. It would round the bend and pull into view exactly one year later. I just didn't know what it was bringing with it.

PART II

4

42nd Street

The Bridge

I made it. *Finally*. My life in the theater big leagues can begin at last.

Is what I thought in 2006.

The theater company I was working with, Theater Mitu, had a reputation in the downtown scene for making bold, if odd, theater. In 2003 we made an original adaptation (a play with music) of Homer's *The Odyssey* for Juilliard; a then unknown Oscar Isaac played the role of Nestor. We were in residence at New York Theater Workshop. We were happening.

In 2006 Theater Mitu made its biggest splash—a complete reimagining of the musical *Hair*, performed at the Skirball Center on Washington Square by students of NYU's Experimental Theater Wing. I was the music director and re-conceiver of the music, taking for inspiration the electronic landscapes artists like Björk and Radiohead were creating on their albums. With the help of my technical-wizard friend Ethan Hein, I updated the orchestrations of *Hair* to match director Ruben Polendo's vision for the show—a dystopian, tech-drenched cult-like future where everything—every prop, every article of clothing, even every microphone on each actor's head—was monochromatically *white*. As if America was in the vise-grip of corporate hegemony, an oppressive place brooking no deviant form of self-expression, a place where the "hippies" revolted against society and its wars and announced their discontent via how they wore their hair.

Which is exactly the plot of *Hair*. Though in our production the hippies were bald.

Every single actor in our production shaved their head. It was brave of them, and it annoyed their teachers and classmates, not to mention the audience—*it's* Hair! *Why are they bald?! They sing an entire song about their hair! A song called "Hair!" Why are you doing that, that's not how it's done!*

Mission accomplished, as far as I was concerned. The show and the hippies and their hair were once again making people uncomfortable and *bothered*.

The only object that had any color beyond white didn't make its appearance on the stage until the final moments of the production: it was the American flag. After two hours of blinding-white sameness and synthesized protest songs, Jeannie and Burger, two hippies, carried the flag on and draped it over the dead body of young Claude Hooper Bukowski, their friend killed in America's "dirty little war."[1] Red, white, and blue were suddenly shocking colors.

James Rado, co-lyricist and co-bookwriter of *Hair*, loved our production, but he told us with a shrug that the show's composer Galt McDermont ". . . would have hated it."

I was so proud of this production and so certain of its impact on the theater scene at large, that I waited by my phone for a week after we'd closed, knowing that the job offers would never stop coming.

When they didn't come at all, I realized I'd made a bigger idiomatic mistake than simply *counting my chickens*, I'd *put all of my eggs in one basket*: I hadn't been working on anything else except *Hair*, and now that my *Hair* was gone, I had nothing to do.

Most theater-makers in New York City have a side-gig. They teach, they wait tables. They have to do something to pay bills. Some, of course, are from wealthy families and don't have to worry about things like rent. Not me. Not most people I know. To make ends meet, I started working at a shop in Williamsburg, Brooklyn, selling hip, designer housewares. I remember calling my mom one day in shock when a customer came in and bought an eight-hundred dollar pillow. It was gorgeous. But it was eight hundred dollars.

Post-*Hair*, for months and months, I took the L train to the Bedford stop in Brooklyn—I was living in the East Village at the time—and I would wait daily for my life to change. This is how it happens, after all, right? You pay your dues, you work hard, you make an exciting piece of theater, people notice, and then you graduate up a level. That's the trajectory. But for months and months nothing at all changed beyond my getting bluer and bluer. My then boyfriend, a man not in the arts at all, had an active drug and alcohol problem, and while I never succumbed to that particular addiction, I did succumb to the sorrow around it. The job at the design shop was fine, I liked the people I worked for, but my life was moving in the reverse flow that I had intended. All of that hard work for nearly a decade in the city, paying my dues, and I felt as if I had not so much as climbed a single rung on a ladder but rather dug a pit in which I now found myself. Even my commute was backwards—one lives in Brooklyn and commutes to Manhattan, I was doing the opposite.

I knew my romantic relationship should end, I just couldn't end it. I didn't want to be alone. Even when he told me, "This career isn't really working

---

[1]Lyric from "Three-Five-Zero-Zero," from *Hair*, lyrics by Gerome Ragni and James Rado, music by Gald McDermot.

for you, maybe you should think about doing something else," I couldn't end it, I didn't have anywhere to go, anyway. No home. My apartment had subletters, the only way I could pay rent since being a clerk at a design shop in Brooklyn didn't bring in enough income. And my boyfriend needed me to carry him. Literally carry him home, drunk, to his apartment that had no walls, he'd had them torn down in hopes of one day renovating. We were holding each other up, he and I, but only by enabling the other's worst impulses. There was no love.

I look back on this as a very dark moment of my life, an especially deep drop from the high of my expectations of life after *Hair*.

The only thing I looked forward to every day was listening to the album *Aerial* by Kate Bush, which I would play on a loop in the design shop, where I was most often alone, save the occasional wealthy customer.

On the darkest day, when I let the thought slip into my head that no one would really even notice if I decided to walk home across the Williamsburg bridge and just disappear, music saved me. I got a call from my acting agent Dianne saying that Kansas City Rep was doing a production of *Two Pianos, Four Hands* and they were offering me a part. It wasn't an audition. It was an *offer*. This had never happened to me before, getting an offer without an audition, so I assumed they were mistaking me for someone else, like the time a bar agreed to throw me a birthday party because they misheard my name over the phone as *Todd Oldham*.

But, no, they wanted me. *Two Pianos, Four Hands*, as the title suggests, is a play that requires two actors who play the piano, and play it well. All of that piano-playing for all of those years in the city, someone had noticed.

I didn't know it was coming, and I didn't know I needed to work so hard to prepare myself for its arrival.

"Yes," I said, "yes, I will do it, yes." I didn't know the play *Two Pianos, Four Hands*. I didn't care. It was a lifeline, I took it.

Dianne told me that the final moment of *Two Pianos, Four Hands* was a ten-minute, very difficult Bach concerto, to be played from memory. Could I play it? I looked at the music for the concerto and saw right away that it was far beyond my grasp as a pianist. I didn't care. I said I could play it, "no problem."

And this is what pulled me out of the pit. Dianne negotiated with Kansas City Rep that they would pay for a rehearsal room for me so that I could learn not only the Bach concerto, but the entire show's-worth of music I would need to play in the production, which was a play about two young men each training to become a concert pianist.

Every day, after my shift at the design shop, I took the train to a small rehearsal room in midtown Manhattan where I practiced. Scales and everything. Like I was a music-school student all over again. The Bach concerto was intimidating, and for months it seemed that I would never get it into my hands, even if I played it very, very slowly. But I kept at it, my life depended on it, working the fingering methodically and feeling akin to the character I'd be portraying in the play, a musician forcing himself, *willing himself* to become a good enough pianist to play Bach.

It worked. Like learning a new language you can one day speak, I could now play the Bach Concerto in D minor. I broke up with the guy and went to Kansas City which had all of these fountains everywhere that felt like renewal. Kansas City Rep put me back on track. And I vowed never to let myself land in that dark place again.

The positive effect of that vow is that I now tend to have many irons in many fires at all times, so that I never feel that I have *nothing* to do. Nothing to do is a dangerous thing for me to have.

The negative side of that vow is that I'm now deeply suspicious of every project, certain that if it even happens, which it probably won't, it will end when it ends, and that is how it is meant to be, there's no changing it.

I didn't choose to be a fatalist, life made me one.

And so 2019 felt familiar to me with respect to *Girl from the North Country*. The show was over. Broadway wasn't going to happen. Don't expect the phone to ring, Todd. Move on.

I did move on.

I dug into a writing project with Kate Douglas, a musical we'd been working on called *The Lucky Few*. Kate and I were on a writing retreat in Saratoga Springs (thanks to Ari Edelson at The Orchard Project) in the summer of 2019 when my phone did ring, a call from my new acting agent, Ben Coleman.

"So, we finally got word about *Girl from the North Country*," he said. "You're going to Broadway."

I thought when this day arrived I would jump for joy; part of me did. But another part of me, the forty-four year old fearful of heights for the falls, said, "That's very exciting news. Thank you, Ben."

BEN COLEMAN (email)

Hi Todd!

Great speaking with you. Per our conversation, I am sending you the opening offer points for the Broadway production of GIRL FROM THE NORTH COUNTRY. Let's digest over the weekend and circle back.

The theatre is the Belasco, and they want to send out a press release announcing the show on Tuesday.

DATES:

- January 6th [2020]—rehearsals begin
- February 7th—first preview
- March 5th—opening night . . .

Congrats!!!

Opening Night

Every moment from here on would be a first for me. My first day of rehearsal on Broadway. My first costume fitting on Broadway. My first preview on Broadway.

My first opening night on Broadway.

JEFF BRANCATO (email)

Dear favorite company,

Tomorrow is the big day!! OPENING NIGHT IS HERE!

We're excited for you all to celebrate with the morning/afternoon off before we gather for a 5:30pm LEGACY ROBE CEREMONY on stage . . .

And FYI, in response to the Coronavirus outbreak, the Shuberts have added extra cleaning shifts in all of their theaters for disinfecting and keeping us all safe and healthy. Let us know if you have any questions.

Rest up and we'll see you tomorrow for a show and a PARTAAAAY!

Love,

Jeff, Laurie, Kaelyn, Sam, and Cheyney

One hour before our opening night performance at the Belasco Theater, March 5, 2020, the cast gathered onstage for the Legacy Robe ceremony. My friend and fellow CCM alum Kirsten Wyatt was there.

KIRSTEN WYATT If you are a past recipient of the robe, you are invited to any other celebrations, any other opening nights. And so that's how I was at the *Girl from the North Country* opening night, because I'm a past recipient. And at that time, too, I was also serving on the Council of Actors Equity as a chorus representative.

The Legacy Robe started as a bit of a joke in 1950 between members of various Broadway musical choruses.

KIRSTEN WYATT It's a way to honor the ensemble of a show. Folks who are in the ensemble—you're part of something bigger than yourself, so sometimes individual recognition is sort of overlooked. You know what I mean? And so [the Legacy Robe] is a way to really honor those who have dedicated their craft to being part of something that's bigger than themselves. That's my take on it. I was a recipient of the Legacy Robe, and to me, it was one of the high points of my career.

The robe itself, a patchwork of Broadway show logos, is awarded to the member of the chorus who has booked the most chorus contracts. The winner dons the robe with the help of its most recent previous winner, stands in the middle of a giant circle formed by the cast, creators, crew, and assembled union reps, and then spins and dances and essentially blesses the entire circle by running its perimeter to great cheering. The whole thing feels pagan and ancient, important and fabulously silly.

KIRSTEN WYATT   It's one of these traditions that has just evolved—going around the circle and blessing and all of that stuff.

John Schiappa was the recipient of the Legacy Robe on our opening night. He played the part perfectly, spinning like a cyclone as we cheered, the robe whipping up the names and images of the shows running in the neighborhood, our neighborhood; a community stitched together, John's impromptu storm-dance lifted and spun us all. I hugged my friend Kirsten, who said she couldn't believe this was my Broadway debut after so many years. She seemed proud of me, and I was proud, too.

As part of the ongoing tradition of the Legacy Robe, it would now be John's turn to pass the robe on to the next recipient at their Broadway opening night.

JOHN SCHIAPPA   It was supposed to be passed to *Diana: The Musical.*

But there was something uninvited attending our opening night that would prevent this passing of the robe; our ceremony had a giant asterisk hanging above it like a cursed star.*

KIRSTEN WYATT   I do remember the pandemic looming. We didn't know.

Diana: The Musical would not open that month or even that year. The next Broadway opening of any show, with chorus or without wouldn't happen any time soon. *Girl from the North Country* was the last show to open before the world shut down just six days later.

OSKAR EUSTIS   It was at the opening night party that I caught Covid.

It all crashed down around us very quickly.

OSKAR EUSTIS   I went into the hospital just a few days later, and while I was in the hospital they shut down the theater. I went in on March 10th, and on March 12th Cuomo[2] shut the theaters. So I walked out of the

---

[2]Andrew Cuomo, Governor of New York from 2011 to 2021.

hospital into this hole in the world, and I was delirious. I didn't clock that the theaters were closing until I was ready to be discharged. And it was horrible. It was horrible.

What ceremony was there for this?

The New Faces: Part 2

Two months earlier, on January 6, 2020, we started rehearsals, over one year after we'd closed at the Public. My phone rang the day before. It was David Pittu, our "Reverend Marlowe," telling me that he was not going to be joining us.

DAVID PITTU It's not that I didn't *want* to go to Broadway. Of course I did, I was planning on it, but when I got this other job, I really had to weigh my feelings about the show. Part of me knew it could never, for me at least, be what it was that first time. Plus when it comes to exciting TV stuff I always feel like I have to get in line behind bigger names than mine, so I was pretty thrilled when this one came my way.

David had been cast in a major role on a Netflix limited series about the fashion designer Halston.

DAVID PITTU And it was a great part with a great cast [including Ewan McGregor], great people. I know I made the right decision. But it was a difficult decision. And it was very important to me when I accepted that job to call all the main people I had scenes with in *Girl from the North Country* and tell them I wouldn't be joining them, because after you work on something over time and develop those relationships, I didn't want them to just hear it from the stage manager.

When a show transfers from downtown to up, it's inevitable that not every cast member will transfer with it. Sometimes, as in David Pittu's case, another opportunity comes along and the actor takes it. Understood. Sometimes the actor is let go for one reason or another. Sometimes the timing just doesn't work out.

For various reasons, in January of 2020 we had a few big cast changes: Joe Scott, the boxer, would now be played by Austin Scott. Nick Laine, proprietor of the inn and husband of Mare's character Elizabeth, would be played by Jay O. Sanders. And David's role, Reverend Marlowe, would now be played by Matt McGrath.

In addition, three new swings joined the company: Jennifer Blood, Law Terrell Dunford, and Chiara Trentalange.

And of course, we'd just lost Artie Gaffin. His assistant Jeff Brancato, whom Artie had mentored for years, would take over as Production Stage Manager.

Broadway dimmed its lights in honor of Artie a few weeks after he died. A group of actors, writers, directors, and designers gathered in front of the Broadhurst Theatre on 44th Street for the memorial. I remember I was sweaty; I rode my bike and it was another warm September. Usually I'd apologize for sweating, but I just couldn't that evening. My hug is damp, so what? No one cared, no one was thinking about my back. We were thinking about Artie.

At Mare's home in Connecticut there is a hawk that returns to her yard every year, and it loves the tree Mare and her husband Tony planted in honor of Artie.

I walked into our first day of rehearsal at the New 42 studios, proud of my lanyard that the security desk had given me, the lanyard I would need to show the guard upon arriving every day to prove that I belonged here.

LUBA MASON   I was so proud of my drumming at that point. I was feeling confident. It was nothing like starting at the Public. We all were coming in with already experience and knowing what we were doing. And I was curious what that rehearsal process was going to be like.

I couldn't have wiped the smile off of my face if I tried, even when I noticed one troubling thing: *That new actor is as tall as I am.*

This is unreasonable of me, but it's just true: I have to be the tall one. I'm 6'6" and it's just kinda my thing. I'm the tall guy. My husband likes to point out in restaurants or airports or on the street (or anywhere really) *tall people*. He'll say, "That guy's taller than you." And my pride (at something I didn't *accomplish* or in any way have control over) overwhelms me and I have to prove him wrong by awkwardly finding a way to stand next to that person, hoping they don't notice me, so Mark can see that *I am taller*. If I am not taller, I don't admit it, I just insist that we find another place to sit.

So, it's day one, and the first thing I do is find a way to stand next to this tall stranger, whoever he is, hoping he won't notice, to prove to myself that *I'm taller*, when he suddenly turns around and looks me in the eye.

"Hi, I'm Austin."

I can't hate him, he exudes pure friendliness. Plus I'm just *this much* taller than he is.

CAITLIN HOULAHAN   Oh my gosh. I think Austin might be taller.

No.

AUSTIN SCOTT   I was nervous for sure. I didn't know what it would be. I didn't know if there would be any room to make the role my own.

PLATE 1 *Jeannette Bayardelle and cast sing "Pressing On" at the Tony Awards. Courtesy Mare Winningham.*

PLATE 2 *John Schiappa spinning in the Legacy Robe.* © *Rachel Stern.*

PLATE 3 *Ovation at the Belasco. Courtesy Mare Winningham.*

PLATE 4 *Marc Kudisch and Jeannette Bayardelle, in her Covid cab, as I called it.*
© *Chiara Trentalange.*

PLATE 5 *Dressing-room roommates, Austin Scott and Todd Almond.* © *Bruce Glikis.*

PLATE 6 *Daily pre-show testing.* © *Rachel Stern.*

PLATE 7 *Closing night party.* © *Chiara Trentalange.*

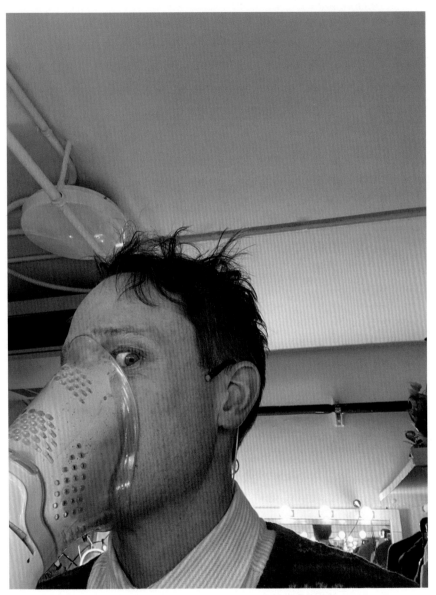

PLATE 8 *Pre "Duquesne Whistle" selfie for my husband.* © *Todd Almond.*

PLATE 9 *First week of rehearsal, Public Theater, August, 2018. © Tom Nelis.*

PLATE 10 *The new world. © Todd Almond.*

PLATE 11 *Anthony Edwards steps into the show at a moment's notice, has one rehearsal.* © *Tom Nelis.*

PLATE 12 *Austin Scott, here rehearsing with Kimber Elayne Sprawl, joins the Broadway company. Conor with his guitar. Courtesy Kimber Elayne Sprawl.*

Austin Scott had come to us directly from playing the title role in *Hamilton* on Broadway, one of the most demanding jobs in our field and surely the peak of the current-day musical theater mountain. I assumed that Austin must have been simply offered the role of the talented boxer "Joe Scott" in *Girl from the North Country*, but that's not the case. Even if you're playing Hamilton in *Hamilton*, you've still got to audition for your next gig.

AUSTIN SCOTT   I went in to audition for the first time between shows on a Saturday. I was exhausted. My voice was totally shot and I looked bedraggled and was feeling so tired. I then had a callback the following Saturday . . . again between shows.

Between shows on a two-show Saturday, all I ever want to do is nap. Austin works hard.

KIMBER ELAYNE SPRAWL   I thought [Austin] didn't like me!

He has movie-star looks and a quietude about him.

KIMBER ELAYNE SPRAWL   But it's just that he's an introvert. He's quiet, he's very quiet, and he doesn't give much unless he needs to. And I was just all over it. Talk about opposites!

Kimber's character Marianne slowly and cautiously falls in love with Austin's character Joe over the course of the play, their happy ending providing that little bit of light that even the darkest of stories needs.

KIMBER ELAYNE SPRAWL   I was just like, "Well, listen, we need to be friends. You have permission to talk to me and touch me any way you want. Let's build a connection." I just wanted the show to be good! And I was just like, "You're my only scene partner!" So I really came on very strong.

Another tall new presence in the room was Jay O. Sanders, taking over the role of Nick Laine.

CAITLIN HOULAHAN   I remember our first rehearsal at New 42, singing through everything and just the joy that people had, and also kind of wondering what Jay O. Sanders was going to be all about. I can't imagine how scary that must have been for him to be the lead of something and join a group that had been together for so long.

JAY O. SANDERS   I feel my size was good, I could see it as a good aspect of using me in this role to be a sort of central tent pole for the piece, which I really felt, it wanted to have something that it moved around.

That first week, Conor auditioned actors to replace David Pittu, so John Schiappa swung into the role of Reverend Marlowe for rehearsals.

> JEFF BRANCATO (email)
>   A HUGE kudos and welcome to Matt McGrath, who joined us at 2pm and has already been in two scenes, done a scene transition, and danced in "Duquesne Whistle." Matt, we're so happy to welcome you to this "dysfunctional Duluth family!"

And just like that, John swung back to his ensemble role.

> MATT MCGRATH   It seemed like a lot of fun-loving people that loved each other quite a bit. And it seemed like a moving train. So I was kind of getting on a moving train, but luckily I wasn't the only one.

My husband remembers seeing Matt McGrath back in 1992 in the Alec Baldwin/Jessica Lange *Streetcar Named Desire* on Broadway and still thinks of him as ". . . that young actor who kissed Jessica Lange."
     We had our new castmates. It was January, 2020, and we were in rehearsals again.

> ROBERT (BOB) JOY   There's a little anxiety about whether we were going to be able to regather the chemistry, the family down at the Public felt extraordinary to me. I think the Public itself is kind of a magical place. Being Off-Broadway is quite different from being *on* Broadway. And so you want to make sure that the feeling is there. And by the end of the first day, I knew it was there.

Bob pauses and adds . . .

> ROBERT JOY   The pandemic was nowhere on the horizon.

> MATT MCGRATH   I mean, we kind of already knew that Covid was coming. It's like *Covid is coming, are you guys up on this? Do you know anything about it, are we being wary?*

"Coronavirus" was somewhere else. Not America. Certainly not Broadway, and most *definitely* not in this seventh-floor rehearsal studio overlooking the giant, weird hovering hand atop Madame Tussauds wax museum across the street.
     We didn't have time to worry about "Coronavirus," whatever that was. We had work to do.

> AUSTIN SCOTT   It felt like, *let's break this thing open.*

Voices

I did something stupid, something I *knew* not to do, not *ever*, and I did it on day one of rehearsal of my Broadway debut: I sang full-voice on no sleep and without warming up.

Rookie mistake.

Only I've been singing my entire adult life, I knew better.

Sleep issues plague me, sometimes manifesting in sleepwalking episodes, like the time I woke up standing in the middle of my hotel room in Philadelphia, lifting up a corner of the couch looking for my husband, who was in our apartment in New York. I have learned to function on just a few hours of a REM cycle. It's not fun, but I can manage.

But under no circumstances should you *sing* on no sleep. Just like you shouldn't lift heavy weights or drive a car on no sleep, it's dangerous. Your coordination is off. You'll injure yourself.

I didn't warm up my voice that morning because I decided I wasn't going to sing that day. I hadn't slept, and I needed to conserve my low energy. And yet, when we got to "Duquesne Whistle" in the read-through, I didn't "mark" the song as I should have—"marking" means quietly singing to *save your voice*. I should have marked, but I sang out, full-voiced. I pushed and shoved and muscled out those forty-two high Gs. And while I was doing it, I knew I should abort. *Stop, stop! Stop singing, no one will care if you don't sing today!* But maybe I wanted to prove something? Justify my presence in a Broadway rehearsal room? Whatever the psychology, I didn't stop.

And I hurt my voice. Bad. I felt it.

Shit.

Changes

What is a "Broadway musical," anyway? Were we one?

> LUCY HIND   I do remember feeling a little bit of pressure to be a "Broadway" choreographer.

I wondered the same thing: I'm a Broadway actor now, should I do something different from what I did Off-Broadway? My performance at the Public felt simple and clean (after my initial over-acting), but was that *Broadway* enough? Was moving to Broadway *upgrading*? Did Elias need *upgrading*? Lucy Hind, also making her debut, asked herself a similar question.

> LUCY HIND   I do remember coming in one day and saying, "Conor, I've just got some changes for Duquesne Whistle," *wink, wink. I'm a Broadway Choreographer now!* And Conor said, "Okay." He was so

sweet. And I put them in, and they weren't massive changes, but it was just a little bit jazzier. It was just a little bit more lined up. And he didn't say anything. And then I think it was either at the end of that rehearsal or the next day we came in to do the number. I said to him, "Conor, the changes I put in . . ." And he said, "You're going to take them out." I was like, "I am." He said, "I'm glad." I don't know what I was thinking! I made those changes to serve me, not the show. I think it must be easy to get into that trap.

What about the show itself? Did it need something more—an upgrade?— now that it was uptown?

CONOR MCPHERSON I remember having a meeting with Aaron [Lustbader, General Manager] . . . and he just said to me, "On Broadway, there's a kind of tradition of a curtain number." He said, "I dunno what it would be in this [show], but if there's something you can think of, it sends people out in a good buzz. And then they tell good friends." He says, "It's kind of useful." I was like, *okay*. And I had wanted to use "Pressing On" somehow. I thought, *oh, it could be good there*. I came in and said, "We're going to try this." It probably wasn't what the producers had thought we might use. But it worked so well.

"Pressing On" is from *Saved*, the second of Dylan's trilogy of "born again" albums. I remind you here of something Conor said:

CONOR MCPHERSON A huge thing for me was coming across [Dylan's] Christian era. That knocked me for six. I loved that. I just loved the passion of his music around that time.

The song had been with Conor since the very beginning. So when Aaron suggested the show add a finale, Conor had no trouble knowing just what that should be, but the task fell to Simon Hale to make it a reality.

SIMON HALE We were in New 42 [rehearsal studio], and Conor walked over to me. I knew that they were talking about wanting to put a song in at the end of the show. And he just gave me a little piece of paper and it just said, "'Pressing on', Saved." And that was it. He didn't say anything. He just put this thing in front of me and walked off. So I went back to the apartment and just put an arrangement together with Jeannette's voice in mind, having heard her sing rather extraordinarily, as we all know, in the room. I made a decent guess of a key, which I think we ended up staying in, and wrote an arrangement. Because I thought, "Let's get something ready just in case we are going to look at this." And a couple of days later Conor said, "Should we have a look at that song?"

CONOR MCPHERSON When we did that, there was something undeniable . . . like a gale-force wind hit me in the face with those voices. People were just, *fuck. Yeah*. It was a very special moment.

SIMON HALE I felt at that point I knew what the show was. And at the beginning, back to 2017, I didn't know what that world was at all.

Voices: Part 2

AUSTIN SCOTT I didn't know if there was really going to be any room to make the character [of Joe Scott] my own. But I realized immediately that Conor was not interested in me recreating what had been done. "*Find these characters in yourself now*." And I was really grateful for that because it helped me feel like less of an outsider.

Broadway rehearsals were the same as Off-Broadway. There was freedom for everyone to make their own decisions about their characters.

AUSTIN SCOTT Everyone was doing their own thing and it became clear that at times we were living in different worlds. I'd enter a scene with the backstory I had created for this Black man living in 1930s Duluth, Minnesota and I'd come up against another (actor) with a different idea of what that looked like. Our perspectives clashed at times but that—that's real life.

One cardinal rule in acting is that you never tell another actor how to play their part. But that rule was broken when one actor offered thoughts to Austin on how he should play his character.

AUSTIN SCOTT There were moments where I had to decide, *I'm going to go with my gut here*. As a director, Conor gave us a lot of freedom and with that came space for a variety of perspectives about character relationships and the world of the piece.

Austin is so kind-hearted in the re-telling, and I appreciate his protective non-name-naming. Rehearsal is a safe space, after all, and with generous souls like Austin Scott, it's even a forgiving space for colleagues who overstep boundaries.

AUSTIN SCOTT I think a lot of those moments ultimately led to realizing the relationships. The characters live in two different worlds. When I leaned into that, I think it was stronger. We don't have to be on the same page about this moment. We just have to live in the same room. We just have to live in the same world.

The line between fiction and reality had already started to blur. After the pandemic and the murder of George Floyd, the line would be nearly invisible.

Changes: Part 2

Literature is my favorite artform, and I believe the true power of any novel lies in the re-read. When you re-read *Les Misérables* you feel again all of the pain that the characters suffer, but their suffering doesn't feel in vain because you know where it's leading. It's already written.

To re-read is to be a fatalist.

And fate seems real to me. I look back at certain choices I made in life that panned out later in unexpected, positive ways, and I do see more than just coincidence.

Then again, maybe fate is really just hindsight with a good eye for coincidence. I don't know. Sometimes I throw my hands up and think *it's all meaningless, nothing matters, who cares?*

I even hear myself say, "I don't care. Nothing matters."

But then I feel an invisible hand guide me, hold me back, deny me something, or nudge me *toward* something, like those holy streetlights did, leading me through snowy Manhattan. And I follow. It's probably just my conscience or my survival instinct or even my laziness; could be my hunger or my narrow-minded comfort-seeking; my habit or desire. But whatever it is, it guides me as if it knows the future and is making sure I get there, and I can't help but think that a similar guiding hand put the song "Pressing On" in front of Conor so that someone years later in that very small post-pandemic audience could hear it.

> CONOR MCPHERSON   Yeah. Bob's determination, almost like he's trying to believe. That's a big tenet of Christianity, too. The leap of faith. Just believe and then you'll believe. He's trying. There's "Many try to stop me, shake me up in my mind." He's struggling with his faith. So it's like, if you're *coasting along*, you're not *pressing on*. I always love those lyrics, and getting Jeannette to sing those lyrics, well that was turbo charged.

I was struggling. My voice was in bad shape, and I worried that I'd fumbled on my first day, fumbled so bad that they were going to send me back down to the minor leagues.

I needed comfort. I needed Bob Dylan's faith. I needed exactly what "Pressing On" was offering.

> CONOR MCPHERSON   I love the imagery and the stories [of Christianity]. Do I think that that's what the universe is? Could it be that there is nothing? Yes, it could well be. And none of us will ever know.

If I liked the Bible, I would have read it every day during that period. I found myself rereading *Les Misérables*.

Even though I was struggling, I knew I was meant to be there, in that rehearsal room, in Conor's play. I felt it. Even if I had messed up, which I had, I was meant to be there.

Back at the conservatory in Cincinnati, I had a similar set-back. At the end of every school year, we had to sing one by one in front of the entire vocal department faculty for what they called a "board" exam. That single "board" performance determined if you would be allowed to continue on as the conservatory the following year. My freshman year, I failed my board. They dropped me from the program.

After only one year, I was out.

Maybe I should study writing? I like writing. Maybe I'll be a writer. Where can I go to study writing? Iowa?

But I knew, *I knew* I was meant to be there, specifically at the College-Conservatory of Music at the University of Cincinnati. This was my path. I was certain. Not Iowa. Not anywhere else. It was written, I could feel it. For whatever reason, the novel of my life says that I graduated with a Bachelor of Music degree from CCM.

I decided to stick around Cincinnati that summer, even though I was no longer a student at CCM. I worked at a music store and took voice lessons, and I did nothing else. When the next school year rolled around, I enrolled as a University of Cincinnati student with no association with the conservatory. At the end of the first semester, I knocked on every voice-department faculty door and explained that I had made a mistake by failing my board, but that I'd been working to correct that mistake. Could I please audition for the department again?

They didn't have to hear me out, they already had and they'd already made their judgment, but for some reason, they were kind enough to give me a second chance. I sang for them in a mid-year board re-do. The next semester I was a conservatory student again.

Now here I was in a similar situation in New York City, years later, as a professional singer. I really didn't want to be dropped from this show because I'd messed up.

Every time Jeannette sang "Pressing On" I felt so grateful to be in the room. I needed to hear it.

CONOR MCPHERSON   In the ritual of theater, you do something like "Pressing On" at the end of it, it feels powerful, and that feeling can keep you going. And you realize, *something was going on.* "When what's lost has been found, and what's to come has already been." That's just like . . . those contradictions! Mind-blowing. I mean, there was *never* a time that I saw [that song] that I wasn't just profoundly moved—I felt so grateful, lucky, humble. And those things are meaningful. Cause you don't come away kind of going, *you know what, maybe it's all meaningless.* You come away going, *you know what? It feels like it means something, it means something.*

It doesn't have to be eternal life to mean something right now.

But even *that*, if it means something right now, that *is* eternal. Do you know what I mean? It's like any moment, once there's one moment, then there's eternity. Because once there's something, what's outside that something? What's the nothing? What is it? Where is it? Once there's something, there is eternity and there is infinite space. There just is. So once there's any existence or any time, it's forever. And it's for all directions.

Once there's something, it's all holy. I mean, it's all meaningful. It's all mysterious and amazing and mind-blowing. And actually for me, the sort of vastness and the sense, the absence even of any meaning, literal meaning, is quite comforting. What's happening to me is the silence. We all just return to the silence. And you were here, you got a little glimpse of it, and then you were gone. That's kind of enough for me. It's hard to reach that place.

In fact the true mystery—the greatest mystery—is non-existence. That's the concept we cannot even visualize. Nothingness. But of course, that is where we are all headed. Existence is necessarily violent. It's an interaction of different energies that all struggle to exist at the same moment. The universe is full of explosions and crushing pressures as all these forms of energy interact. And our little lives are also consequently full of pain and conflict. But ultimately this coming together of the elements, all the atoms that make each of us a human being with consciousness for a fleeting moment, will dissipate and dissolve. And we will return to the silence from whence we came. That's our eternal destiny. I find that more dignified than some notion of "eternal life." And in a weird way—more holy. Or at least that's the way I like to think about it all anyhow.

Amen.

Voices: Part 3

Each day I woke up hoping my voice would feel better, and each day I thought it did, but then I would sing, and . . . *splat, crack, horror.* My voice, that I know so well, that had felt free and open at the Public, was now a stranger to me, clamped down in my throat, caught up in a prison of knots and out of my control.

I didn't know what to do. Our new castmates, Austin and Jay and Matt, were bringing all of this new life to the room, they were so good, each of them; Jeannette's performance was blooming in front of us into something magnificent; Mare and Kimber and Colton, Marc and Luba, Tom, Bob, everyone was deepening and growing. And I was fumbling. I didn't want to be, I wasn't meant to be.

I should have asked for help straight away, but I didn't. Not for weeks. I kept pushing through rehearsals and slamming into my solo, horrified at how badly it was going. My trust that it would get better was wrestling with a dumb stubbornness. Marco called me in for a few one-on-one rehearsals and I kept insisting I was fine, just needed to find the right vocal placement again after a year of not singing.

He didn't seem panicked, honestly, and there was no reason for him to be. I had been fine at the Public, why wouldn't I be fine now?

It was all fine, it was all going to be fine.

But my panic was growing. I knew how relentless the preview period would be, with rehearsals every day and shows every night. Maybe my voice could recover if I had a week of no vocal rest, no speaking or singing, but that wasn't an option.

When in the third week of rehearsal I *again* cracked on all of my high notes and saw Conor's face fall, if only slightly, betraying a bit of worry, I came to my senses and realized *I need help and I need it now.*

Who could help? Experts. I made two calls.

First, Liz Caplan, Broadway and film vocal coach. She said she could squeeze me in next week.

Second, Elliot Fishbein, functional manual physical therapist. His office said he had nothing available until late February. Shit. By then we would be deep into previews. His office put me on the waiting list.

Thankfully Liz could see me after rehearsal that Monday, but I wasn't sure if it was advisable for me to even sing in a lesson without physical therapy first. Luckily, I got an email from Elliot Fishbein's office saying he had a last-minute cancellation and could I come in this morning?

Perfect, except it was impossible. "I have rehearsal, can he see me after?"

"No. Only this morning. His next availability is next month."

I told his office *yes, I'll be there*, knowing full well that I couldn't be because we were doing a final run-through of the show in the room first thing that morning, top-to-bottom and I couldn't miss that. The designers were going to be there to watch, so were the producers. It was a big day.

But opportunity was reaching out a helping hand, and I needed to take it. And as any good musical theater fan knows, "Opportunity is not a lengthy visitor."[3]

When I got to rehearsal, I pulled Conor aside, and trying not to seem overly needy, I quietly explained the situation, that I had injured myself, that's why I had been struggling, that I needed help, and there was someone who could help me today, and could I possibly miss the run through of the show so that I could get that help.

---

[3] A line of advice to Cinderella in Sondheim and Lapine's *Into the Woods.*

Without a moment's delay, Conor said, "Of course. Take care of yourself, I'm not worried about you."

I jumped up, forgetting to say "Thank you," grabbed my bag and coat, ran down the seven flights to the street level, unlocked my bike right there on 42nd Street, the heart of Times Square, and zipped down to Chelsea to Elliot's office.

I must have looked like a wild animal when I walked into Elliot's office. Desperate. *Mean*. A cat at the vet in one of those videos.

Elliot used his hands to release the gnarls I'd manifested in my vocal muscles. Liz led me through a series of exercises to reignite my vocal technique now that my instrument was functional again.

It wasn't fate, it was *other people* that saved me that day. I texted Conor "Thank you."

After a day of silence and sleep, my voice was closer to feeling like mine again, and I knew I would recover. And when I did, Jeannette put her hand on my shoulder after my solo, and with eyes that said *I know you've been struggling*, said, "You sound great!"

She's such a good person.

So it was hard to see *her* struggle vocally immediately thereafter, only for a completely different reason. Fucking Covid.

The producers flew Jeannette to Lincoln, Nebraska to do a pre-Broadway-opening press event for our show.

JEANNETTE BAYARDELLE   You guys were in rehearsal. And so I flew out there, and I remember when I was flying back on a plane, there was a guy next to me, and I remember him coughing and stuff. And this was very, very, very early on with them talking about Coronavirus. Nobody was really, it was like you had to be watching the news or you had to be in the know to know about this thing. And I remember thinking in my head, *this man has Coronavirus*. So I get back, I did this new thing with my song where I took the octave up.

Go immediately to minute 3:30 of track twelve on our original Broadway cast recording of *Girl from the North Country* to hear what Jeannette is referencing here. In the song "True Love Tends to Forget," embedded as it is in this arrangement between bookends of Luba Mason's killer rendition of "Sweetheart Like You," Jeannette, as Mrs. Neilsen, lays her emotional state bare to her lover, Nick Laine. That vocal line she sings on "I was lying down in the reeds . . ." is not what is written in the score. That's all Jeannette.

When she was in Nebraska for the press event, she thought she'd give this new melodic idea an inaugural go. Lincoln would be an out-of-town tryout.

Lincoln loved it.

When she came back to New York, she sang it for us—the climactic chorus *a full octave higher* than written, creating this dramatic angst that matched the moment perfectly. We held our breath, transfixed, and then erupted into ecstatic applause when she'd finished.

Jeannette had just lifted the entire room the metric equivalent of that octave right off the ground.

Conor and Simon beamed.

JEANNETTE BAYARDELLE   They were like, "Yes, put it in a show."

But Jeannette's trip to Nebraska gave her something more than a new "moment."

JEANNETTE BAYARDELLE   A week later we had to do that event at the Bitter End, in the West Village.

The marketing team put together a New York press event at Dylan's old stomping grounds, the Bitter End, the West Village bar still coasting on the association with B.D. It was a cool idea, to sing where Dylan had begun his career in the city, and instead of dressing in the period of the play, we dressed in the period of Dylan's heyday there, the 1970s. There is a YouTube video of the event, and if you go 20 seconds in, you'll hear Jeannette sing that same incredible climax of "True Love Tends to Forget."

JEANNETTE BAYARDELLE   I normally never struggle vocally. I'm not one of those people that gets sick and is like, "Oh, I can't sing." That's not me, I can tell you on one hand how many times I've gotten sick. Where I can't sing.

Yet, you'll hear in that clip that Jeannette is uncharacteristically . . . struggling.

JEANNETTE BAYARDELLE   And I noticed in the Bitter End when I was singing and you go back to tapes, it just was feeling a little somewhat . . . . this ain't right. And then from there, it just got worse. I remember I was in rehearsal and I was like, "I have got to go to the urgent care tonight" because I just felt—I was tired, so long. I went to urgent care that Saturday night and then Sunday I didn't come in. Then Monday we were off, and Tuesday I came back. But when I came back, my voice wasn't back.

This was how it started. Our cast's spiritual leader was the first hit. And in our first several weeks of previews, with our Broadway audiences filling up the house, Jeannette sang the climax of her big song in the lower octave, where it was originally written. And though she sounded fine down there, we all *knew* what she could really do; Jeannette could lift the Belasco Theater twelve feet off the ground.

JEANNETTE BAYARDELLE My voice wasn't back and my body wasn't either. But at the time, I didn't care about the body. When you are a singer, you don't care. You could be like, *my back, my stomach*, you don't care about that. You worry about this.

She points to her throat and sighs heavily.

JEANNETTE BAYARDELLE   And that was the beginning.

And that was the beginning.

5

44th Street

F#

January 29, 2020

We're two blocks north on 44th Street now at the Belasco Theater, which, being near 6th Avenue instead of 8th, is on the *wrong side* of Broadway, according to some. It's true, most of the theaters sit to the west of Times Square and get more foot-traffic than those on the *east* side. But like all fabulous outsiders from the wrong side of the tracks, the Belasco is the most beautiful one of all.

January 30, 2020

We're teching the show and Jeannette is still sick, but surely it's not . . . *that*. Most of us just ignore *that*. *That* is in other places and it's never going to affect Broadway.

But Jeannette has doubts.

JEANNETTE BAYARDELLE   When I went to the urgent care [during rehearsals], I was like, "Listen, could it be Coronavirus?" And they say, "No, it's not in this country now, blah, blah, blah, blah, blah."

What can she do?
She shows up to work and presses on.

February 6, 2020

I'm so in love with our new home at the Belasco that I tell my friend who is coming to our dress rehearsal tonight to get there early so she can take it all in. There's no lobby to speak of, just a box-office and a door to the auditorium, so it's not that I'm recommending she generally mill about. No, I text her "Get here early and take your seat immediately so you can *look up*. And then *look around*. Tiffany glass light fixtures and ornaments throughout the house! You can almost make a game of trying to find them all, like you're on some fantastical glass-butterfly hunt."

She texts back: "K."

I'm out of control with happiness. And I don't care who knows it.

February 7, 2020

JEANNETTE BAYARDELLE   This is how bad my sickness was: my left eye had a yellow haze over it. It looked like a scary movie. It was a yellow film over my eye. Went to the eye doctor and everything. I was coughing so hard that my back went out.

But the show must go on, we're in previews now and there's a real Broadway audience in the house tonight.

I will die, only now I will die on Broadway. After this performance, whatever happens next, I will forever be able to say that I've performed in a Broadway show. At forty-four years old, this is a major life accomplishment.

My parents are in the audience. So is my husband.

Preparing for my "Duquesne Whistle" entrance, I put on the crisp-pressed white-linen three-piece suit ensuring, because we want the moment to be perfectly *angelic*, that I am wrinkle-free. To that end, I have devised a system for putting on the suit: First, I strip down to my underwear and put on only the socks and shoes, which is quite a look, so I make silly poses in the mirror. I can hear on the monitor in my dressing room Jeannette and Luba singing "Sweetheart Like You/True Love Tends to Forget."

Poor Jeannette, she must have a sinus infection or something.

Next, I put on the shirt, then the pants—stepping into them with an exaggerated lunge like the Minister of Silly Walks to avoid putting a crease anywhere. Now the vest, which is snug, I'll need to watch what I eat, and lastly the bow tie, which I put on upside down as a kind of good luck talisman. Stage management will help me into the jacket when I get to the stage left wing (and they'll button it for me so I don't lift my arms and get creases at the elbows).

I snap a selfie and text it to my husband with the message: "About to die!"

Then I remember he's in the audience. I hope his phone is off.

I head down to the stage-left wing from my dressing room much earlier than necessary because I want to watch the two scenes that precede my big song: "Hurricane" and Thanksgiving.

JEANNETTE BAYARDELLE   I was so messed up. I felt like this is the worst thing ever. I've never been this sick before. And I just had to push through it.

"Hurricane," Dylan's ode to Rubin Carter, the champion boxer unjustly accused of murder and imprisoned in New Jersey, whips the stage up into a fever-storm, the entire ensemble dancing and shaking like a people possessed, possessed by America's roiling racial and economic disparities. I sing along, full-voiced from the wing, even though my microphone isn't on because I'm not in the scene.

Jeannette pushes herself to get through the performance . . .

JEANNETTE BAYARDELLE I understand to folks out there in the audience, Broadway is the highest level, it's the highest platform where we present what we do as a theatrical performer.

. . . and is now certain that despite what the doctors told her, *the coronavirus is here,* and it's exactly what she's dealing with.

Next is the Thanksgiving scene, long and hyper-realistic, played out in real time, as if from a Robert Altman film, with multiple conversations happening simultaneously and multiple story-lines intersecting over a loud meal of actual food and drink; the band plays in the corner and the ensemble laugh and eat and dance, adding to the chaos.

JEANNETTE BAYARDELLE I wanted it to be this big gospel, full-voice number, but I got sick and I couldn't hit those notes.

Somehow Conor has managed to create not a representation of real life but real life on the stage during the Thanksgiving scene. I'm taking it all in: the noise of people, the tangle of desires, the addictions and the secrets, the music, the bursts of anger, singing, all happening at once.

JEANNETTE BAYARDELLE Of course, I have an "A" show, I have a "B" show and I have a "C" show. But I really try not to steer away from what we know the show to be.

Watching from the wing, I feel like Emily in *Our Town,* who gets a chance to take in one more full-sense immersion into life before she must go to her grave. "One more look!" she begs.

My father blustering, my mother unraveling. They are so beautiful.
I can't look at everything hard enough.

JEANNETTE BAYARDELLE My goal is always an "A" show. But being that I did get sick . . .

So much life with death so near, my death! I have died, but no one at this Thanksgiving meal knows. Not yet. Nor do they know that one of our cast, Jeannette, is struggling mightily with an infection that will take us all down.

JEANNETTE BAYARDELLE   . . . I think I did a "C" show for a good month in previews.

I hear my cue, I make my entrance, stepping in front of my first Broadway audience, as Elias's ghost.

"Listen!" I sing on an F#. I always loved that the note was F#, just one half-step away from G, and Elias himself is just one little half-step away from G-d.

My voice is ringing throughout the house as I sing.

JEANNETTE BAYARDELLE   Sometimes we take that for granted, we think we are talented, but it's a collective. Yeah, you sound good, but Scott Sanders [audio engineer and board op] got us sounding real good on that audio, you know what I mean? These are people who have worked on their craft for years. You don't just jump on the stage and sing and you sound like that. Yes, we sing nice, but we've got some juice and some help.

Listen to that Duquesne Whistle blowin', blowin' like it's gonna sweep my world away.

So much life with death so near.

I'm here now!

Cruise Ship

My real-life mother and father, earlier that day, were sitting on a cruise ship docked in Bayonne, New Jersey. They had decided to kill two birds: get some sun in the Bahamas and then swing up to New York City to see their son's first performance on Broadway.

I woke up that morning, February 7, to headlines like:

4 passengers on a cruise ship docked near New York City are getting further evaluation for coronavirus[1]

"Oh, no! My parents have brought the coronavirus to the city," I said to Mark.

They were meant to stay with me and Mark in our guest room, but we decided it would be bad if I got sick, so, in case they'd been exposed, *could they stay in a hotel that we've arranged and paid for?*

---

[1]Croft, Jay, *CNN*, February 7, 2020, cnn.com. Accessed October 9, 2023.

They said that as soon as they were allowed to disembark, which could be days from now, staying in a hotel would be "No problem."

Luckily, they made it off the ship that day Covid-free and to my first preview, which my sweet mom kept calling my "opening night."

The Forbidden High-Five

Mid-February, somewhere in the middle of previews.

I'm happy. And feeling healthy again.

I bike to the show every day, but sometimes I feel like walking. It takes fifteen minutes. I head right through Times Square, crossing from the Northwest corner to the Southeast, and while the throngs of tourists feel suffocating, I enjoy noticing fellow actors or musicians in the crowd, on the way to their respective shows. I don't necessarily know them all personally, but I know we're in the same tribe. I give them the secret nod. They nod back.

We are starting to hear more troubling reports of the coronavirus:

Global death toll from coronavirus exceeds 2,100[2]
Coronavirus outbreak "getting bigger": All the latest updates[3]
US prepares for possible coronavirus pandemic[4]

Maybe we should all start sanitizing our hands more frequently. Maybe don't shake hands with people, or hug people, or touch people. Just to be safe. Just for now. Okay.

On one of my walks to the theater for a preview performance, I pass my friend Elizabeth Stanley, who is playing the lead role in *Jagged Little Pill* at the Broadhurst Theater (on the *right* side of Broadway).

ELIZABETH STANLEY   I have a vague memory of that moment on the street with you.

I cannot shake the novel-thrill that I'm now performing on Broadway, so I'm really bouncing as I walk, which I can see in the reflections of store windows makes me look a bit over-eager. Actors should look cool, *pull it together Almond*. I smile at my friend Elizabeth walking toward me, she smiles back, I raise my palm up as we pass each other, and Elizabeth slaps me high-five.

---

[2]Jiang, Steven, *CNN*, February 19, 2020, cnn.com.
[3]Siddiqui, Usaid, *Aljazeera*, February 28, 2020, aljazeera.com. Accessed October 10, 2023.
[4]Feuer, Will, et al., *CNBC*, February 21, 2020, cnbc.com. Accessed October 10, 2023.

ELIZABETH STANLEY   That's always so fun when you're like, "Oh my God, we're both on Broadway!" It's so rare when you're doing a Broadway show to see other people [you know] who are having that moment.

But as soon as we slap our very cool high-five, I immediately think: *I shouldn't have done that. I shouldn't have touched her hand. We're not supposed to touch anyone's hand. That's how you get coronavirus. And people are dying from this thing.*

I get to the theater and I immediately wash and sanitize my hands, annoyed that I can't just enjoy the moment. It's tainted now if I can't slap a high-five with someone in my tribe. Little do I know that this will be the smallest of joys to be denied us.

I am reminded of another virus that made touching anyone in my tribe feel dangerous. Coming of age in the late 80s/early 90s, there was added terror for gay men like me. It was hard enough living in a small town hostile to anything not cis-gender or heterosexual (how many times did I erase the word "fag" from my locker?), but since this was pre-internet, there was no way to connect with other kids feeling the way I felt, and the main story on the news about gay people was that they were dying horrible deaths because they had sex. I knew I was gay, and like any kid going through puberty, my hormones were activating. But according to the television, my only window to the world beyond Nebraska, sex equaled death. I think a lot of gay men my age have never been able to disentangle those two things.

And now the phones in our pockets were telling us touch equals death.

White House advisor Dr. Fauci says handshaking needs to stop even when pandemic ends—other experts agree.[5]

There's a great tradition in the theater of "going back." You'll hear it after a show if you eavesdrop on certain audience members, "Are you going back? We're going back." It just means going backstage to the dressing rooms to see the actor(s) after the show. You have to be on the list at the stage door to get backstage, they don't let just anyone "go back." To be on the list, you have to know one of the actors. So saying, "We're going back" is a little bit of a name-drop.

And dammit, I wanted people dropping my name so they could "come back" to my dressing room! That is part of being a Broadway actor!

Luckily, before Jeff announced the moratorium on "coming back" in the name of safety, I did manage to eke out two backstage visits from friends who came to early previews: My sweet friend Ken whom I'd met in Kansas

---

[5]Scipioni, Jade, *CNBC*, April 9, 2020. Accessed November 14, 2023.

City when I was doing *Two Pianos, Four Hands*. I credit him with helping to pull me out of the dark place I was in, largely through karaoke. And Cathie and Taylor from New Hampshire, a jovial couple who have been together for years and still make each other laugh.

But that's it. Just Ken and Cathie and Taylor.

No more friends backstage. No more high-fives in the streets. No more shaking hands. No more touching.

Over at *Jagged Little Pill*, Elizabeth Stanley got sick.

ELIZABETH STANLEY   I am definitely of that old school Broadway work ethic where I was just like, unless I really cannot do it, I will be there. I will do the show. And so I had missed maybe one show. I mean, it might've been two, but I think maybe it was just one. And then I came back, I was like, *I still feel really tired, but also better.* So I'm sure I was just continuing to spread it around. I mean, I'm sure we all just had it.

Her experience at *Jagged Little Pill* would be like the experience at every show on Broadway. We didn't know how prevalent Covid already was within our ranks, and there was nothing at all in place like a ten-day mandatory quarantine.

ELIZABETH STANLEY   And then I just remember when the producers came and said, "Hey, we're aware that this is kind of becoming a thing, just so you know we're going to be safe." But of course, no one really knew yet. So we all went, *oh, okay.* But I remember the ensemble really being [upset] because they were all sharing dressing rooms, and I was kind of isolated in my own [dressing room]. There was already a divide like we see in our country. I mean, it's fascinating, but even in our cast, some people were saying, "Everyone calm down. It's just people getting sick. It's fine." And then other people were saying, "No one's paying attention. This is serious. We shouldn't be here. At what cost are we doing this?"

It wouldn't be until March 11, the day before the shutdown, that we truly felt the threat on Broadway's doorstep. It took the *New York Times* putting the words Broadway and coronavirus in the same headline to make it real for us:

Broadway Usher Tests Positive for Coronavirus[6]

---

[6]Paulson, Michael, *New York Times*, March 11, 2020, nytimes.com. Accessed October 10, 2023.

Here Comes the Story of the Hurricane

March, 2020

JEANNETTE BAYARDELLE My sister and I were a part of this prophetic group. And in this group they were warning us, "Listen, a virus is coming," and this is before anybody was talking about it.

JEFF BRANCATO We're in previews and it's going well, we tech quicker than we'd planned, we're selling out . . .

JEANNETTE BAYARDELLE And so I'm trying to prepare for opening night, I'm trying to do my thing and my sister's calling me, *Go get groceries, go get groceries, go get this, go get this.* I'm like, "Leave me alone!"

AUSTIN SCOTT Jeannette, she was the town prophet. She read every article and seemed to have insider connections with scientists. She just knew everything.

JEANNETTE BAYARDELLE I remember going to Jeff. I was literally going into that office. Conor was there one time. Tristan was there. And I said, "Guys, we need to film this [show] because when they shut Broadway down we need to have *content*."

AUSTIN SCOTT She would speak from fact. "Listen, it's going to hit in a week, it's going to shut everything down and sports will be first."

We're a week away from opening night, and I'm following the rules: I'm washing my hands and taking my vitamins and not touching anything and reading the news online.

It's a nuisance. Jeff and his stage management team launch into slightly skeptical action backstage.

JEFF BRANCATO We aren't going to do backstage visits anymore. We *are* going to sign autographs, but each actor will need to have their own Sharpie. And stage management will have to label the Sharpies.

Meanwhile, my religious experience *onstage* is getting deeper and stranger. In the dark wing in my white suit, I sing along to "Hurricane" with my arms raised as if it were a hymn of praise—wrinkles be damned!—and Austin Scott is the preacher riling up the congregants.

Covid creeps its way into the theater like a sentient, invisible fog from a horror movie.

JEFF BRANCATO I remember, I'm like, *I'm not fucking labeling Sharpies!*

Like any good horror movie villain, it moves silently, making its victims doubt its presence.

JEFF BRANCATO   People can wipe their own Sharpie down with a Clorox wipe if they care. I'm not wiping down *wipes*!

Covid is still not *real*. It's in the US, sure, but we're fine. We have a show to do.

JEANNETTE BAYARDELLE   And Conor said, "Jeannette, do you really think this is a thing?" I'm like, *yes*. I remember telling Jeff, "We need hand sanitizer."

I'm fixated on "Hurricane," I can't figure out how on earth it was even rehearsed, it's such an unusual number. It feels supernatural, like when someone starts speaking in tongues.

The song comes out of nowhere in the second act. Joe Scott, the boxer, takes center stage . . .

AUSTIN SCOTT   I was given the structure of ["Hurricane"] as a million different things, and also none of those things. And what is it? Here's this wild, beautiful fever-dream of a number: *make sense of it, find a way to get behind it and embody it.* And we spent a ton of time on finding the dance moves.

. . . and he sings lyrics that don't push the play forward or make complete logical sense within the story; the song is about a real-life person in another decade. Another reality. It doesn't add up, but it's undeniable that it's *doing something* to the audience. It's doing something to *me*. It's stirring something up, something potent. Austin glides and spins, and everyone else on stage catches a fever that sets *them* spinning too, and shaking and dancing or in Luba's case *kicking* and *stomping*.

It's wild. And I'm glued to it, standing right in the path of stage management, who are now bustling around backstage a bit more seriously now, whispering intense whispers to each other.

JEFF BRANCATO   Jeannette asked if we had hand sanitizer and we were like, *yeah*. And she said, "You should go and buy hand sanitizer now. It's all going to be gone."

The slow train was rounding the bend at last, and it was pulling a hurricane with it.

And Joe Scott, the play's version of "Rubin Carter," a man defamed, imprisoned, oppressed, and maligned, is whipping it up.

LUCY HIND   "Hurricane," that is the fever-pitch for me when I talk about that number. It's about those characters yearning. Aching.

AUSTIN SCOTT   Lucy's vision was that it was like a folk dance and I think somehow I just never quite got into that.

It wasn't dancing, it was conjuring. Fate was at work again, here.

LUCY HIND   And then one day [Austin] was just doing some moves, his arms above his head and kind of stamping . . .

Fate and Austin Scott were stirring up through Bob Dylan via Rubin Carter something that's been blowing unheeded in America for centuries, something that would churn itself up to a gale force in the summer of 2020 with the murder of George Floyd.

Here is a Black man in 2020 singing Dylan's lyrics from 1976 about a decade-old injustice borne of American racism; lyrics that *even then* felt 200 years overdue:

When a cop pulled him over to the side of the road
Just like the time before and the time before that
In Patterson, that's just the way things go
If you're Black, you might as well not
Show up on the street, less you wanna draw the heat.

Meanwhile, in the wings, the fog of Covid is thickening, waiting to make its entrance. Just as Jeannette, still struggling with the virus's symptoms, had warned.

JEANNETTE BAYARDELLE   I didn't want to be the bearer of bad news, but I had the people at home saying, "Listen, it's coming. It's coming. It's coming."

Marco and the band are steamrolling their heavy groove; Robert Joy is jerking his feet back and forth on the ground in this like he's trying to make the earth turn faster; Luba Mason is stomping and wiggling like an electric current is catching her; Chelsea Lee Williams leaps into the air like she's almost free of gravity.

If this is a church service, this is where the spirit descends.

AUSTIN SCOTT   It became something else for me. It was less-literal dance moves, and more body movement . . .

This is the divine fire. I can't look at everyone hard enough. They are so amazing.

AUSTIN SCOTT   . . . it was an expression of emotion that had to come out.

The song runs out of words, ending instead on a group guttural "Ahh!" everyone's arms raising up in a way that suggests both railing to heaven and a pulling of something from the earth.

As the lights go down on the scene, Jeannette lets out a heavy sigh and leans all of her weight onto the dining table down center. Exactly how a prophet would do, exhausted from having warned everyone that something was coming, something everyone was ignoring, something she'd already encountered.

JEANNETTE BAYARDELLE   And then it came.

March 4, 2020

JEFF BRANCATO   We're walking to dinner between shows on Wednesday. And [assistant stage manager] Laurie says, "My husband just said that they were shutting down the N.B.A. and the *Today Show* is not having visitors anymore."

March 5, 2020

MANDY HACKETT   What we do on opening night is we sit and read the reviews and we pull quotes. It was me, Patrick Catullo, Aaron and Tris, and all our whole marketing and press team. We were all there. I have the best pictures! Everyone had left except the producing team, and we had this amazing dance party. We danced all night at Bryant Park. Danced and danced.

March 7, 2020

AUSTIN SCOTT   I remember having talks with Kimber and saying, "Surely not *Broadway*. Right?" And if it did shut down, it would be for a few days or a week. But it's *Broadway*. There's so much money at stake and so many jobs on the line.

March 8 and 9, 2020

JEFF BRANCATO   We recorded the cast-recording on Sunday [the 8th] and Monday [the 9th]. A cast member called me before he was supposed to come [to the studio]. He said his partner was coughing a lot and has a fever. And we said, "Don't come, don't come, don't come."

March 10, 2020

JEFF BRANCATO   And then two of our swings got the flu, so they were out Tuesday.

March 11, 2020

JEFF BRANCATO   And then Wednesday night [the 11th], Bob Joy called me and said, I'm really, I felt like I was losing my voice during the show. I'm really not feeling well. I really think I probably shouldn't come in tomorrow.

March 12, 2020

JEFF BRANCATO   We had our first understudy rehearsal Thursday [the 12th]. We got there, we're rehearsing, we're doing the opening number. And usually the way [associate director] Barbara [Rubin] and I would run [an] understudy rehearsal is I would give the understudies their staging and then Barbara would come in and give acting notes. I think we were in the breakfast scene . . . I remember Barbara hovering behind me and she said, "Did you see this?" and she showed me her phone.

   NEW YORK TIMES
   Broadway, Symbol of New York Resilience, Shuts Down Amid Virus Threat

JEFF BRANCATO   I called Ashley, our company manager, and she didn't answer. And then I called her back again and she said, "I know we're figuring it out" and hung up on me.

There would be no show that evening.

JEFF BRANCATO   And, so yeah, we ended rehearsal, did some cleaning, waited till everyone got to the theater who wanted to get their stuff and then went home.

We wouldn't return for over a year and a half.

Idiot Wind

Now everything's a little upside down
As a matter of fact the wheels have stopped
What's good is bad, what's bad is good
You'll find out when you reach the top
You're on the bottom[7]

---

[7]From "Idiot Wind," Dylan, *Blood on the Tracks*, 1975.

Flowers: Part 2

AUSTIN SCOTT   I remember the plants.

He laughs.

AUSTIN SCOTT   I remember thinking, what's going to happen to our plants?

In addition to the opening night flowers we received as gifts, Austin and I placed plants around our dressing room, as well as a large print of a photograph of a wide-open field. With a big sky and what we imagined was very fresh air. Our dressing-room window opened to a New York City alley, we had to do *something*.

AUSTIN SCOTT   Can we leave the plants here? Will they survive two weeks?

JEFF BRANCATO (email)
Hey all!
We are at the theater now. If you would like to come in to grab anything, you are welcome to do so. Please be here by 6:30 (your half-hour) if possible.
If you do not want to come in, let us know if you have anything in the dressing room that is perishable that we should trash.
As of now, it looks like we have a month-long break, but we will keep you posted, of course! But as of now, everything cancelled until April 12.
Please keep April 2 open for [Good Morning America], if that still happens . . .

Sending love from our lonely theater!
Jeff xx

AUSTIN SCOTT   It was scary and surreal, getting that email, "*come get your stuff and take it all.*" I wonder whether in other industries it was really that abrupt and unsettling. But something about working on Broadway felt like we were untouchable.

JEANNETTE BAYARDELLE   And I remember when it was time to go and get our stuff my sister said, "When you leave, take everything." So when I left my dressing room, I took everything. And when I tell you Marc Kudisch was like, "Jeannette, why are you doing this? It's only two weeks we'll be back." I said, "No, we're not coming back. We're not coming back."

The Jeep

"We're coming back in a few weeks," I said to Mark at home, "because we have to rehearse for an appearance on *Good Morning America*."

Mark and I got engaged in 2011 on a little island off the coast of Maine. Every summer since we first met in 2008, we've tried to get to the island for at least a couple of days. We'd just take our work with us and try to spend as much of August there as we could.

It's a humble place, a small town, the industry is lobster; it's gorgeous, a bit wild, unspoiled and private-plane free. Every summer after 2008, we would drive our rented car around the island looking at houses, hoping to find a place we could make a home. Nothing could compare to the house we had been renting, and when we returned to it after every fruitless search, we agreed that *this house* felt like our home. If only we could explain that to the people who owned it.

Friends would often visit us on the island and we'd tell them, "We're going to die here, just not this summer."

In 2019 we didn't go to Maine because we were invited on a trip to Europe with our best pals Meredith and Yvonne, to whose four children we are the donor-dads. Sitting in the south of France, the kids swimming, Yvonne asked us if we were still hoping to "buy something on that island." We said, "Always." That evening, Mark pulled up the real-estate website Zillo on his laptop, and gasped.

"What?!"

It was our house. The house, *our* house, was listed. It was for sale.

We couldn't sleep.

The next morning we went online to show Yvonne and Meredith the house but when we opened Zillo, it was no longer listed. Someone must have bought it.

Shit.

But now Mark was determined to find something for us. This was our dream, to own a home, and we felt like it was time; we'd worked hard for decades, Mark had just turned fifty and I was well into my fourties. So that evening, he hopped on Zillo again to look at what was available on the island and he gasped.

What?!

The house. *The house was back.*

Really?

And the price had dropped.

By late October of 2019, we owned the house. The house we loved and that had always felt like home. I was just about to start my year-long contract on Broadway with *Girl from the North Country,* so we wouldn't even be able to *go* to the house until 2021. We didn't care. It will be waiting for us, because it's our home now.

So you can imagine the first thought that popped into our heads on March 12, 2020, when Broadway shut down.

Let's go to the house.

At the time, Mark was working for a big agency in New York City, and his office closed, as did most every office in the city. Neither of us needed to be in New York. The dogs preferred the grass in the country. So did I. What if we throw some things in the car and drive up to Maine, is that too outrageous? Let's do it!

But then we remembered, *we don't have a car.*

This is the magic of my husband, Mark Subias. He said, "I'll be right back," and he left the apartment. About thirty minutes later my phone rings. It's Mark. "Hey, come over to the Jeep dealership on 11th Avenue, I think we've got a car."

By the time I got there—it's a five-minute walk—he had worked out the details on a new-but-last-season black Jeep. These things shouldn't surprise me, Mark negotiates for a living, but they always do. His way through the world is effortless and gorgeous.

We drove our new Jeep back to the apartment, threw in some clothes, some books, our computers, some things for the kitchen, some toys for the dogs, *the dogs*, and by the weekend, we were on an island off the coast of Maine, an island roughly the same square mileage as Manhattan, in our new home.

On Sunday, March 15, *the ides of March*, at 2:55 p.m., I looked at Mark and said, "I have a matinee starting in five minutes."

Impossibly, we were staring at the Atlantic ocean, over 400 miles away from New York City.

Interlude

Sleepwalking

I took a selfie almost daily during the pandemic, thinking it would make an interesting record. What you would see if you looked through those selfies is nearly the same expression on my face, the only thing that changes is my hair. It grows and then it is cut, my beard grows and then it is cut.

In a major way, the photos are completely uninteresting. I measured my days in hair growth, but I traveled the universe in my sleep. If only my phone took pictures in there.

Composer Andrew Gerle asked me to write a song for a collection of songs about life during that time. Amber Gray recorded the song for the album *Artists in Residence,* which Andrew produced.[8]

"I Don't Know About You"

I don't know about you
But I've been having all sorts of crazy dreams
Maybe it's just the isolation
I don't know about you
But every night my mind goes tumbling to extremes
Pretty sure it's Covid bifurcation
Pretty sure it's understimulation
Makes me crash around the mirror's other side

> *Goodnight, my love.*
> *Pleasant dreams.*

Oh, no, I'm waiting tables
And I can't find the door to help the guests outside
Then suddenly, there's Marilu Henner
Takes my tray and tosses me a tenner
Says, "Walk with me through the wall."

We do just as she says
And in the empty streets we pass a TV star
It's Tony Whatshisface from that one show
She says, "That's someone I used to know."
But I wake up just before she spills it all.

---

[8]Amber Gray was nominated for a Tony Award for her performance as Persephone in *Hadestown.* She was also in *Natasha, Pierre, and the Great Comet of 1812* and Sondheim's final original musical *Here We Are.*

The days are so long
The days go nowhere
But the nights, the nights . . .

There's a giant in a tree
And he says to me,
"You wanna know how to transcend?"
I say, "Of course! Of course I want to know!"
He says, "Okay, just close your eyes real slow
And say 'My name is the wind.'"

And so I do, I do,
I do just what he says
Because I'd like to transcend
I close my eyes and say,
"My name's the wind!"
And, poof, I wake up in my bed again.
And I wonder, *Is this what he meant by transcend?*

The days last all day
The days sit so still
But the nights, the nights . . .

My husband wakes me up at three
He says, "You're sorta scaring me
You're talking in your sleep
But in a voice that isn't yours"

"It's the socks," I say
"They found a portal
Through the dresser drawers!"

I don't know about you
But I've been having all sorts of crazy dreams.

It's likely all the social isolation
It's prob'ly just a lonesome aberration.

Maybe I'm just missing everyone.

Come meet in my dreams.
It's wild, it's wild in here.
I'll see you in my dreams.

6

Hospital

Chelsea

After her 2018 run in *Girl from the North Country* at the Public Theater, where she was a member of the ensemble, Chelsea Lee Williams went directly to Broadway, making her debut covering multiple roles in Daniel Fish's daring production of *Oklahoma!* During *Oklahoma!*'s run, *Girl from the North Country* announced its Broadway transfer, and when it started rehearsals in January of 2020, Chelsea found herself doing double duty: rehearsals for one Broadway show during the day, performances of another at night.

CHELSEA LEE WILLIAMS   Towards the end of the run [of *Oklahoma!*], I started to have health issues. I didn't know what was going on. *Maybe it's just stress*, I thought.

Chelsea has the face of a golden-age silent-film star. She's timeless. Compelling. It's not hard to understand her immediate success after graduating from Juilliard's drama department.

CHELSEA LEE WILLIAMS   I definitely feel like the stress of the work schedule played a part in it.

In *Girl from the North Country*, in addition to her ensemble track, she covered both Jeannette Bayardelle and Kimber Sprawl. Over at *Oklahoma!*, she covered the actresses playing the roles of "Laurie" and "Ado Annie." So when rehearsals for our show overlapped with performances of her other show, Chelsea was carrying no fewer than five full roles in her mind and body. Any of which she could go on for in a moment's notice.

CHELSEA LEE WILLIAMS   Just sitting backstage and hearing a show night after night that you're not necessarily in each night, it takes a certain level of mental stamina to be able to do that. And that's when I think the reality of eight shows a week comes into play, especially for standbys.

In the big picture, *this is success*, working on two Broadway shows simultaneously, almost immediately after graduating from one of the most prestigious acting programs in the world.

CHELSEA LEE WILLIAMS   And I interact with people in other shows who are [covering roles], who are really fighting mentally. *I want to go on, but I can't.* I heard some say they feel like they're getting paid not to perform.

Day to day, however, it's a lot to manage. It's hard work.

CHELSEA LEE WILLIAMS   It's very strange, very, very strange being paid not to perform. But you *could* perform, you could go on *right now*, it could happen, this very second.

There's an old joke: What's the quickest way to make an actor complain? Hire them.

Fine, it's funny. Actors can be whiny. But there's a dark kernel of truth buried in that joke. The stage-actor's schedule is famously punishing, especially for understudies and covers. Eight shows a week, one day off, *Monday*, rehearsals most afternoons, shows at night. They have no evenings free. No weekends free—those are two-show days. Holidays are not a break, in fact, holidays are the *busiest* time; most shows add *extra* performances over Christmas. If you know an actor or have an actor in your family, no doubt they couldn't come to your party, they couldn't meet you in the park, couldn't take that quick getaway, and probably RSVP'd *will not attend* to your wedding announcement.

The term "Broadway widow" refers to the spouse or partner of a working actor, another joke with a bitter truth; it's as if the actor has died, because they're never home, they're eternally "at the theater."

Cue the sad music.

It's the actor's life, it's what they've signed up for, *no whining*. Everyone's life is hard. Fair point. But where this joke turns from something funny to something serious is when the actor has a health issue.

CHELSEA LEE WILLIAMS   Before we started [Broadway] rehearsals [for *Girl from the North Country*], I started having weird symptoms in November.

Getting to the doctor, already difficult for anyone, can be nearly impossible for an actor on this schedule. So actors typically ignore warning signs. They focus on work, on getting *work*; even when you have an acting job, you have to find another one, because the show you're in is going to end, they all do, eventually. There's a relentless focus on *getting a job*, even when you have one, even when you have *two*.

CHELSEA LEE WILLIAMS   There was a talk about whether or not I was even going to be able to do *Girl from the North Country*. If we would've extended *Oklahoma!*, I wouldn't have been able to do our show.

It's hard to recover if you are unwell because you just don't have the time, and calling in sick is not something actors do, traditionally.

CHELSEA LEE WILLIAMS   So I had it worked out where I could be in rehearsal all day at *Girl*, and then at night do *Oklahoma!* And there were times where I went on. So it was, they were very long days. And I wasn't well at all.

After a show opens and has been running for a determined number of weeks (giving the understudies time to rehearse), actors are then allowed to "call out," meaning *miss a performance*. People call out only when they're too sick to sing. My husband loves to tell the story about actress Marian Seldes never missing a single one of *Deathtrap*'s eighteen-hundred-something Broadway performances, even when she had double pneumonia. The double pneumonia part might be apocryphal, and so too might be the near-Tallulah-Bankhead-level-of-camp response she supposedly had in defense of performing while being so sick: "Darling, if you can crawl, you can act."

CHELSEA LEE WILLIAMS   I remember having conversations with friends who are in other shows: "I can't believe so-and-so called out." It was forbidden.

There's a lot of pressure for an actor not to "call out," especially when the show is still in previews, because the understudies haven't rehearsed yet (they don't get to be onstage until after the show has officially opened). The show can't go on if people call out during previews, and as we know, *the show must go on.*

CHELSEA LEE WILLIAMS   And then I remember having to call out in February. We had just started previews and my body ... I remember calling Jeff and I was like, "Hey, I'm calling out." And his reaction was like, "We're in previews." I said, "Listen, I'm at the ER. They're not letting me go. I have to stay here."

So Chelsea missed a preview. And the show was fine, Chiara Trentalange made her Broadway debut going on for Chelsea's ensemble part.

CHELSEA LEE WILLIAMS   I ended up being in the ER, I think it was a Sunday.

Chelsea sighs.

CHELSEA LEE WILLIAMS   Looking back, I will never do that again. Ever.

Never do what, double-duty?

CHELSEA LEE WILLIAMS   I will never not listen to my body, I won't ever push myself to that point. Because during that time, before the pandemic—*the show must go on.*

That phrase can be triggering for actors. It's meant to bolster team spirit, but it can also mean: your health doesn't matter, the show does.

CHELSEA LEE WILLIAMS   The idea of calling out!

She laughs and shakes her head.

CHELSEA LEE WILLIAMS   It was still *that* Broadway.

That Broadway. That's the Broadway that shut down on March 12, 2020. And now suddenly nobody was working, and nobody was focusing on finding work. There was no work. When Chelsea was forced to sit still for the long moment of the shutdown, the symptoms she had been setting aside became impossible to ignore.
Though the hospitals were overburdened with the sick and the dying, this was the opportunity for Chelsea to get the help she needed to heal something that, on that old Broadway schedule, would never have gotten better.

CHELSEA LEE WILLIAMS   I was able to have surgery. So that's the silver lining of the pandemic for me, because otherwise it would've been just eight shows a week and I probably would've either tried to work through it, or I would've eventually had to leave the show.

Chelsea's story is Broadway's story. The sickness we'd been ignoring, be it Covid or the systemic racism that the murder of George Floyd laid bare for the world to see that awful summer, would no longer be ignored. We were sick.
Would we seize the opportunity to heal? Could we heal?

CHELSEA LEE WILLIAMS   I know a lot of stuff happened to a lot of people during the pandemic, and I don't ever want to take away from that. I don't ever want to go back to that time, to what we all saw on tv, that definitely changed me, my perspective of life. It is a blessing to be able to get up and walk around and go perform.

It is a blessing to be able to get up and walk around and go perform.

7

The Real World

The Empty Stage

For the sleepwalker, there is a disorienting moment of crossfade between dream and reality. Just when the dream is at its most immersive, waking-world objects begin to appear, faintly at first, as if reality were a transparent image overlaid onto the dream. Chairs, walls, the floor, all of the mundane things concretize around him like something from a scene in an old science-fiction movie where invisibility wears off, while the dream collapses and dissolves into such complete oblivion that the dreamer can't even remember what it *was*.

There is a moment, mid-crossfade, when reality and the dream hold equal strength.

I'm falling between green petals above a city of old men;
I'm standing in the cold hallway outside my bedroom.

It's a bright afternoon;
It's the middle of the night.

I'm there;
I'm here.

Both are true. One on top of the other.

Like the brief, perfect alignment of a solar eclipse.

Every time I pass through that moment, I am overwhelmed with the thought that there's some truth I should grab on to and that this is the only moment I can grab it.

But I can't. Because reality crushes it and oblivion takes it. And it's gone.

The closest I've come to experiencing this sensation in my waking life was in October of 2020, seven months into the shutdown, when I found myself onstage at the Belasco Theater making a music video for "Duquesne Whistle."

My castmate Kimber Sprawl directed the video-shoot from LA via Facetime, and Jim Glaub, under the aegis of the creative-marketing company "Super Awesome Friends," produced.

There was no sign of Broadway returning, but there *was* something for the theater community to celebrate: the announcement of the 2020 Tony nominees. Shortly after the Broadway shutdown on March 12, the American Theater Wing announced that they would postpone their annual Tony ceremony from June 7 to a yet-to-be-determined date in the future.

After a summer with no word from the Wing, the nominees were finally announced on October 15, 2020, though the ceremony itself wouldn't be held for another frustrating eleven months. Kimber thought the nominations were something worth celebrating, and to that end she asked if I'd be interested in filming a music video of "Duquesne Whistle" in the streets around Times Square; the idea was that I would pass by all of the shuttered theaters as I sang, highlighting everyone in our community who had been nominated for a Tony. It's a joyful song, after all, and joy was scarce. I said, "Sure!"

Girl from the North Country had not been nominated for a single Tony but only because we were found to be ineligible. We had opened, yes, and *opening* is the requirement for nominations, but we simply hadn't run long enough before the shutdown for nominators to see our show. So the powers-that-be determined that we would be eligible for the *next* Tonys, whenever those would be. If ever those would be.

After a Zoom meeting between Kimber, Jim Glaub, and myself, we decided that filming a music video inside our empty theater, the Belasco, might produce a more powerful visual—instead of focusing on awards, we would focus on the survival of our industry, showing an empty theater waiting to be filled with people again, hopefully sooner than later.

Fine by me. Though I'm an actor, I'm introverted, and the idea of dancing and lip-syncing through the streets around Times Square in front of strangers filled me with dread—I would have done it, but I would have died a little.

So we worked out details with the Shuberts to film on the Belasco stage.

"Protocols" had already elbowed their way into life by that fall. I had started work on a television series in early October that year and, *oh, boy*, did I encounter "protocols." Every morning we filled out a self-report health form: do you have a fever?, are you coughing?, etc. Upon arrival at the set we reported to a nurse who administered the deep-nasal cotton swab Covid test. Traveling from the hair and makeup trailer to set, we wore hospital gowns over our costumes and plastic shields over our faces. On set, in between each take, we put masks on only to take them off moments later to resume filming. We were encouraged not to socialize on breaks, or if we did, to maintain a safe social distance. I don't actually know what most of the crew look like from the eyes down, they all wore masks all day every day.

Apparently I took all of this very seriously, because in looking back at emails to Jim and Kimber, I see that I insist on "protocols" being "rigorous" for this video shoot.

I got an email back from Aaron, our general manager.

AARON LUSTBADER (email)
  Hi Todd,

  Yes, we will have vigorous Covid safety protocols in place. We worked through our plan with Equity and got their approval (which is a very real process these days as you might expect).

When I walked through the stage door that day, the emptiness of the theater knocked me for six, to use a phrase of Conor's. Since Kimber was in LA, it was just me and Jim and director of photography David Givens on the stage. The Belasco felt abandoned. Eleven-hundred empty seats. No actors in the wings. No band at the music stands where the scores still sat open to the last page of the last song, "Pressing On." I could feel everything that wasn't there, could see the traces of missing people, hear the music-lessness. Like what's left behind by a civilization that vanished one day with no signs of a struggle. Not the same thing as a ruin, this was the remains of something interrupted.

The Belasco is a union house, so anything technical like lights or sound must be handled by members of the stage-hands union, IATSE. We weren't able to have any IATSE folks for this video shoot, so the space felt *even emptier* when building management turned on the "work lights," the utilitarian overhead-fluorescents, making the stage feel like an examination room.

Since we couldn't use the sound-system, Jim played "Duquesne Whistle" on his phone. I was to lip-sync.

Here's where the sleep-walking feeling comes in. I'm half in a dream (the play) and half in reality (the present day). I'm acting, trying to be Elias in 1934, but the harsh lights are ruining the illusion. I can hear my song playing, but it's from a tinny speaker on a device. There's no one playing any of the instruments that I see in front of me: a piano, a drum kit. I'm opening my mouth to sing, but my voice is coming from somewhere else.

It's dream-logic. Only I'm awake.

I get that sensation that there's some truth here that I need to grab on to. But what is it? I can't feel the religious feelings I'd felt. Hadn't I been here before, worked up into a hurricane by holy fire? Didn't I see God? I've forgotten how to transcend. I can't feel it. But how could I expect to? This isn't a performance. The stage lights aren't even on, the horrible work lights are. I'm not in my costume, I'm in jeans and a Bob Dylan tee shirt. The cast isn't here, the band, the audience. There's nobody on this stage but me.

Maybe that's the truth I need to grab onto: heaven is other people.

Theater is other people.

And everyone is gone.

I lip-synced through the song half-a-dozen times or so on the vacant stage, recreating the basic patterns I'd made in the show, which I was surprised to discover I couldn't remember all that well. When Jim and Kimber felt like we had enough footage, we just stopped. It was all very informal. Uneventful. Not theater.

Someone turned the work-lights out, leaving just the ghostlight burning center stage.[1] Kimber signed off from LA, I put my mask back on, and Jim and David and I bumped elbows goodbye.

When I left the theater, I remember feeling tired. Why? That hadn't been hard work. Probably I just hadn't slept well the night before in anticipation of filming, but my eyes were heavy like I'd been crying all morning, which I hadn't been. I walked my bike home.

There's a trick shot in the music video, which you can see online; from the back of house, the camera shoots over the empty seats. Kimber and Jim have superimposed actual footage from the show onto the stage so that it looks like the ghost of the musical is still performing itself for no one, with full lights, costumes, sound, and actors. It blinks in and out of existence.

Whenever it goes, it leaves only me on stage reenacting the memory of it.

Emails

Life during the shutdown existed inside my computer. My friends and family were in there, my collaborators were in there. *Girl from the North Country* was in there.

Broadway was emails now.

Emails from my union, Actors' Equity, about unemployment benefits and how to apply for funds.

Emails from our press team with interview requests from news sources.

Emails from theater companies hoping for online content. I made videos for several companies including a cross-country collaboration for the Public Theater with Lindsay Mendez, who was living in LA; Lindsay, who has a Tony Award for her performance as Carrie in the 2018 revival of *Carousel*, is a marvel. She played Hermione in my musical version of *The Winter's Tale* for Public Works, so we recorded an at-home version of one of the songs.

Emails from Tristan Baker, our producer.

---

[1]A "ghost light" is a single bulb on a stand that every theater leaves burning onstage whenever all other lights in the theater are turned off. I've heard from some people this has to do with actual ghosts, and I've heard from others that it has to do with demarking the edge of the stage, lest someone enter in the darkness and fall off the edge.

TRISTAN BAKER (email)
Dear GFTNC Family—

We hope you are keeping safe and well.

We simply cannot believe that a year ago today we were getting our glad rags on for the most wonderful opening of our beautiful show.

What an incredible night that was!

Who could have known that while we twirled around Bryant Park until the small hours, only a few days later we would be on pause. For a year and counting.

But we really do think we can see the light and are hopeful that the good vaccine news continues and we are on track for a September return.

So, this is just a short note to say we are thinking about you, we are sending love, and please raise a glass to yourselves and each other this evening.

And let's look forward to when we are all back together and can bring this show back to where it belongs at the Belasco.

Stay safe.

With all best wishes,

Tris, Charlie & Aaron x

Emails from my husband, who was just downstairs working in the dining room—I had claimed an upstairs guest room as my office. "Shall we take the dogs for a walk?"

I found out I had landed a role on the *Gossip Girl* reboot on HBO Max. Neither Mark nor I had ever watched the original series, so we binge-watched every season. There are six seasons. There are 121 episodes. I know a lot about Blair Waldorf and Serena van der Woodsen. And I know the identity of "Gossip Girl" because I watched the series finale.

It's Dan Humphrey.

My old self-preservation technique that I learned after *Hair* kicked in. *Broadway is not returning, Todd. Move on.*

I tried to focus on writing projects, like my adaptation of *A Tale of Two Cities*, which I had worked on for nearly a decade with director Lear deBessonet. It was programmed for the 2020–21 season at the American Repertory Theater, A.R.T., at Harvard University with a built-in transfer to Playwrights Horizons in New York City; obviously, this show was no longer going to happen in 2020 or 2021. And, sadly, it would never happen. Like a lot of projects I heard about from writer friends, Covid killed it.

Having no idea if things would ever go back to "normal," I let myself accept the fact that I lived on an island in Maine now, and I took care of dogs, I wrote songs, read books, watched *Gossip Girl* and deleted a lot of emails.

ACTORS' EQUITY ASSOCIATION (excerpt of email)

Dear Todd,

At Actors' Equity, we've spent much of the summer hard at work to establish safety standards for theatre across America. Earlier this month, we announced new safety standards for LORT[2] as well as updated standards for fully vaccinated companies at a single venue. **Today we can share that we have reached an agreement with the Broadway League on safety protocols for Production Contract shows including returning and new Broadway productions as well as sit-downs across the country.**[3]

One key element of the protocols is updated guidance relating to Heating, Ventilation and Air-Conditioning (HVAC) systems. The League has also determined that they will mandate vaccines for the full workforces on these productions, with specific exceptions for those who cannot be vaccinated, such as children and those with health restrictions. The protocols include additional safety measures for unvaccinated personnel in the workplace.

Workers who are vaccinated will not only protect themselves, but others, including those who cannot get the vaccine at this time.

I refused to get my hopes up.

Our company manager Ashley Berman sent updates which were reminiscent of our final weeks at the Public, when I did get my hopes up after the many meetings teasing a transfer to Broadway. I wasn't going to do that again.

ASHLEY BERMAN (email)
Dear GFTNC Cast –

As you know, we had previously checked availability to potentially start rehearsal as early as June as we were cautiously optimistic a summer return might have been possible. Sadly, that would have required a vaccine roll out that was pitch perfect – and while things are improving on that front rapidly, it is not practical to return that quickly as an industry.

Emails like this didn't upset me, because, without being pessimistic about it, I just wouldn't let myself believe that it was ever going to happen. Of course I wanted nothing more than for *Girl from the North Country* to come back—I had barely gotten a taste of my Broadway debut—but my soft

---

[2]League of Resident Theatres, an organization of regional not-for-profit theaters around the country.

[3]Emboldening in original.

heart had built an elaborate safe-room over the years, and for better or worse, it had locked itself inside.

ASHLEY BERMAN (email, continued)
We still hope to be one of the first shows back when Broadway returns, and we presently anticipate that will be in September (with rehearsals preceding).

Sure.

I focused on other things. And I was *lucky*, I had work. I had a whole new character to create for the *Gossip Girl* reboot. Most actors did not have work, and to add to their troubles, their healthcare was ending.

ASHLEY BERMAN (email, continued)
In the meantime, we realize that many of you may be facing the termination of your healthcare eligibility in the coming months. The good news is that the current iteration of the Federal Stimulus Package (American Rescue Plan Act) includes an 85% subsidy on Cobra health insurance (as well as an extension of unemployment benefits) for all impacted employees. We expect this will be retroactive to January and should be in place until at least September. We expect this positive news to hopefully be confirmed this week. If you have questions about how to navigate Cobra plans, we will be able to provide you with resources via the Actors Fund that should be of assistance. We are grateful the government is stepping in to help the arts sectors in ways it hasn't in the past and hope this provides a bit of relief in such stressful times.
We encourage you to call your Senators and urge them to vote to pass the American Rescue Plan Act as soon as possible. In addition to the cobra subsidies mentioned above the American Rescue Plan Act would increase the federal weekly unemployment supplement to $400 and extend the Covid-19 unemployment programs through the end of August; provide direct payments of $1,400 for those making less than $75,000/yr, based on 2019 or 2020 taxes (depending on whether you've filed 2020 taxes); and appropriate $135 million in emergency supplemental funding for the National Endowment for the Arts and an additional $1.25 billion for the Shuttered Venue Operators Grant Program (Save Our Stages).

The way insurance worked before the pandemic for Equity actors was that an actor had to work eleven weeks[4] in a one-year period on an Equity contract to get six months of health coverage. Which is much harder than it sounds. Of the more than 50,000 members in Equity, fewer than 7,000, or

---

[4]It is now sixteen weeks.

14 percent, qualify for insurance. Obviously, after a year of not working, every actor's insurance lapsed, and so COBRA, the government program that allows individuals a limited, self-funded extension of the health coverage they've lost, which can cost upwards of $1,100 per month, was the only option for many. Even with the government's help, it was a high out-of-pocket premium, especially when unemployed.

In the twenty-two years I'd lived in New York City, I'd aged exactly twenty-two years.

That obvious math came as some surprise to me when I considered that my body was no longer the body it had been. My physical health wasn't something I ever worried about in my first decades in the city. For years, I lived uninsured and carefree. Smoking. Drinking. Avoiding doctors. Only getting my teeth cleaned (and drilled) by students at the NYU school of dentistry because it was free (more of a barter; I got a cavity filled, they got a guinea pig). I was young and broke and being healthy is expensive in America.

It wasn't until I was forty years old, when my husband Mark introduced me to a strength coach named Hannah Fons, that I thought *I should take better care of myself*. I asked Hannah right then and there if she would take me on as a client.

Slowly over the course of the pandemic, Mark turned the small barn on our property in Maine into a home gym. During that year-plus of the shutdown, he and I would work out (or "train" as Mark would say) via Facetime with our respective trainers (Mark with his long-time coach Tim, me with Hannah); nothing felt better than throwing open the barn doors on beautiful summer days and swinging kettlebells where sheep used to sleep.

In May of 2021, I got an email from our producer that was positive, more than positive, it was a near-certain confirmation of our return.

But I couldn't get my hopes up. I wouldn't.

Because I'm an expert at finding the phrase that lets doubt in. Here are the important parts of that email. See if you can find that part that made me doubt. Hint: It's one word.

TRISTAN BAKER (email)
Dear GIRL FROM THE NORTH COUNTRY team –

As always, we hope this email finds you well and safe. We write today as Broadway is clearly on a firm path towards re-opening this fall and to reconfirm our personal commitment to each of you that GIRL FROM THE NORTH COUNTRY <u>will</u> re-open as part of Broadway's relaunch ... We presently are aiming to begin rehearsals in September ahead of an early Fall performance start, but we won't be able to confirm these details until we have a better sense of everyone's plans. To this end, we will be reaching out in the coming weeks to you (or your representative(s) as appropriate) to confirm your intentions to re-join the production and hope to be back to you all with a production calendar by the end of May.

Did you find it? It's in this phrase: "We presently are aiming to begin rehearsals in September ahead of an early Fall performance start, but we won't be able to confirm these details until we have a better sense of everyone's plans."

The word: *but.*

Whenever I read that word, or hear that word, something in my brain slams shut. *I was right to doubt,* I think. And because I've taught myself over the years to avoid falling into despair because of a "but," I immediately turn my attention to something else creative. It's a defensive move.

I know what I'll do, I'll write a song.

But then we had a cast Zoom meeting with Tristan and Conor and Aaron, with concrete plans and dates, a rehearsal schedule, costume fittings, etc., and okay, well, fuck it, my hopes went up. Way up. Dammit.

This is only going to break my heart, I thought, but I unlocked the little safe room and it peered out, curious.

Like Pee Wee Herman said to Simone in that giant dinosaur's mouth when she was too afraid to follow her dreams because there was always a "but" that got in the way, I said to the universe, "Let's talk about your big but."

The universe answered by email.

TRISTAN BAKER (email)

We are presently planning to make our return announcement in the press and put tickets back on sale on Monday, May 24th (Bob Dylan's birthday!) . . .

We plan to begin rehearsals on Monday, September 20 – Our first public performance/re-opening will be on Wednesday, October 13, 2021 . . .

Of course, we are hopeful that everyone will be coming back . . .

Information regarding Covid protocols are very far along between the various unions and the Broadway League but not yet finalized . . .

While the return of Broadway is sure to be a brave new world on many fronts, we cannot wait to be back together in person at the Belasco this fall!

As always, please feel free to reach out with any questions you may have.

Warmest wishes,

Tris, Charlie and Aaron

After eighteen months of sleepwalking, reality was concretizing around me.

A Man Behind a Curtain

While I had been "crashing around the mirror's other side" in Maine, industry insiders in New York were working to get Broadway's lights back on.

How did they do it?

The truth is: I have no idea.

I've served as a juror on two trials in New York City. The trials were different in almost every aspect, but I walked away from each with the same belief: there is no such thing as the truth.

Individual perception exists, personal narrative exists, persuasion exists, but "the truth" is too complex a thing to grasp, it would require that an amalgamation be created of every individual point of view that led us to the event we are hoping to label "the truth."

There's a scene in *The Hitchhiker's Guide to the Galaxy* by Douglas Adams where a super computer is asked to find the "answer to the ultimate question of life, the universe and everything." After over seven million years of thinking, the super computer comes up with the answer, and the answer, which the computer warns no one will be happy with, is "42."

That scene feels like what "the truth" means to me. It's practically incalculable, and probably unsatisfying. The problem with "the truth" or "the answer to the ultimate question of life, the universe and everything," or even just the number "42" is that those things are all answers, so *what is the question?*

Broadway shut down in March of 2020 and reopened eighteen months later in September of 2021. That is the answer to the question, but what is the question?

"How did this happen?"

To answer that would require over seven million years of thinking about the personal narratives of the over 117 billion people that have ever lived on Earth, or at least the almost 97,000 people in the Broadway industry, or at the very, very least the over seven-hundred individual souls that make up the Broadway League.

So I thought I'd start with Tom Schumacher.

Tom Schumacher is the president of Disney Theatrical Group. He wears an array of playful, circular, high-end designer glasses, giving him a single visual characteristic that an animator might give to a Disney character. You can't mistake Tom.

He's a powerful figure on Broadway, and I like him very much. I was curious—what was it like for him and his many productions on Broadway leading up to March 12, 2020?

TOM SCHUMACHER   As Chairman of the [Broadway] League[5] it was my responsibility along with Charlotte to organize a series of meetings in

---

[5]The Broadway League is a "trade association representing commercial theatre in the United States and around the world," according to the League's website.

response to the threat posed by the Covid outbreak. We didn't know what would happen because the news was breaking very fast. I had Bob Wankel from the Shuberts and Nick Scandalios from The Nederlanders (both of them former League Chairs) at my side at the conference table for a series of meetings. The first was with the security leads for the various Theatre Operators—both for-profit and non-profit. We needed an operating plan for all of the theaters in the event of a closure.

By the 9th or 10th of March we had all of the Broadway Unions to the League office to advise them of the potential impact on the workforce. We didn't know if we'd be closing the Theatres, but we needed to have conversations to make sure everyone was aware that we were facing a potential "temporary" shut down. There was a lot of anxiety but not yet a lot of dialogue or information.

Then on Thursday March 12, we had your producer Tristan Baker along with all of the other Producers, from shows like Stepppenwolf's *The Minutes*, which had just opened, to shows that were waiting to open, and of course the long running shows, all together at the League offices. I asked everyone to turn their phones off and I told them "we have to be confidential here because something serious is going on and we may be on the brink of closing." We needed to control any rumors in the press until we were 100% sure of what we were going to do and how we were going to do it. Misinformation would be worse than no information.

One producer said, "I have a matinee today and I don't have enough cast to get the show on stage. I don't know what they're sick with, but I have people calling out that are very sick." They had the symptoms: fever, body ache, loss of taste and smell and the rest of it. And he said, "I just can't get the show on today. We'll have to cancel."

And then another Producer said, "My cast doesn't *want* to go on stage. They are refusing to be backstage at all." And it was clear this was heating up very quickly.

And at the same time we have the Governor's office on the line in the other conference room. We are running back and forth to the phone asking ourselves the question, "what are we going to do?" I said to our group, "It could be just a week or two that we shut down, but it looks like we'll have to."

Girl from the North Country's lead producer, Tristan Baker, recalls this meeting.

TRISTAN BAKER   All the producers were brought into the Broadway League. We all sat around the table all day together. That was the day it shut down.

Broadway is a $2 billion dollar industry, and, according to *Forbes*, it "contributes $14.7 billion to the economy of New York City on top of ticket sales and supports 96,900 local jobs."

No one wanted Broadway to shut down. It's the city's life-blood.

TOM SCHUMACHER   So while the Producers are in one room, we have the Governor on the phone in the other room and we say, "Mr Governor, *you* have to tell us we're closed . . ."

And unless the government called an emergency shutdown, the producers were going to be on the hook for untold losses.

TOM SCHUMACHER   ". . . You don't have to tell us when we reopen because you don't know, but tell us we have to have an emergency closure because we'll have to activate our insurance."

Governor Cuomo agreed to announce the closure. The producers could expect their losses, which at this point they were thinking would amount to only a week or two of canceled performances, to be covered by their insurers.

TOM SCHUMACHER   I come back into the room with the Producers and I say, "Folks we have to stay tight. We're all locked in this room together. The Governor told us we're closing. We have a press release ready and we're about to have someone run to press send." And then someone holds up their phone and says, "Broadway closing" is already on *Deadline*.

Somehow, in the few moments between Tom's phone call with Governor Cuomo confirming a mandated Broadway shut down and the League's press release being prepared, the news leaked to the press.

The room then filled with tension.

TOM SCHUMACHER   Someone in the room leaked it and right off the bat we had "trust issues."

It's unclear how this breach happened, who leaked the news, and if the leak even came from this closed room, but it immediately sowed distrust in the ranks of the producers, and would lead to a lack of a unified response in the months to come.

A small group of League producers who trusted each other (or perhaps just wanted fewer voices in the room), powerhouses Sue Frost, David Stone, Jeffrey Seller, Kevin McCollum, Barry Weissler, and Scott Rudin, formed with Tom a smaller breakout group that met nightly by phone or by Zoom.[6]

---

[6]Sue Frost, producer of *Come from Away*; David Stone, producer of *Wicked*; Jeffrey Seller, producer of *Hamilton*; Kevin McCollum, producer of *Six*; Scott Rudin, original producer of *Book of Mormon* (since removed).

Functioning as an ad hoc advisory committee, this group called themselves the "Little League," and took it upon themselves to strategize Broadway's return.

It would prove nearly impossible, as information about the virus kept changing.

We are living in what some call the post-truth age. A time of "alternative facts." As a friend of mine would have it, there is today "a problem for every solution."

Not only was the virus evolving, so too was the information about it.

Consensus could not be reached, even within the focused and like-minded "Little League," on how to combat the coronavirus and open theaters safely.

TOM SCHUMACHER   My days began about 6:00am. I would take a walk a couple of miles in the morning and I would talk to folks like Scott Rudin. I'd call Andrew Lloyd Webber and Cameron Mackintosh about what was happening in the UK. I'd ring Carmen Pavlovic for news in Australia—which was in a totally different situation than we were. We were all talking globally about what was going to happen. And then I'd come back to the house and get on Zoom by 9:00am. Those calls went until about 6:00 and then we'd have what became known as the "Little League" meetings.

For many people in the industry, workdays during the pandemic were long. My husband had this experience. He started Zooms with his clients in the early morning and maintained a series of them through the day and evening. All in the name of *the future* and how we could get there.

Meanwhile I was in my office writing songs about *my dreams*, for heaven's sake.

But to my earlier point about multitudinous narratives, a single "truth" about how to reinstate life as we knew it never appeared. Not for Broadway. Not for New York City. Not for America.

At the height of the pandemic, FEMA, the Federal Emergency Management Agency, issued to the country what they called "Coronavirus Rumor Control" to give the public tools to "distinguish between rumors and facts regarding the response to the Coronavirus."

I think we all remember that there was no rumor control. We couldn't agree as a nation—as a world of nations, really—on what the coronavirus even was, let alone how to deal with it. The comparatively small world of Broadway, a niche market of like-minded people, was no different.

Some rumors suggested that we'd achieved "herd immunity" as a species, and we should just "let Covid run its course." Translated to Broadway, that would mean *open the theaters now*. But no union was going to allow that option. As World Health Organization Director-General Tedros Adhanom Ghebreyesus said in a press briefing October of 2020, "Allowing a dangerous virus that we don't fully understand to run free is simply unethical."

Some rumors suggested there would be at least another year of Covid outbreaks, so strict protocols should be extended. Translated to Broadway, that would mean *do not open the theaters for another year*. Basic economics wasn't going to allow that. New York City depends on tourists—66.6 million of them visited the city in 2019 according to the office of the State Comptroller—and tourists come to New York City to see, among other things, Broadway shows.

That's not even taking into account the actors and other union professionals who depended on Broadway for employment. Government help with insurance and extended unemployment ended in the summer of 2021. People needed to get back to work.

Okay, so then what about allowing half-occupancy in the audience? That was one proposed solution. While that was working for some limited-run shows at not-for-profit theaters—Aleshea Harris's fantastic *What to Send Up When It Goes Down* at BAM, for example—it was unsustainable for Broadway. As Mark Kennedy said in an article for NBC, "The average operating costs for a play are about $300,000 per week, while weekly costs run $600,000 for musicals. Conventional wisdom is that many shows need to sell at least 80 percent of tickets just to break even."

Producers don't open Broadway shows to break even. 50 percent audience occupancy was not an option.

What if we attack the virus itself? Grignard Pure, makers of the dramatic haze you see in Broadway musicals like *Phantom of the Opera* (or *Les Misérables*), suggested that they could do just that with their product: the haze itself.

In an April 2021 article for *Politco*'s "E&E News,"[7] authors Ariel Wittenberg and E. A. Crunden report, "In January, Grignard Pure became the first EPA-approved antiviral treatment used in air—rather than on surfaces. Internal tests reviewed by EPA show the product is 98 percent effective at deactivating viruses when it has reached a 0.5-milligram-per-cubic-meter concentration in a space for 30 seconds."

This idea got no traction in the industry.

No solution could.

Just like in America.

Some rumors suggested Ivermectin, a horse-deworming medication, could cure Covid. Some rumors suggested bleach.

Some even suggested Covid wasn't even real.

The truth of the matter was ungraspable, because it didn't exist.

TOM SCHUMACHER   It was clear no one in New York had a clue on how to re-open theaters. There was no information on HOW we'd actually do it.

---

[7] E&E stands for Energy and Environment.

Broadway was closed and it needed to reopen. That was the answer.

What was the question?

It would turn out to be an ancient question that the Greek playwrights thought up.

Dreamland

I'm dreaming. Sleepwalking.

But dreamland is crossfading with the real world.

Ugly truths are crashing in. I slam into them like walls.

We all do.

The real world is awful.

Nick Cordero, a working Broadway actor whom I didn't know, has died of prolonged, agonizing Covid complications. He was forty-one years old.

More and more stories of people hospitalized, close to dying. Danny Burstein, beloved Broadway actor, has a harrowing hospitalization and near-death experience. Healthcare systems overwhelmed, collateral tragedies. Rebecca Luker, beloved Broadway singer, and Danny Burstein's wife, passes away from complications with ALS.

Weddings and funerals are super-spreader events.

Maine Wedding Gives Half Of The Guests Coronavirus,
   Outbreak Leads To 177 Covid-19 Cases And 7 Deaths[8]

My niece dies in a tragic accident; my parents, in their seventies, can't even go to her funeral.

Friends' stories. Castmates. Matt McGrath suffering Covid symptoms in a Manhattan hotel, afraid of going home and getting his elderly mother sick. A stranger brings him food.

Many shows will not reopen.

Many debuts will never happen.

Young actors showing up to New York, like I had done twenty-some-odd years earlier, will turn around and go back home. Their dreams crushed.

Reality overwhelms.

Like an alarm.

The Minutes

Wake up.

The long dream that felt like seven million years was ending.

Wake up, Todd.

---

[8]*Forbes*, November 12, 2020, Victoria Forster

I hadn't sung in over a year, so my voice was a bit rough. My body was in pretty good shape thanks to Hannah and kettlebells, but I needed to start singing every day, which I did, mostly in the shower.

It felt good.

It felt so good to be awake again.

August 3, 2021

JEFF BRANCATO (email)
Hi all!

Here are the notes from yesterday's meeting . . .

We all had a lot of questions, which Jeff, ever the stage manager, anticipated. He laid out all of the answers in beautifully organized minutes from a cast Zoom meeting.

Here are some salient bullet points. (Jeff's minutes in italics.)

Minutes from Cast Zoom Meeting, 8/2/21 at 12 noon
– Welcome to the company, Colin [Bates], He will be our new Gene Laine. Colin played the role of Gene in Toronto and the second West End productions.

Colton Ryan would not be returning to the show. He had been cast in the Hulu series *The Girl from Plainville*, starring opposite Elle Fanning, and his schedule wouldn't allow both.

My husband once had to get oral surgery and the surgeon gave him an anesthetic that made him a little loopy, even for a short while post-surgery. In the recovery room, I asked my loopy husband how the surgery went, and he kinda slurred "Fine." And then he said, "The nurse asked me how to make it in show business." I asked, "Well, what did you tell her?" And Mark said, "I told her, 'Be special.'"

Colton is special. He started his career on Broadway covering the title role in *Dear Evan Hansen*, a gig he landed while still in college, and in 2023 was nominated for a Tony Award for his performance in *New York, New York*. What an entrance.

Colin Bates, an American actor who, like Chelsea, was a graduate of Juilliard, would play "Gene Laine" upon our return.

COLIN BATES   It was super easy because I mean, the group, everyone was super familial and no, it was much easier than I thought it was going to be.

Colin's been making professional theater since he was a child when he played the eponymous Billy Elliott on the West End, and as an adult he rides an electric scooter all over the city. His frenetic energy parkours around any room he's in.

COLIN BATES   I arrived and that day was like, I already felt a part of the family. Yeah, I mean, you guys took me in and it felt very good.

– *PT will be starting up again the week we start rehearsals.*[9] *We will also be having another Rake Workshop since it's been a minute since we've been on stage.*

Our stage for *Girl from the North Country* was "raked," meaning it tilted forward for better audience sightlines. Upstage (the area toward the back of the stage furthest from the audience) is a bit higher than downstage (the area closest to the audience).

What that means for the actors is that we stand and dance on a slanted floor, some of us in heels (not me). Imagine doing your job, whatever it is, but you're on a little hill the entire time. The cumulative effect of weeks and months like this is rough on one's body, especially the back.

A "rake workshop" is a session with a physical therapist who teaches the actors ways to counteract the effects of the rake. A lot of it comes down to basic stretching before and after the show. But there are also things an actor must do while performing to protect themselves.

When Kimber sings, "Tight Connection to My Heart," I enter from stage right with a small group to sing backup harmonies in silhouette; I stand facing directly stage left, my gaze perpendicular to the audience, so the rake tilts me slightly sideways. To counteract the effect on my back that standing at a sideways tilt for an entire song might have, the physical therapist taught me to soften (slightly bend) up upstage-knee, which would take the tilt in my body away.

Throughout every performance, during every scene, depending on which way I was facing, I would make these slight physical adjustments. Part of me is singing and acting, but another part of me is thinking about what to do with my knees.

– *We would like everyone to know that we are changing the "Show must go on" mentality. We want everyone to feel comfortable deciding to call out of the show if they don't feel well without the pressure of worrying about coverage. This is the reason we are adding swings.*

This is a significant change to the ethos of Broadway. In my experience, it brought to bear two very positive things: actors taking better care of themselves by calling out when they aren't well, and swings showing the world how wonderful they are.

---

[9] Physical Therapy. Productions usually hire a physical therapist who comes to the theater on two show days. Actors can sign up for twenty-minute sessions.

Of course, there are stories of certain actors in certain productions taking advantage of this change, refusing to go on, piling up "personal" days, forcing canceled shows because they "can't go on." But like any system meant to help everyone, *some* people mistreat it, and while that stinks, the new system is still an improvement.

> *– We have hired a third-party HR company called K&K Reset. They will be a great asset to us as management (and have been on other shows like "Phantom" and "Moulin Rouge"), but especially to you as company members. We will be introducing them to you all shortly.*
>
> *They will also be helping us with our anti-racism/unconscious bias/ anti-harassment training. We will have several of these trainings with the full company (cast, band, and crew). One will be over Zoom before we start back up in the room, and two sessions will be held in-person during rehearsals.*
>
> *§ We want these trainings to be more of a "town hall style" where these discussions can be held in a safe space, rather than the "check-the-box, we did it"-style presentations of the past.*

The anti-racism sessions we had were eye-opening and long overdue. Broadway couldn't ignore its own racism any longer, and I'm proud to be a part of an industry that at least attempted to address this. I say "attempted" because I know we didn't "solve" racism. Not even close. We think because we're in the arts we're inclusive, and we're not. We think because we're artists we're different, and we're not. We have the sickness.

KIMBER ELAYNE SPRAWL   It was such a revolutionary summer with George Floyd and the spotlight that we're shining on our own industry.

AUSTIN SCOTT   It had to be done. And it was so great that it was being done. And at the same time, everything got torn open, and torn open again. Like an exposed raw nerve. I was carrying everything I had experienced over the pandemic: the lockdown, George Floyd, and walking around white neighborhoods and having visions of being shot at, all of these horrible things. I was then bringing that into this room. It just didn't feel as much like a family to me, especially when we were doing those K and K meetings, because a different part of me got stirred up.

> *– Covid protocols:*
> *– The company will receive a manual for all the protocols we will need to follow in the next few days.*

"Protocols" would add hours to our days and tens-of-thousands of dollars to the show's budget.

MARE WINNINGHAM   I think we were all just so freaking grateful to be back that we just were like, "Okay, tell us what to do and we'll do it."

There were testing sites installed in unused spaces around the Times Square area, and each show was assigned to one of them.

Alecia Parker is a Broadway producer and general manager. Alongside Barry and Fran Weissler, one of Alecia's biggest shows is one of Broadway's most successful: *Chicago*.

ALECIA PARKER   The expense [of Covid protocols] was big. We didn't have a choice. It was the only way you could reopen, so you had to add the expense on. Daunting, because at times we were buying pallets of tests. That was the only way to get them. Other times, I literally paid people going to drug stores and buy as many as they could because you had to have the tests and they weren't regularly available.

Our testing site for *Girl from the North Country* was the lobby of the Music Box theater, which was available because its occupant, *Dean Evan Hansen*, wouldn't reopen until December of that year. The results of the antigen test took about thirty minutes, and since we weren't allowed into the Belasco Theater until we had a negative test result, I got pretty good at killing time by walking my bike around Times Square and people-watching.

– Mare and Tony's House Event!
        *We have decided on the date of **Sunday, August 29th** based on everyone's availability. We hope everyone can make it. And thank you again to Mare and Tony for hosting. It is going to be a very special day!*

Mare Winningham and her husband Anthony Edwards invited the entire cast to their home outside of the city for an all-day barbecue and swim. We sang, and swam, and ate, and it felt like a family reunion.

All to celebrate one thing: We're back!

A Man Behind a Curtain: Part 2

The Greeks invented theater, and with it a classic plot device called *deus ex machina*.

God in the machine.

Deus ex machina, per Merriam-Webster is "A person or thing (as in fiction or drama) that appears or is introduced suddenly and unexpectedly and provides a contrived solution to an apparently insoluble difficulty."

Most often, this "person or thing" is an actual god. This time, it was a government official.

In May of 2021, New York Governor Andrew Cuomo unexpectedly lifted the capacity restrictions on indoor venues, which included Broadway. Essentially, he proclaimed that Broadway was now *open*.

Just like that. A "solution to an apparently insoluble difficulty."

Ta-da!

"But," as NPR noted, "the reality is that Broadway shows need time to rehearse, recast and develop safety protocols onstage, backstage and for the audience."

No show was ready to just *open* in May of 2021. Except for one: *Springsteen on Broadway,* which is exactly what it sounds like: A Bruce Springsteen solo show. It had been an impossible ticket when it originally ran in 2017–18, and since it was a relatively simple show to remount (and a sure thing for the box office) it reopened on June 26 for a limited run.

What about the forty other Broadway houses? Broadway was "open," but how to get shows up and running?

A kind of panic set in.

ALECIA PARKER We were never going to have a consensus on an exact date that every show is going to be open, because every show was in a different state. So that didn't make any sense. I think it was just that it was critical to get the industry reopened for the employees, for the public. We had to make sure we were doing it safely. I was part of the protocol committee and just we knew it was critical that this was the moment to do it.

Producers met with each of the unions associated with Broadway . . .

ALECIA PARKER Fourteen of them, by the way!

. . . about how to do this quickly but safely for actors, crew members, musicians, theater staff.

ALECIA PARKER There were groups of us that were assigned different pieces of it. I think two people in the industry, Maggie Brohn and Anthony LaTorella, really led the way 90% of the time with Jason Laks at the league. But one of the things that kept us busy during the pandemic was our constant calls about protocols; we had an epidemiologist that worked with us and all those things.

Eventually, the "Little League" sub-committee with Tom Schumacher et al. opened back up to include all of the producers in the Broadway League. If the entire industry was going to open, there had to be some kind of inclusive, organizing principle . . .

TOM SCHUMACHER When meeting with the larger group of Producers I said, "Folks, when we come back we're going to be crowded for who gets rehearsal space, who gets shop space . . . so just share with me your dates and I'll help you coordinate."

. . . not to mention, *money.*

> TOM SCHUMACHER We began the process of how to navigate the economics of a return. And out of that grew a conversation about how can we engage in a national conversation to get funding to support the industry so we could keep our productions together and come back. And that's the conversation that led to hiring two really key—one Republican and one Democrat—lobbyists. They were a huge piece of what became the national effort for SVOG—the Shuttered Venue Operators Grant.

The Shuttered Venue Operator Grant, per the US Small Business Administration, is a program that was ". . . established by the Economic Aid to Hard-Hit Small Businesses, Nonprofits, and Venues Act, and amended by the American Rescue Plan Act."

> ALECIA PARKER Without support, nowhere near the number of shows would have reopened. The producers just wouldn't have had the money to make it happen.

"The program includes over $16 billion in grants to shuttered venues, to be administered by SBA's Office of Disaster Assistance." Venues like museums, movie theaters, and live performance venues could apply and receive up to $10 million dollars to defray costs accumulated by the shutdown.

The play *Pass Over* by Antoinette Chinonye Nwandu was the first play to open on Broadway on August 4, 2021.

Waitress and *Hadestown* reopened in early September, 2021.

So, one show, *Springsteen on Broadway,* had completed its "limited run" and three others, *Pass Over, Waitress,* and *Hadestown,* were already up and running when Broadway officially "reopened" on September 14, 2021.

> TOM SCHUMACHER   And then we reopened. You recall in September of 2021, *Hamilton* and *Wicked* and *Lion King* all opened on the same night. We had Stephen Schwartz, Julie Taymor, and Lin-Manuel Miranda visit each of our three shows together. Jeffrey Seller, David Stone and I planned it to stagger the curtain times so they could speak to the audiences at each of the "re-opening" performances. It had a major press impact and it was an unofficial way to say, "Broadway is back."

So, Broadway was open again. And that was the end of Covid.

> TOM SCHUMACHER   And then of course Omicron hit that December and set us back again. Whatever ground we'd made we was killed again by Omicron.

Shit.

What I'm Always Afraid Of

The day before we started Broadway rehearsals for the second time, I had a troubling thought: *What if no one comes to the show?*

But that's silly. Of course they'll come, it's Broadway, they always come.

Back in March of 2020, we had full houses. Every night. They'll be full again.

Sure, we weren't *Hamilton* or *Wicked* or *The Lion King*, we weren't a *legacy*, but we were Dylan. We were cool. We were different.

They'll come.

But something about that big reopening of Broadway in September focusing on the massive commercial hits triggered a life-long personal struggle with doubts. Doubts about my being a part of the club. Real or imagined, my experience had always felt like that of an outsider looking in. And now I was feeling all of those doubts again; maybe this was all just a larger-scale version of calling home to tell my parents that I was going to be in *Les Misérables* only to find out that wasn't true at all.

Les Misérables never needed me.

Did Broadway need *Girl from the North Country*?

I kept reading article after article about Broadway's exciting return with *Six* and *Moulin Rouge* and *Book of Mormon* and the "Legacy Shows." Bright musicals. Comedies. Romance. I heard people saying they wanted "escapism." Like the screwball comedies of the 1930s after the Great Depression. People didn't want reality, reality was depressing.

In an article for the *Los Angeles Times* in 2009, responding to the state of the arts after the economic downturn, Morris Dickstein noted that, "Studies of the 1930s have shown how the economic meltdown was accompanied by psychological depression: loss of morale, a sense of despair, grave fears for the future."

Post-Great-Depression, we Americans wanted Fred Astaire and Ginger Rogers. We wanted Myrna Loy and William Powell in *The Thin Man*.

Even in the play *Girl from the North Country* itself, Marianne wants to see a romantic comedy with famous movie stars.

MARIANNE: You wanna see a movie? You know, those things you should be writing.

GENE: Eh. Movies. They're so commercial. What's on?

MARIANNE: You see *It Happened One Night*?

GENE: Who's in it?

MARIANNE: Claudette Colbert. It's goofy. This guy is helping this girl run away from getting married.

He smiles mischievously at her.

GENE: You'd go and see it again?

MARIANNE: Sure if you wanna . . . I got nothin to wear.

Maybe audiences would want a musical version of *It Happened One Night*, and why not, it's a fantastic film, someone *should* make a musical of it.

But, as Morris Dickstein pointed out in the same article, escapism was not *all* that Americans wanted after the Great Depression. What about *The Grapes of Wrath*? That was popular, too. And being about the Great Depression, it spoke directly to the circumstances that everyone had just survived.

Matt McGrath was on Broadway the only other time it semi-shut down for two days.

MATT MCGRATH   I happen to have been the M.C. in *Cabaret* when September 11th happened. I was with Brooke Shields, we were the leaders of the cast, and we had to make a decision of, do we do the show on Thursday night when we're back? Maybe we should tell everybody we know that this horrible thing happened. And I thought, *we can't apologize for what we're doing here*. We're here to let them forget just for a second. And if we just let them escape for a second somewhere else and give them that experience, maybe they'll not think about what just happened just for a second.

The post-9/11 audience wanted *Cabaret*. What was the post-pandemic audience wanting to see? I had to believe there was room, even desire, for social commentary.

The first play to open on Broadway post-Covid, *Pass Over* by Antoinette Chinonye Nwandu, would be the test.

Pass Over, a serious play using religious imagery and tackling the current racism epidemic, a play that received glowing reviews and featured two of New York's very finest actors, John Michael Hill and Gabriel Ebert, and one of Chicago's very finest, Namir Smallwood of Steppenwolf Theatre Company, closed after little over a month of performances. They couldn't get an audience.

Damn.

We were a serious play with religious imagery and glowing reviews. I looked up the reviews to remind myself.

They weren't *all* glowing, it turns out.

Helen Shaw at *Vulture* hated our show. She liked the cast's singing, but that's it. In fact, all of the things I loved about *Girl from the North Country* annoyed her.

HELEN SHAW (*Vulture* review)

And there's something perverse about the way Dylan's lyrics are handled. We are kind of meant to pay attention to them, kind of not . . . The push-me-pull-you annoyance of it leaves you unwilling to parse the lyrics at all. This reaches its absolute peak when the wonderful Luba Mason—a hotel tenant with secrets and woes to spare—sings "Señor" glumly, but with intensity. "Señor, señor" she croons, scuffing the floor with her shoe. *What?* You have to laugh.

I shouldn't have read that. Dammit. There's a saying about reviews, "If you believe the good ones, you've got to believe the bad ones." That is why you shouldn't *read* reviews, Todd. And definitely don't read the comments in the online theater chatrooms.

I read the comments in the online theater chatrooms.

Some of them were about *me*. And my "offensive" portrayal of a neuro-divergent character. Shit. Exactly what I was trying to avoid.

Don't look at these things, Todd.

Just show up.

MARE WINNINGHAM   I started to feel like when we come back, this is a different play we're doing. It's going to be hitting so many levels.

My anxiety was pushing all of my own buttons. As if I was standing outside the room of that Keith Haring audition again, listening in to someone else get the job. My early days in the city haunted me. *Girl from the North Country* should go sing its sad songs in the streets, moping around the city, that's where it belongs, that's where I belong, it's where I've always belonged. Twenty-two years in the city at this point, hadn't I at least figured that out?

The Tony Awards finally happened on September 26, celebrating all of the shows that had opened before the pandemic. Except for us. I knew that it was because we hadn't run long enough to get nominators in, but it still felt like we had been left behind. Like we weren't a part of the conversation anymore.

That "you're not good enough" feeling again. I was old enough to understand that "the call was coming from inside the house," as a friend of mine would say. My feelings were not corroborated by reality, this was my own psychology provoking me.

But even if I'm gloomy, which I admit I am, I'm not a self-saboteur, I'm a hard worker. I tucked all of my doubts into my pocket where I know they're nice and comfy, and I pressed on; I worked out with Hannah, I sang every day to get my voice back in shape. I found Elias again.

I was ready, I was just afraid—not afraid of *Covid*, I was afraid of what I'm always afraid of: *Relevance.*

JEFF BRANCATO (email)

Hello NORTH COUNTRY Broadway Company!

It has been A WHILE since I've gotten to send a schedule to this group ... *547 days*, to be exact ... and how wonderful it feels to not have to wait one day more!

I hope this email finds everyone healthy, happy, and EXCITED to be returning to our home-away-from-home at The Belasco! As our amazing production team and crew are back in the theater waking "the boarding house" up from 18-months of hibernation, and our talented cast and band are gearing up to join us next week, here is some information for everyone:

> **Production Calendar**, through Jan. 2022. Of course, this is a general outline and subject to change.

> **Cast List** and **Face Page**, including our FIVE new cast members—Colin Bates (Gene Laine), and Alex Joseph Grayson, Housso Semon, Edward Staudenmayer, and Anastasia Talley (Swings)

There wasn't time for my fear. As they say in the opera world in lieu of "Good luck": *In bocca al lupo!* Which means: *Into the mouth of the wolf!*
My best friend Markus used to always respond: *Senza paura.*
Without fear.

8

The New World

How Does It Feel?

Girl from the North Country felt even stronger as a work of art after the pandemic.

MARC KUDISCH   I remember taking video of Times Square in early October and it felt like New Year's Eve, it was packed. People were out. I just thought, *this is so exciting*. The people are out. Everybody's here. Anyone who thinks New York is dead is crazy. Look at this!

It felt as if the play was meeting the moment perfectly.

JAY O. SANDERS   This stuff we talked about in the play was about our feelings, about what we'd gone through, and people were just in tears and saying afterwards, "Oh my God."

It was relevant . . .

JAY O. SANDERS   Because it was a reflection of what we were all going through. It was so important.

. . . even if our audiences were small.

AARON LUSTBADER   The presumption was the shows that would do well with a local audience would succeed. And the long running tourist driven musicals were dead in the water because who would possibly be coming to see them? . . . [But] the industry-wide conventional wisdom was not correct. That people actually were very excited to come revisit the shows that they knew and loved.

Wicked and *Hamilton* and *The Lion King* had audiences right away. We struggled. But it still felt important.

JAY O. SANDERS   It could have been five people out there; I felt the enthusiasm at our show was just as great with the smallest houses. And it was all about the same thing. Even though it wasn't set in Covid, it was set in survival time.

When Mare Winningham sang "Like a Rolling Stone," I could hear the audience hearing the song anew and recognizing something of themselves in the lyrics, seeing their own recent struggle through Bob Dylan and Elizabeth Laine.

> People call say "Beware doll, you're bound to fall"
> You thought they were all kidding you
> You used to laugh about
> Everybody that was hanging out
> Now you don't talk so loud
> Now you don't seem so proud
> About having to be scrounging your next meal[1]

It was shocking, the relevance. How does it feel? *I know how it feels.*

At the Public and early in our early Broadway run in 2020, we had been playing at history, *acting* history, imagining the lives of the people we were portraying, these long-ago people who had shared a long-ago struggle.

And now we didn't have to try so hard to relate.

> How does it feel?
> To be on your own
> With no direction home
> A complete unknown
> Like a rolling stone

Life for everyone over the past year had been uncertain and frightening. *Girl from the North Country* was an acknowledgment of that. If I liked church, this would have been my church. Mare showed us all our own bruised selves with "Like a Rolling Stone"; Austin shook us with his "Hurricane" like he was exorcizing the terror; Luba let us cry for what we'd lost with her "Love in Vain"; Kimber gave us courage to hope with "Tight Connection to My Heart"; And Jeannette got us up on our feet, ready once more to walk into the difficult world with "Pressing On."

JAY O. SANDERS   I felt that the backstage was as alive, if not more so than out there with the audience, because all of us were aware of what we were putting up with, what we needed, how glad we were to see each other. And we were the audience ourselves.

---

[1]"Like a Rolling Stone," Dylan, *Highway 61 Revisited*, 1965.

The daily testing was frustrating, a never-ending doctor's appointment, but the show felt worth it, the show felt important. Covid-tests became a necessary daily chore, completed with pride.

LUBA MASON   I found it to be a pain in the neck. I have to say, I was definitely one of those people who was not paranoid about covid.

The masks and no-backstage visitors, the rules, the distancing; all of it was dispiriting. I've been around Broadway for twenty-plus years, I've "gone back" countless times, I've been to openings, and previews, and dress-rehearsals, opening night parties, the Tonys, etc., I know how much fun it is to be on Broadway. I've seen it. But as an actor, *Girl from the North Country* a year-and-a-half later was *still* my debut. And it wasn't fun.

RACHEL STERN   I think we were so happy just to be back. But, I mean, since everyone was masked and we weren't allowed to have people backstage, we were missing one of the greatest parts about being on Broadway!

But it felt important. And important things aren't always fun. Press on.

Austin Scott and I, as dressing-roommates, got along very well. Neither one of us is particularly chatty, but we managed to have some deep conversations. But now, post-Covid, we were wearing masks around each other, even in our private dressing room, which gave our pre-show time together a sterilizing effect. What had been casual and friendly and intimate was now veiled and mute.

SCOTT SANDERS   Coming back, it just felt like it was just harder. With all the testing, the isolating, the lack of fellowship, the small audience, it just really felt hard. It was a struggle.

The audiences were not growing in size.

LUBA MASON   That's what was really depressing. It was really hard to get up the energy for a hundred people, two-hundred people in a twelve-hundred seat house. And the drudgery of the testing and just seeing how our show was missing its timing.

The memory of the full audience was more vivid with each small audience we had.

LUBA MASON   We opened in March of 2020 to the rave reviews. We finally get on Broadway, finally get on Broadway, and then we're shut down again.

Sometimes it felt like we should just cancel, there would be so few people in the audience.

> CHELSEA LEE WILLIAMS   I was like, "You guys are we really about to do this show?" But then part of me thought *why am I mad at the people who showed up?* These people actually are here. They bought their tickets. We've got to give them the show.

Chelsea was right. Ironically, we needed to revive for ourselves the just-retired phrase: *The show must go on.*

The audience needed it. *We* needed it. *I* needed it.

The religious feelings returned to me.

As I watched the nightly Thanksgiving celebration, I could feel above me the spirits of God and Elias and Bob Dylan. I realize Bob Dylan was very much alive and *not a spirit*, maybe it was the spirit of his music, or maybe the spirit of *music* itself, but it sat in a trinity with God and Elias, the father and the son, above me.

Over all of that shared food and the particulates flying from laughing mouths, on a stage where it was impossible to stay six feet apart, I knew that some of my castmates were uncomfortable. Covid was still killing people, after all. We weren't *safe* from it.

> CAITLIN HOULAHAN   It felt serious. It felt life or death, and I didn't know if we were exposing ourselves to something that we shouldn't be exposing ourselves to. So I had a lot of anxiety about that. And I remember at one point, I was around Aaron, our GM [General Manager], and I just burst into tears and he said, "Oh, can I give you a hug?" I think I was just so stressed, and I didn't know how to express my emotions, especially around how most people were so excited to be back. And I didn't know how to describe how stressed out I was.

"How does it feel?"

I knew that some at the Thanksgiving dinner had complicated feelings about the post-murder-of-George Floyd environment America was in. We'd talked about racial bias as a cast, we'd completed our trainings with K & K Reset, but *how did it feel* actually being back? Was this a new Broadway? Were we changed, as a culture? As a theater community? Or were we just performing change?

> AUSTIN SCOTT   I remember thinking: *there's a billboard in Times Square with me and Kimber holding each other. And there's another one of the two of us kissing.* But if you come to see the show, that's not the main story. That's not what the show is really about. It's a piece of the show. And I remember feeling "Are they putting the two Black characters on a billboard to advertise this show has Black characters . . . to meet the

moment?". Now I am very grateful that my face is on a billboard in Times Square. I am so grateful that you've chosen to showcase us. But I'm also feeling "*Why us? Why are we up there?*"

"How does it feel?"

I knew that many at the Thanksgiving dinner had been experiencing the *othering* of racial bias long before the summer of 2020.

MARCO PAGUIA   When we had the training, do you remember when we did that training? People who identify as Black people, who identify as white. And then it's "Other, Asian and Latinx," and there were three of us, so I think about that sometimes. And you know, *embrace your specialness*, but it kind of leaves you on an island a little bit. So I've always felt like a little bit of an outsider, always, always.

"How does it feel?"

The question "How does it feel?" no longer felt rhetorical. I half-expected someone to stand up in the audience and answer Mare when she sang it.

Do you really want to know?! Because I can tell you! This is how it feels!

The Belasco Theater was emotionally charged at every performance. Offstage, the real world was clinical and no fun. Tests and social distancing. Suspicion and isolation. Stripped of emotion that had to go somewhere, so it was injected into this two-and-a-half-hour thing called *Girl from the North Country*. The play was bursting.

JEANNETTE BAYARDELLE   The world had changed. Our minds had changed. Our perspective on life had changed. We had been through something so traumatic that it's amazing that we didn't kill each other. I mean, because we're in a different world. We're on edge in a different way.

I felt it at the breakfast scene. I heard it in Mare's voice. I saw it in the audience's eyes—the only things exposed because of their masks.

I saw it in the way the characters devoured that Thanksgiving meal.

ROBERT JOY   I'm pretty much a vegetarian. But I thought, *I'm going to enjoy this turkey and stuffing and cranberry sauce every single night and the potatoes.* I just thought *let's go for it.*

The Great Depression had starved everyone, and so had the pandemic.

JEANNETTE BAYARDELLE   *Oh, God, where are we?*

I don't pray, typically. But with the Trinity above me and a vision of life in front of me, I found myself praying every night during that Thanksgiving scene where these humans, both characters and actors, who had been starved by circumstances, feasted.

JEANNETTE BAYARDELLE   We came back to a world of uncertainty and fear.

Wearing my pressed-linen Sunday best now hopelessly wrinkled at the elbows.

Even though I knew the pain so many of us were feeling, the uncertainty and fear, the frustration, the anxiety, and the doubts.

Even though I knew that although we were not suddenly *better*, at least we were together.

Even though I knew that the answer to the question "How does it feel" was "It fucking hurts," I still found myself praying, "Thank you."

The Variant

AARON LUSTBADER   Jeannette told me at Mare and Tony's summer party in August that something very bad was going to happen in January or February, but that it was all going to be okay.

Omicron started so sweetly for us.

MARE WINNINGHAM   I invited everybody in to sing "Happy Birthday" to my mom.

It started with a song. In early December, the entire cast crowded together in Mare's dressing room to make a video for Mare's mother. We sang and waved at the camera and blew kisses and threw our arms around each other. A giant group hug.

The next day, Mare tested positive for Covid.

MARE WINNINGHAM   And then when I got Covid, my first thought was, *what have you done?*

My brother Travis and his wife Penni were in the audience that night. They had traveled from South Dakota to see the show. I was half in my costume and slicking down my hair with the goopy product provided by the wig department when I heard the news: *Mare is out.* I texted my brother.

TRAVIS ALMOND   We thought, well, *bummer.* You know, because she's one of the actors you want to see!

Just a few hours earlier, Jeff had gotten the news about Mare's positive result.

JEFF BRANCATO   I remember going back to Jen Blood and I was like, "Hey, can you come downstairs with me for two quick seconds? I have a quick question for you."

JENNIFER BLOOD   I had just finished a bag of chips, the full bag. Not even a healthy-ish chips—just, not food that I would eat if I was going to do a show!

Because Covid is a health issue, there were rules around sharing someone's infection status. Mare had tested positive on the antigen test prior to half-hour, and because the antigen test can be inaccurate, a PCR test was necessary. In the hour-or-so between those test results, Jeff needed to discuss what happens if Mare doesn't go on without discussing *why* Mare wouldn't go on.

JEFF BRANCATO   You weren't supposed to tell wardrobe or sound. *Nobody*. And I went downstairs to Mary [Johnston Rutherford, wardrobe supervisor] and I was like, "Hey, is Jen's costume for Elizabeth accessible?" And then we went to John Sibley [Audio] and I was like, "Have you had a mic fitting for Jen Blood before as Elizabeth?" He was like, "Yes." And I'm like, "Cool, okay, just asking." Meanwhile, Mare is standing in the alley outside waiting for a test result.

BARBARA RUBIN   I happened to be at the theater and Jeff was standing with Mare in the alleyway, and I was coming up to Mare to hug her. And so they kind of had to [puts her arms up in an X shape] clue me in to what was going on. And so it was totally nuts, the call was literally being made right there.

JEFF BRANCATO   And then so I say to Jen Blood, "If you want to start putting on makeup, you can, but please don't tell anybody what's going on."

Meanwhile, Mare is dealing with the fact that she has Covid and the fear that she'd spread it to the entire cast when we gathered in her dressing room the day before.

MARE WINNINGHAM   How will I be able to handle the shame if it's a domino thing?

Jeff assured her that he had followed the guidelines; we were in her dressing room for under five minutes.

MARE WINNINGHAM   It has to be longer than fifteen minutes [to be transmissible].

But no one *really* knew how this thing was getting passed around. Mare had been diligent in her mask wearing and hand sanitizing.

MARE WINNINGHAM   I have no idea where I got it. Nobody does.

Naturally, the cast was a bit troubled by the news. Would we all get Covid now?

AUSTIN SCOTT   We all crowded in [her dressing room]. And what are the odds, the next day she got it!

Suddenly *every* interaction with our fellow actors felt risky. Was every interaction risky? There were no answers, only more and more questions.

AUSTIN SCOTT   How soon are you actually contagious? Meanwhile, I'm on stage kissing Kimber, though actually at that point we had changed it to a hug. But it was an emotional show, and there are a lot of times where you are five inches away screaming at someone's face. And then there was a lot of spit flying and stuff like that.

During the breakfast scene, Luba and I shared a bowl of oatmeal and ate from the same spoon.

AUSTIN SCOTT   We had become a family and so close, and then all of a sudden there was this danger. You know what I mean? We couldn't hang out in each other's dressing room between shows and talk. Or if we did, we didn't tell anybody. And having to wear masks when we were together sitting in our dressing room.

JEFF BRANCATO   We weren't supposed to say someone had Covid, but Mare had given me permission to tell everybody. I announced over the page-system what was going on, and everyone was a little panicked. I was panicked. It was our first time. It suddenly felt like you had an intruder in the house, this virus is here.

MARE WINNINGHAM   Barbara walked me to an Uber. And I was watching the audience going in [to the theater]. And I was just devastated. It was awful. It was so awful.

JENNIFER BLOOD   They brought me down to [Mare's] dressing room.

And suddenly it was *places*.
The audience is seated. My brother is out there. Here we go.

TRAVIS ALMOND   After the show, we were so blown away that we thought, "Well, geez, how good must Mare be if *this* is her understudy!"

The audience loved Jennifer.

JENNIFER BLOOD   God, what do I remember of that first night? I remember getting to act two and feeling things went off the rails a little bit.

But she would get a rare gift for a swing: the chance to do several shows in a row. Covid protocol was clear: when an actor tests positive, they are out for a mandatory ten days.

JENNIFER BLOOD I had gotten used to the idea of doing these jobs and never going on and kind actually being okay with that.

Jennifer would play Elizabeth Laine for the next ten days.

MARE WINNINGHAM And then of course, Jen was a complete and utter triumph, which is so wonderful to think about. She doesn't even have a run-through! I mean, I know that she's ready, but still, you don't have a run through and boom, you're going on and you nail it?! Incredible. So I'm back at home, crying and saying to Tony "I'm jealous. I'm just really jealous." And he says to me, "Mare, don't you want her to be good?" And I'm like, "Of course I want her to be good! It's not even about wanting, I KNOW she's good. It's not about that. It's some weird combination of just hating missing out, and knowing you're replaceable."

While Mare's dressing-room singalong didn't itself cause Covid to spread, the virus would eventually spread through the cast that December, as it would spread through every cast on Broadway.

AUSTIN SCOTT Covid became a part of the show. It became a character, a cast member, a member of the company. And it was always looming, always present, and always a kind of "divider" between us. It made it hard to do the show. It made it hard to find that "fire" that we had before. And we weren't getting the same energy from the audience. The audiences were much smaller, and scared. It was very hard to find the same thing, at least for me, interpersonally within the cast. Because there was always just kind of a sense of, as soon as I go off stage, I have to put on a mask. And I, there's just this danger looming the entire time.

We started to hear about other shows canceling performances last minute because too many in the cast had tested positive. On December 15, 2021, Michael Paulson of the *New York Times* reported: "On Wednesday, 'Tina,' a jukebox musical about Tina Turner, canceled both of its performances; 'Harry Potter and the Cursed Child,' a stage sequel to the novels, canceled its matinee, and 'Hamilton' canceled its evening performance. A new musical adaptation of 'Mrs. Doubtfire' had already canceled four performances between Sunday and Wednesday, while Lin-Manuel Miranda's improv troupe, 'Freestyle Love Supreme,' canceled three, and 'Ain't Too Proud,' the Temptations jukebox musical, canceled one. At an Off Broadway theater down the street, a strong-selling revival of 'Little Shop of Horrors' scrapped four shows last weekend."

ALECIA PARKER   I got a call that *Chicago* may not be able to go on, and I was like, "That's not possible. You can't be serious. We have a line around the block outside. You've got to open the doors. We've got to do a show." But we didn't. The fact that Omicron hit us so soon after we were just getting our footing was also really tough.

Actors again found themselves sitting at home, helpless, wondering if their jobs would disappear, if our industry would shut down, maybe this time for good, something that two years prior had seemed impossible, but now felt terrifyingly likely.

MARE WINNINGHAM   When I had to miss shows, I hated it. I sat there on my couch doing nothing from 8 to 10:45. *The show is happening right now, and I'm not there.* It just felt awful.

Jeannette Bayardelle had predicted this.

JEANNETTE BAYARDELLE   I told Ashley [Berman, Company Manager], "It's going to come back. It's not over." Ashley's like, "Okay, but Jeannette, we have the vaccine." I said, "I know, I know. But it's coming back. I'm telling you, it's not finished. It's going to be the worst. It's coming back." *Okay, Jeannette. Okay. Okay.* And then it came back.

LUBA MASON   We would have meetings about Covid and I'd be like, "Jeannette, what's really going on" 'Cause she always knew.

JEANNETTE BAYARDELLE   At some point Jeff [Brancato] came over to me, he said, "Alright, what's going to happen? Should I pray to you or should I pray to Jesus? Who am I praying to?" So it was kind of hard being that person because people were just rolling their eyes at me.

We were absolutely rolling our eyes at Jeannette, especially when she showed up backstage in full plastic armor that looked like a transparent, one-person carriage that covered her from her head to her hips. But she continued to be right about everything, so the laugh was on us.

JEANNETTE BAYARDELLE   Poor Luba, [she's] in the dressing room with me. I'm having these conversations on the phone, she's like, "Wait, *what's* happening?!" We got close, me and Luba. She was just so gracious.

Omicron was affecting the audiences, too. Dessie Moynaihan of the Shuberts understands New York City's need for tourists, and tourists' needs for New York City.

DESSIE MOYNIHAN   We were ruining people's vacations because they had come [to New York] to see shows and the shows weren't going up.

Broadway had already suffered huge losses during the shutdown.

DESSIE MOYNIHAN   And now we were going through it again.

This Ain't a Dream No More

There's a phenomenon known as "the actor's nightmare." It's an anxiety dream that many performers have, similar to the common anxiety dream that most *people* have—the one where you're back in school and didn't study for the test or you're in your underwear and can't find your locker—but in the actor's nightmare, you're onstage in front of an audience performing a play only you don't know your lines or even what play you're in. In my actor's nightmare, which you'll be unsurprised to learn I have frequently, I'm onstage and the curtain is just about to rise, any second now; I can hear the audience anticipating the performance, and I know that I have a major role in the show they're about to see, but I also know that the show is in German, and I have no idea how to speak German.

In December of 2021, when the Omicron variant was causing a massive Covid resurgence, I inadvertently made the actor's nightmare a reality for a sweet young man named Aidan Wharton, who had joined the cast in December as a "vacation swing."

AIDAN WHARTON   The original plan was I would rehearse for two weeks.

A vacation swing is an actor who joins a cast for a limited time, to help cover roles while a certain actor is out for "vacation."

AIDAN WHARTON   And then Omicron hit.

Aidan's a quick study. He's sweet and easy to like.

AIDAN WHARTON   I'd been there for a week. Jeff said, "We have finished [learning John's track], let's just look ahead at the Gene track."

This was on a Tuesday afternoon. Forty-eight hours later, Aidan would make his Broadway debut in a role he'd not yet fully rehearsed.

Omicron hadn't forced us to cancel any shows, but that was a very real concern. If the right combination of just a few actors called out, we wouldn't have adequate coverage to go on.

The weekend prior to Aidan being thrust unexpectedly into his Broadway debut, I caught a cold the same day I got my Covid booster and had a terrible reaction to this one-two punch. Fluish and miserable the entire two-show day on Saturday, I pushed my way through the matinee on Sunday, barely making it to the curtain call.

The next morning I had no voice, couldn't make a sound. My husband teases me because every morning, the first thing I do is make a little high-pitched humming sound to check what shape my voice is going to be in that day. I don't think I'm the only one who does this. That morning, the only sound I could generate sounded more akin to *The Exorcist* than to music. Even Mark noticed and said, "Are you okay?"

Because it was Monday and therefore a day-off, this normally wouldn't have been an emergency. I would have just stayed silent all day, steamed, relaxed, and recovered. But I couldn't rest that particular Monday because I had a solo concert that evening at Chelsea Table and Stage, a concert to celebrate the release of my Christmas-themed album, *A Pony for Christmas*, and my guest star was Broadway legend Betty Buckley.

I needed my voice.

Like most singers, I have an ENT (ear, nose and throat doctor) who will squeeze me in if there is an emergency. This was an emergency. I taxied immediately up to her, and she prescribed a steroid that would take the swelling down to get me through my concert that night.

It worked well enough. I did the concert, never mentioning to the audience that I was sick, who wants to hear that? We were celebrating! Betty Buckley *sang a song I'd written*, which was a dream come true. I've loved Betty Buckley's voice since I was in college—my friends and I would compete with each other over who could lip-sync to her live version of "Meadowlark" better. Markus always won.

The next day, Tuesday, I was still miserable, the cold had settled in my throat and I was swollen and coughing and truly unable to sing.

I called out sick.

And then I called out Wednesday, both shows.

And then I called out Thursday, but not before phoning Tristan, our producer, to apologize. The optics were bad for me. I'd performed a concert on our day off, and now I was calling out sick. That looked irresponsible.

AIDAN WHARTON My boyfriend [Casey] was in *Mrs. Doubtfire*, they were also experiencing their own Covid crisis. Casey called me to tell me that his Covid test had come back inconclusive. And at that point, how they tested meant that he would be positive by tomorrow. So, he came to see me [in Bryant Park], and I triple-masked and hugged him and comforted him outside on the sidewalk. And then I went to have dinner before the show. As I was walking back to the stage door about to open it, I see that Jeff was calling me and I was like, *uh-oh*. I opened the door, and he was standing right there.

Colin Bates had tested positive for Covid. The perfect combination of actors. Out sick. We would have to cancel the show, maybe multiple shows, unless . . .

AIDAN WHARTON   And [Jeff] looked at me with a smile, sort of apologetically, and just said, "Are you ready to make your Broadway principal debut?"

Suddenly, this brand-new actor, whom the cast had just met a few days ago, and with whom no principal had ever rehearsed, was going to be onstage, in the show. On Broadway.

AIDAN WHARTON   Jay offered to run lines with me. Everybody was just so accommodating. And I think the entire company was holding space to prepare because they're like, *we don't know you. We haven't seen you in rehearsal.*

What about Gene's song "I Want You" with Caitlin, had Aidan ever even sung it with her before?

AIDAN WHARTON   Ten minutes before the show.

Aidan was living the actor's nightmare in real time. The curtain was about to go up on a show he'd never done.

AIDAN WHARTON   The part that I freaked out about is [Gene's] little snippet in "Señor," because I realized during act one that I had *never* sung it. I had never talked about it. I didn't even know what the words were.

I invite you to imagine yourself in this situation. You're moments away from performing a song you can't remember the lyrics to. On Broadway.

AIDAN WHARTON   And so during intermission, we ran through it a couple times, and then I wrote the lyrics inside Gene's little notebook and on my hand and was like, *okay, okay, okay.*

Ironically, the lyric Aidan couldn't remember was, "He said 'Son this ain't a dream no more, it's the real thing.'"

AIDAN WHARTON   When my agent told me I got the show I was relieved because finally, after being a struggling actor, after being an *aspiring* actor, I was like, *I have booked this show. I have booked a Broadway show. I did it. No one can take that away from me.* And so to perform that first night and sing, "He said, 'Son, this ain't a dream no more, it's the real thing.'" I just was smiling: *I'm singing this to a Broadway house. I'm singing these words, I'm doing well.* And then instantly got the note after the show: "You are too happy. You can't smile during that moment."

By all accounts, Aidan was great as Gene that night. I don't blame him for beaming.

> AIDAN WHARTON   The biggest mistake that I made that night was that Marc Kudisch gave me a shot of espresso, and I took it at intermission. Should not have done that. Terrible idea. I don't think I fell asleep till three-thirty just lying there. I was on such a high . . .

As for me, I woke up the next morning feeling better, finally, and I knew, after making my little high-pitched hum in bed, that I could do the show that night and weekend.

But this incident, with its last-minute on-stage cast replacements, raised a fascinating question for me and for everyone else: Whose role is it, anyway?

When I had fantasized all those years ago about being on Broadway, I didn't fully appreciate just how difficult the job is, both technically and emotionally. Seeing the swings in action made it clear to me. There is something bigger than each one of us, and that thing is *the show.* We are all in service of *the show.* I felt secure having a featured role that was mine. But in all honesty, Elias wasn't *mine.* Elias belonged to *the show,* Elias belonged to Conor. I was just playing Elias every night. And there were other actors who were in line behind me to do it when I couldn't.

For the swings, this feeling is even more acute. Every choice made was in the interest of *the show,* and that's how it should be, that's why we were all there. For *Girl from the North Country.* It's like being a soldier in an army. It's not about *you.*

That was the hardest month, December, 2021. We hadn't gotten our audience back, our cast mates were getting sick with Covid, and now there was this tension in the air about not only who is calling out, but *who is going on in their place?*

> AIDAN WHARTON   There was a lot of dialogue going on at this point about what the actor's responsibility is to their own health and then how that affects the wellbeing of the show . . .

Omicron set a new tone that would stick with the company through the end of the run. Covid infected not only our bodies but our atmosphere. Every day, especially over that holiday season, felt like an emergency. There was anxiety and frustration in the air. Favoritism and rivalry. Territorialism and fear.

We were a family, after all, and it was the holidays.

> BARBARA RUBIN   Around the holiday period, I felt like we were on a kind of emergency hamster-wheel for a while. And I remember by the time we got to New Year's Eve I was just like, *oh my God, I have to figure out a way to handle the stress.* I can't even imagine the anxiety level of the

actors during that time, onstage unmasked, never knowing if they'd be next.

"Ladies and Gentlemen, for the second act, the role of 'Marianne Laine' will be played by Housso Semon."

Barbara Rubin, the show's Associate Director, watched the show most nights and gave us notes to keep us on track.

BARBARA RUBIN I remember the afternoon—and I remember it specifically because for whatever reason wasn't called in that day—that Kimber was taken off at intermission and Housso was put on.

Housso Semon had joined our company as a swing that fall, when Broadway reopened. She would go on for the role of Marianne one night when Kimber got the results of a Covid test in the middle of act one.

HOUSSO SEMON Luckily I felt ready because Anastasia [Talley, a fellow swing] and I did a lot of extra work. We came in early. We would go downstairs in the green room, we would set up around the table, we would rehearse before rehearsal. We would do everything so that everything landed so that we weren't so panicked when we had to go on.

One of the first lyrics Housso sang when she jumped into the show mid-performance was from Dylan's "Jokerman."

You were born with a snake in both of your fists
While the hurricane was blowing[2]

That's what December felt like. Standing in a hurricane with a snake in both fists. Struggle from within and struggle from without.

AIDAN WHARTON There was a little tension, but the tension came from every single person in the building not knowing what was going to happen.

BARBARA RUBIN The tensions that were building up about just being at work every day and who was going to be next and how that was being managed and ever going to, people would say, *Are we not going to cancel? Are we ever going to cancel? How many people will be out before we cancel a show? What is the policy? Do you know the policy?* And I don't know. I think we were just . . . everybody was trying to do the best that they could under the circumstances.

---

[2] "Jokerman," Dylan, *Infidels*, 1983.

We told ourselves not to take it personally; *we're struggling through a crisis, after all, it is out of our control. We're just trying to get through each day. It's not personal.*

But it all felt personal.

Showing up. Pushing through. Pressing on. And it didn't seem to matter; Covid was still winning. It wasn't fair. Nothing was fair.

Of course it was personal.

Bodies

After the Omicron struggle, I became aware of bodies. My body, all of our bodies. When so much of my experience up to that point had been about souls.

When you act in a show eight times a week, your body begins to recognize the pattern, muscle-memory it's called. *I enter here, I step left, I sing this, I carry this chair.* The show becomes a ritual, a prescribed set of gestures and incantations that can at times feel sacred and meditative and at other times feel oppressive and imprisoning.

Your body just knows how to do it, even if your mind resists.

I had no autonomy over my body.

It was a positive feeling: *Here comes the downbeat of that song, I am compelled to move.*

And it was a negative feeling: *Here comes the downbeat of that song, I am compelled to move.*

I became aware of Marc and Luba's bodies during our fight calls. In the show, the moment Mrs. Burke learns that her son Elias has died by Mr. Burke's negligence, Luba, as Mrs. Burke, has to physically attack Marc, punching him, slapping him, screaming at him. It's an explosive moment and every day, before a performance, they had to rehearse it at fight-call, to keep it safe. I could see it taking a toll on both Luba and Marc, practicing and then performing this minutely detailed violence coupled as it was with such extreme emotion. They offered their bodies.

The swings' bodies. Stepping in to cover for someone else whose body was under attack by a virus.

All of these bodies. With lives outside of this theater. Full, complicated inner lives that they had to check at the door, bringing only their bodies inside.

Marco Paguia was our music director. He played the piano and harmonium at every show, and led the band. One day, the entire cast and crew gathered onstage for a conversation with Marco, led by Conor. I didn't know that the conversation was going to be about Elias, and specifically Marco's experience with the character.

MARCO PAGUIA   When Mr. Burke talked about Elias "howling in the night," and all these images, nobody in the cast or with production knew how much I knew what that was like.

Marco shared with all of us that his son Landon was not dissimilar from Elias.

MARCO PAGUIA   Coming away from it, from *Girl from the North Country*, from all the four production openings and closings of the show, the most growth I had was through being the father of a disabled person, coming into my own as a father, really. I think I mentioned this in that group, just how I started, I'm at the point in my life where I identify more with [the fathers] Nick Laine and Mr. Burke more than I do with [the sons] Joe and Gene.

All of our bodies in a giant circle onstage, learning something new about our musical leader, Marco, who had been struggling unseen for the now three and a half years we had been together as a company.

MARCO PAGUIA   And so I felt like I definitely grew as a leader of adults, not just with music, as a person in the room. And a lot of that growth had to come with me being able to address my own, I guess, *grief* in a way with Landon, having a son that you find out early on is not going to be the son that you are necessarily anticipating you're going to have. And since that afternoon that we had that conversation, I had a whole, it was definitely, it was a catharsis for me. And it continued to have a positive effect for me. And I feel like I don't necessarily always bring him up as much as I would like, to be comfortable with other folks, but I don't shy away from it. I used to just run from it in conversation, because sometimes it's hard. It's like, where do you start?

Marco is a calm person. Even when playing the flashiest bit of music on the piano, he sits unagitated and still, but not emotionless. He radiates empathy.

MARCO PAGUIA   Did you see *Cost of Living*?

I did see it, and it was astounding. Per David Rooney at *The Hollywood Reporter*: "Martyna Majok's *Cost of Living*, [is] a haunting, rigorously unsentimental identity play that refutes stereotypes about people with physical disabilities and their caregivers."
The play won the Pulitzer Prize for Drama in 2018.

MARCO PAGUIA   It was definitely the first show I saw with people with disabilities represented on stage. But it was also one of the first shows that I saw that I really understood the power of theater. And it was because we were all in a room, a small room of human beings observing one person taking care of another person. So it was like this group empathy, you could feel people feeling what it was like that group connection, that, I don't know what that is. And it wasn't an entertainment, right? I mean, yes, I guess on some form, but when you think of musicals, you think at first it's got to be entertaining, right? But that to me was profound. What would make theater different than going to a movie or listening to an album is sharing the space with other human beings, bearing witness to this story that involves caregiving.

In that circle, Conor asked me to speak about Elias. About my approach to the character; Elias was being played with *my* body, my able body. This was concerning to some others who would have to potentially play Elias with *their* bodies in the future.

I choked up to the point where I could barely speak.

I love Elias. Elias sits next to God and the Holy Spirit.

All I could say was that I didn't know what Elias's "diagnosis" was and I didn't want to know. I did no research. I took Elias at his word. He is exactly like the rest of us in that he knows what he knows, nothing more, nothing less. The same is true for me and for you.

When people ask me, "How did Elias die?" I answer on behalf of Elias: "I don't know. I was with my father and then suddenly I was in the cold water." Elias doesn't know, and so neither do I.

It's personal to me, my connection to Elias. Every day during the run, I worried that I was offending people; I am a person who does not identify as neuro-divergent. Marco was characteristically generous about it.

MARCO PAGUIA   We can't pretend that there aren't disabled people in the world. We can't keep filling them with Dustin Hoffmans and I've said this many times. I think there are exceptions that are incredibly beautiful and moving and just right. And I think that yours in the show was one of those.

This whole conversation had me by the throat.
I said to Marco:

TODD ALMOND   I worried that I was offending people, and I tried not to look at what they were saying. Online. And I have looked since, and I see now that I *did* offend some. I've looked, I did offend some people both as Elias before he died, and after he died; one or both of those things offended some people. And I have to say, that day that we were sitting in the circle, I didn't know that conversation was coming. And what I appreciate about it and about you and about Conor, is that it so slowly and beautifully unfolded the entire time, however long we sat there. I mean, it was maybe an hour. It just felt like it was this thing coming from compassion and connection and sharing and not, *we have a problem and we need to address it*. It felt almost like a microcosm of my experience of the play where I didn't know what was coming, and I kept getting better as a person. I kept opening up, and I'm really grateful to you for that. I think about that day a lot, it meant so much to me just as a person. And I'm really grateful that you led that the way you did. So I just wanted to, I guess, say thank you for that day.

MARCO PAGUIA   I had written a couple things down that I just want to make sure I didn't forget to say. I definitely didn't come from *we have a problem*. If anything, it was like, "I have something I'm dealing with and I don't know how to continue dealing with it unless I share." It came with the BAC[3] training about [the expectation of] leaving yourself at the door when you walk into the theater and how we got used to doing that, and with all these, all this police brutality that was happening. And how as a Black person—can they come in and do a story with violence or something and not feel like you have to check it at the door? Do you always have to check it at the door? Or do you check part of it at the door? Or what's the math? I don't understand the math. What are we supposed to do? And for me, I was checking it like a hundred percent at the door on some level. And that's what that conversation was about. You just never know what people are going through at work.

I think about this conversation with Marco almost every day. All this time, I'd been waiting for the slow train coming, but I realized that day that the train had come, and I was on it. This whole time, I had been traveling; the slow train had picked me up and taken me somewhere new. That's why I can't let go of the experience. By the time *Girl from the North Country* was over, my world was different.

---

[3]Broadway Advocacy Coalition. An organization formed to help Broadway fight systemic racism. We had two days of training with them.

Conor's Speech

In January of 2021, Tristan flew to New York from London to tell us that we would be closing.

Part of me was relieved, this had been so difficult.

But a larger part of me was sad. I couldn't help but feel like we'd never actually arrived on Broadway. The door slammed shut in March of 2020, and when it reopened in 2021, we didn't recognize the place anymore.

We were to reopen again in May to both film the show and to give the show one final, limited run leading up to the Tonys. And though that six-week period would be its own chapter in the story of *Girl from the North Country*, it would feel like an epilogue.

As a writer, when I feel lost, I go back to the beginning. The prologue. It's helpful to reconnect with the original source of inspiration. Our source was Conor. The man who *maybe at some point had thought of becoming a preacher*. Conor, who was knocked for six by Dylan's album *Saved*.

> I know all about poison
> I know all about fiery darts
> I don't care how rough the road is
> Show me where it starts[4]

We needed Conor. He would know what to say to us.

On a particularly dark day in May after a sloggy run-through when we were back in rehearsals for our final limited run, Conor gave an impromptu speech. Mare happened to record that speech, and she read to me when I interviewed her.

CONOR (Read by Mare)

I was thinking this might help. It might not, but the story of the play, the nativity and the strange things happening in this house. Where's the baby come from? And there's no room at the Inn. And Matt's character, the preacher, coming in, very strange biblical feeling going on there. The Burkes coming in with Elias, and Elias means lamb. And Matt, the preacher, says to them, "There's a family called Shepherd." So all that stuff is playing under the surface here of the story. And what's happening in a good way is that we are the human part of the story. And humans don't know anything. It's a very, very difficult struggle. Our struggle is intense. And we got Joseph here . . .

MARE   And he gestured to Tom.[5]

CONOR   . . . and then we have another Joseph over there . . .

---

[4] "What Can I Do for You," Dylan, *Saved*, 1980.

[5] Tom Nelis's character was named Joseph Perry.

MARE   And he gestured to Austin.[6]

CONOR   ... and they're coming, Josephs are coming at us. Josephs are being sent to sort of try and make something happen here. And we're all at the mercy of a bigger thing. That's the story. I mean, you don't have to believe in it or anything like that, but that's the story. I mean, it's based on that story, which is very resonant in all kinds of ways. I mean, if you want to look at it this way, that story is merely an articulation of an acknowledgement of nature itself, which is that things are renewed, things are resurrected, winter comes, but the sun comes back, warmth comes back, the baby will come. There's a redemption in the cycle of nature if you want to look at it that way.

But we are all just tiny little ignorant beings within that huge big cycle. We can be aware of it, we can worship it, we can think it means something, we can acknowledge it and we can just say, "Well, it's all a mystery," but it's a cosmic situation, this story, this show. It's a cosmic situation. There's no question Bob's God, Dylan's music in this show as far as I'm concerned, is God. Right? Everything that's flowing through here through his music and which is coming through him is all the things that we can't understand. I'm not sure he even understands it. He often says that he doesn't know where his songs come from, but they are hugely resonant, meaningful, universal and deep. And that stuff is flowing through the play. That's where the opportunity for meaning and resonance is coming into the play. And we got lots of it.

And it's keeping the story buoyant and it's bringing us to the stars and you guys as musical talent, you're just all doing an incredible job. And so my point being the human beings in the middle of this mystery who don't know what's going on, have a lot of fucking problems. Basically that's all they have in this story. It is not our job to redeem these characters. It is not our job to show that they have any depth of understanding. It's our job to show that they kind of don't, and that the only hope we have is for grace to flow in through this music, this kind of God-like surrounding that holds us all together in the show. And so in a sense, the show for me is a big ritual and a ceremony based upon all the things I was taught as a kid when I was growing up.

Do I still believe in them? Can I accept them all as literal things? I don't know. But what I do know is I live in a mystery. That's all I know. And I'm an artist and I'm just trying to celebrate that as best I can. Well, I think in order for us to do that, we got to go hard and we got to go deep and we got to go down into the darkness always. And the way we do that is by showing that these people are troubled, and they're having struggles. And not only that, their struggle is biblical. It's a struggle with God we're dealing with here. These people do not know what's going on

[6]Austin Scott's character was named Joe Scott.

and it's God's plan that's going on. And in a way we suggest that maybe it is what's going to happen here. Maybe God is coming into the world we don't know.

So if that helps with the sense of just pushing through and saying this struggle, this struggle is biblical. That's how ignorant these people are. This is biblical stuff. It's not like, *Oh, I'm wondering what, who I should vote for* . . . It's crazier than that. *I know nothing and I don't know if I can live and I cannot fucking do it anymore. And I don't want to be around these people anymore. They're driving me fucking crazy and how can I help them? I'm just sick of it. And Jesus Christ, what are we going to do?* That's the struggle. So the more we plow into that and what these people are doing in their ignorance, the better this thing sits together. Right? If we do the same thing as the music, all we're saying is, "Hey, here's some music." That's what we're saying. And I think that's not good. What really works is when our story is the opposite of music. The music is beautiful but the story is mean and it's ugly. Because that's what life is like sometimes—maybe a lot of the time for a lot of people—but then when we hit them with the music—it's such a beautiful relief! It's like honey and vinegar. Bob Dylan brings the honey and we bring the vinegar. If it's all honey it's just boring. So we have to be mean as hell—to balance it out—we bring the vinegar—the meanness. Light and shade right? It's the same thing. So if that helps in any way, what I always look for and what I loved about the Saturday matinee, and you're all going to think I'm mad, is I just look to see if the timing's going down because then I know we're doing it. We're not taking the time to "emote." The music takes care of that. So we don't do it. We do the opposite. We just tell the story. We knocked three minutes off the show on Friday and Saturday matinee, and we felt it in the audience. I don't want to see us going anywhere back. There's no reason that anybody here can say, "I got to have a big long moment here." There's just no reason. Because the show feels better when we push on and when we let them decide and we let the music be the provocative part.

So what that is, is a great opportunity for us as performers, I think because we got to bring our A game. We can't rely on any kind of easy little things. We always are on our A game and Marc and Luba doing that Thanksgiving scene, that shit is so fucking hard. But you guys are doing it right. Luba, what Marc's doing is really hard. But what *you're* doing is fucking crazy hard going on and off there, pushing against each other. And you always give it to me and you always do it. You're not hanging about, and the audience are like, why is this happening? But they cannot look away. They just cannot look away. And then boom, we hit them with "Duquesne Whistle" and then boom, the sky opens up and they're like, what the fuck is going on here? But we have them. We have them.

So you're doing a great job, guys. That's all. That's my big note.

EPILOGUE: THE STREETS

December, 2023

I hopped off my bike and locked it to a steel, rainbow-shaped rack just outside of Mare's New York City home near Washington Square Park. Because I was ten minutes early, I stood on the sidewalk and stared at my phone. A deluge of emails hit my inbox, all with the same subject line: "Your quotes for the *Girl from the North Country* book."

These were responses to the emails I'd sent the day before to each person quoted in this book; I wanted everyone I'd interviewed to read and approve their own words and memories.

It was overwhelming, all of these names suddenly pouring into my inbox. Marc Kudisch. Austin Scott. Kimber Sprawl. Colton Ryan. Luba Mason. Rachel Stern. Conor McPherson. Tristan Baker. Simon Hale.

Jeannette Bayardelle.

The flood overtook me on the street corner.

Sheila Atim. Shirley Henderson. Jennifer Blood. Matthew Warchus.

Bob Joy and Tom Nelis and Matt McGrath. Jay Sanders.

I don't know what I must have looked like to a passerby, but I stood there gasping as the names kept coming, rising waters.

Marco Paguia and Jeff Brancato and Ben Mayne. John Schiappa.

Mare Winningham.

Pouring in fast now.

David Pittu. Chelsea Williams. Caitlin Houlahan. Chiara Trentalange.

Housso Semon. Scott Sanders. Colin Bates. Lucy Hind.

I had spent the previous year with all of these people's memories, reliving our time together like that ghostly image of us all dancing in our costumes from the "Duquesne Whistle" video, fading in and out of existence on a stage we'd long ago left. But now here they were, my friends and castmates, in the present tense, flooding their way to me *now*.

I closed the mail app, put my phone in my pocket, and took a moment to catch my breath, maybe let the flash-flood of emotion recede.

Time travel seems absolutely possible in moments like this, when the past overwhelms you.

I shook my head clear and walked into Mare's building.

In her apartment, we sat in the living room and discussed this very book. I'd asked her to read the current draft because I had questions. Questions like, "Is this how you remember it all?" and "That's what happened, right?"

She said yes and yes.

I told her I had planned on telling our story all the way through the Tony Awards, because so much more happened after Conor's incredible speech to us, but that the book felt done at that point. It was a sad ending, maybe, but that's how I felt. I felt sad.

Mare said she felt sad, too.

"Conor told me he felt sad, too, when I interviewed him!" I said.

Why were we sad? It was a wonderful experience.

I shouldn't be sad. It changed me. For the better.

I said, "I should write about how we made a film of the show." Which we did. The week before the show reopened for the third time on Broadway, in May of 2022, we shot a film-version of the stage show. Over several days, with close-ups and multiple angles. Crane shots and audience reactions.

"And what about Craig Bierko?!"

Craig joined the cast for the final six-week run leading up to the Tony Awards, taking over the role of Mr. Burke, my father, when Marc Kudisch left the show. Craig's first time performing the show was for the film version—he'd had two days of rehearsal. He was brilliant.

"I could write an entire book about Craig!"

Mare and I laughed because there was still so much story to tell.

Like the time Mare's husband Anthony Edwards—*that* Anthony Edwards, from E.R., from *Top Gun*!—stepped into the show when Covid swept through Broadway *yet again*. We would have had to cancel a week of shows in our final run if Anthony (Tony), who was not a member of our cast, hadn't stepped in to play Doctor Walker.

He had a few hours' notice that he would be going on that night for a play he'd never rehearsed ever.

ANTHONY EDWARDS   I drove up to [our house] because it was time to take the storm windows off. By about twelve o'clock or one, I was hot and sweaty, and I thought, *I'm going to take a picture of myself to send to Mare:* "Look, it's done!" And then she called back and she said, "Conor has a question for you."

Conor's question was: *Do you think you know the show well enough to play one of the principal roles this evening?*

The next thing Tony knew, he was at the Belasco Theater, at a rehearsal, walking through Doc Walker's staging.

Right before the who started that night, Tony, in costume, looked at me wide-eyed through his Doc Walker glasses and said, "I'm living the actor's nightmare. *Right now.*"

Mare and I laugh remembering this. I say, "I should write an entire chapter about that alone!" She says, "Oh, Tony won't mind if you don't include that in the book." And I say, "No, I want to! I have to! It was one of the strangest parts of our story. He wasn't even in our cast and he went on, on *Broadway*!"

We are cackling now. Remembering.

I say, "Or remember when we went to the Tony Awards rehearsal and they were announcing the winner for Best Actress and it was *you*?"

Mare did not win the Tony for Best Actress in a Leading Role in a Musical, nor did Jeannette for Best Actress in a Supporting Role in a Musical,[1] but at the rehearsal for the Tonys, Mare *did* win. Kind of.

What I never knew about the Tony Awards is that the entire show is rehearsed early in the morning, the day of the broadcast. It's like a dress rehearsal, complete with the full performances, celebrities announcing the nominees, commercial breaks, and the "winners" giving acceptance speeches.

That morning, a beautiful June morning in New York City, when our cast walked into Radio City Music Hall, the dress rehearsal of the Tony Awards was in full swing and up to the "Best Actress in a Leading Role in a Musical" category. The stand-in celebrity presenter said, "And the winner is . . . Mare Winningham, *Girl from the North Country*!"

There was Mare's name, projected in big letters on the backdrop.

And then the strangest thing happened. A woman we didn't know, presumably an actress hired for this gig, this early morning dress rehearsal of the Tony Awards, jumped up from the audience and made her way to the stage as music from our show played from the orchestra. This actress was playing the role of "Mare Winningham," and she bound onto the stage to accept her Tony award.

I was standing next to the *actual* Mare Winningham watching all of this play out like some scene from a David Lynch movie. I saw Mare watching herself give a speech about the privilege of singing Bob Dylan's music each night onstage, how this had been her dream since her childhood, and how grateful she was to the voters and Broadway community for this moment.

"Thank you, I'm so touched!" the actress playing "Mare Winningham" said as she was escorted off the stage and the Tonys dress rehearsal continued on.

Then the real Mare sat down with the rest of the cast and we waited until it was our turn to perform our number. It was bizarre.

We can hardly breathe, Mare and I, remembering this and laughing.

"That's a chapter! How weird was that?"

But, no, it wasn't going to be a chapter, just saying all of this out loud with Mare was enough. The story was over.

---

[1] Though Simon Hale did win the Tony for his orchestrations.

I wasn't on the slow train any longer, it had carried me to this new place, and those final moments of *Girl from the North Country's* run—when we filmed the show, when Craig Bierko took over as my father, when Tony Edwards stepping into the show for a week, when Mare kind of won the Tony Award in the bizarro dream universe morning rehearsal–were just the final stops on the journey, the last stations before the train finally, gracefully, let me off.

I no longer feel it coming, that slow train, I feel it out there somewhere. Traveling on.

Jennifer Blood, John Schiappa, Chiara Trentalange, and Aidan Wharton are currently on the national tour of *Girl from the North Country* as I write this epilogue. Covid is sweeping through the cast again.

JOHN SCHIAPPA (email)
We just got to DC, and have 3 people out with Covid! (This whole thing is surreal and just a tiiiiiny bit of PTSD!)

Otherwise all good.
I hope you are having a wonderful holiday season.
I miss you like crazy—difficult not to look for you in the wings or on the stage every night.

Best,
John xo

Someday I hope the train will swing by and pick me up again. Take me on a long and challenging trip. Drop me off at a newer, older version of myself.

On my birthday this past year I walked uptown to meet a friend for dinner. I passed the Beacon theater, the place where Mare and Jeannette sat backstage with Bob Dylan back in 2018, and the marquee outside said, "Bob Dylan: Rough and Rowdy Ways."

He was inside. Onstage.
Bob Dylan.
Right now.
Still making music.
Still pressing on.
Still singing and searching and being Bob Dylan.

I took a picture of the marquee because it felt like some kind of secret birthday gift to me from what guides me, leading me down this road tonight.

As I walked past, I nodded hello like Bob Dylan could see me from the stage, outside walking the streets of Manhattan in the snow, trusting the lights and believing in the streets' holiness just like I had done before, just like I would always do.

AFTERWORD

Beth

In March of 2024, I got a call from Aaron Lustbader's office—would I consider stepping into the national tour of *Girl from the North Country* for one week? The show would be in Boston, and Aidan Wharton, who was playing Elias full-time now on the road, would be taking a week's vacation. Could I fill in for him?

My immediate thought was *no*. Not because I didn't want to, but because I didn't think I *could*. I hadn't sung regularly for over a year (those forty-two high G's were out of reach) and I'd put on some pounds in an effort to lean into my midwestern farm-stock build instead of shying away from it as I always had. I simply would not fit into my old costumes.

There was no way I could pull myself together vocally and physically in two weeks.

But my husband gently insisted that I do it because he knew I secretly wanted to, and he secretly wanted to see me do it one more time anyway. Did I mention he loves the show? Did I mention he's the greatest man in the world?

So I prepared as best I could, and two weeks later I took a slow train up to Boston which obviously seemed appropriate.

After my first return performance as Elias Burke, which went better than I'd expected, I texted Mare Winningham who had asked how it was going: "The physical and emotional recall has been overwhelming. And also the calm I feel—didn't know that maybe before I had some level of anxiety? Overall, it's thrilling and like a gift; I get to have another encounter and a unique farewell."

What I never could have expected happening was that my mother called me the day after my second return performance with tragic news. My cousin Beth, who was my age and with whom I'd grown up, had been found unconscious in her home. Because her oxygen levels were so low, her brain had suffered damage, and she was already in hospice care.

It was a matter of time, now.

Just like that.

I sat in the lobby of the hotel the cast and crew were staying at and just cried on the phone with my mom. Images of Beth from childhood lighted up the deepest corners of my brain—Beth and I along with my brothers and her sisters grew up one block away from each other in Nebraska, our dads were brothers, they both worked for the railroad. Our lives were filled with trains. Her mom, my Aunt Kay, was like a second mom.

And so that's what *Girl from the North Country* unexpectedly became for me, that week in Boston: a show about my cousin Beth. A ghost story about my own family.

Every night for the entire run of *Girl from the North Country,* all the way back from the first days at the Public Theater through Broadway, right before I stepped onstage in my white linen suit each night, I quietly dedicated "Duquesne Whistle" to someone important to me, and I sang it to and for them. It could be someone nearby—maybe an actor onstage—or someone far away—maybe one of my brothers or a friend I hadn't seen. I would thank God for them in my life and sing the song to them. It made me feel less nervous and more purposeful when my ego wanted to buck and worry about what people thought of me and my singing.

For the remainder of my run in Boston I sang each performance of the song to my cousin Beth. We hadn't spoken in years, I've never been good at keeping in touch with family and friends. But Beth and I were children together, teenagers together, and young adults together. She's at the root of my existence. I thanked God for her every night and sang my best for her.

It's not how I imagined this story ending.

Sometimes I get this existential dread—Why are we here? What are we, anyway? Why is there anything?

And on a smaller scale—Why do I sing? What does music mean? What is the purpose?

And a still smaller scale—What do I do now? Today?

I don't have any answers, probably never will, but I can tell you that I felt *Girl from the North Country* departing from me throughout that week. Like the heavenly cloud above me upon which sat Conor McPherson, Elias Burke, and Bob Dylan—the father, the son, and the holy spirit—finally decided to pass over and beyond me and to some other lucky souls.

And I had to let it go.

The struggles and joys of the real world would return. I would go back to my life. My life that I love so much and can't hold onto hard enough.

My sweet husband would say, "Let's call your Aunt Kay and see how she is doing," and he'd already have her up on speaker-phone. Aunt Kay would tell us that Beth was comfortable, thanks to the good people taking care of her.

On April 3, 2024, my mom would call me to say that Beth passed away at 5:15 p.m.

I didn't know this would be the end of my book, but it is, and I'm dedicating it to her memory.

Maybe that's what I can tell myself in those moments of existential dread: just dedicate all of this to memory.

May God bless and keep you always
May your wishes all come true
May you always do for others
And let others do for you

May you build a ladder to the stars
And climb on every rung
May you stay forever young.[1]

---

[1]"Forever Young," Bob Dylan, from *Planet Waves,* 1974.

WORKS CITED

Chapter 1

Armitstead, Claire. "Stars aligned: Sheila Atim and Ivanno Jeremiah on reviving a mind-bending classic." *The Guardian*, June 20, 2021. Accessed June 30, 2023.

Billington, Michael. "Girl from the North Country Review—Dylan's songs are Depression-Era dynamite." *The Guardian*, July 26, 2017, www.theguardian.com/stage/2017/jul/27/girl-from-the-north-country-review-bob-dylan-conor-mcpherson. Accessed June 14, 2023.

Brantley, Ben. "In 'Girl from the North Country' Rolling Stones gather regrets." *New York Times*, 26 July 2017, www.nytimes.com/2017/07/26/theater/girl-from-north-country-review-bob-dylan.html. Accessed June 14, 2023.

Cox, Gordon. "Carole King musical 'Beautiful' turns a profit on Broadway." *Variety*, Sept. 15th, 2014, https://variety.com/2014/legit/news/carole-king-beautiful-recoups-broadway-1201306008/. Accessed June 12, 2023.

Flanagan, Bill. "Q&A with Bill Flanagan." *BobDylan.com*, March 22, 2017, www.bobdylan.com/news/qa-with-bill-flanagan/. Accessed July 6, 2023.

Heylin, Clinton. *The Double Life of Bob Dylan*. Back Bay Books; Little, Brown and Company, 2022.

Internet Broadway Database. "Conor McPherson." *IBDB | The Official Source For Broadway Information*, 2022, http://ibdb.comconor-mcpherson-4900. Accessed June 9, 2023.

Kozinn, Allan. "Matthew Warchus will lead Old Vic Theater." *New York Times*, May 22, 2014, https://archive.nytimes.com/artsbeat.blogs.nytimes.com/2014/05/22/matthew-warchus-will-lead-old-vic-theater/?searchResultPosition=3. Accessed June 30, 2023.

Nobel Prize. "The Nobel Prize in Literature 2016. NobelPrize.org. Nobel Prize Outreach AB 2023. Sat. June 10, 2023. www.nobelprize.org/prizes/literature/2016/summary." *The Nobel Prize in Literature 2016. NobelPrize.org. Nobel Prize Outreach AB 2023. Sat. June 10, 2023.* www.nobelprize.org/prizes/literature/2016/summary/, 2016, www.nobelprize.org/prizes/literature/2016/summary/.

"Noel Coward Theatre History." *noelcowardtheatre.co.uk*, www.noelcowardtheatre.co.uk/#theatre-history. Accessed June 16, 2023.

"Oliver Awards 2018: Winners in Full." *bbc.com*, April 2018, www.bbc.com/news/entertainment-arts-43668013. Accessed June 15, 2023.

Paulson, Michael. "No more 'groundhog day' for one powerful producer." *New York Times*, www.nytimes.com/2016/06/07/theater/no-more-groundhog-day-for-one-powerful-producer.html?searchResultPosition=1.

Sands, Roger. "Broadway: The engine that helps fuel New York City's economy." *Forbes*, 2023, www.forbes.com/sites/rogersands/2023/01/20/broadway-the-engine-that-helps-fuel-new-york-citys-economy/?sh=10fcc91f53cc. Accessed July 10, 2023.

"The Times They Are A-Changin.'" www.ibdb.com/broadway-production/the-times-they-are-a-changin-423560, 2006, www.ibdb.com/broadway-production/the-times-they-are-a-changin-423560.

Bennett, Bija. "10 rules for life: John Cage." https://www.bijab.com/wellness-blog/10-rules-for-life-john-cage/.

Chapter 2

Christgau, Robert. "The answer, my friends, is still blowin' in the wind." *New York Times*, 27 June 1971. Accessed August 30, 2023.

"George C. Wolfe." *ibdb.com*, www.ibdb.com/broadway-cast-staff/george-c-wolfe-5792. Accessed July 13, 2023.

Heylin, Clinton. *Trouble In Mind*. Route, 2017.

McElvaine, Robert S. *The Great Depression: America, 1929–1941*. Times Books, 1984.

Chapter 3

Brantley, Ben. "Review: 'Girl from the North Country' sets the darkness aglow." *New York Times*, October 1, 2018. Accessed July 3, 2023.

Fleming, Melissa. "September 2018: Unusually Warm and Wet in NYC." *The Weather Gamut*, 2018, www.weathergamut.com/2018/10/01/september-2018-unusually-warm-and-wet-in-nyc/#:~:text=September%202018%20was%20another%20temperature,won%20out%20in%20the%20end. Accessed July 2, 2023.

Rigg, Diana, editor. *No Turn Unstoned*. Arrow Books, 1983.

Chapter 5

Croft, Jay. "4 passengers on a cruise ship docked near New York City are getting further evaluation for coronavirus." *CNN*, February 7, 2020, cnn.com. Accessed October 9, 2023.

Feuer, Will, et al. "US prepares for possible coronavirus pandemic." *CNBC*, February 21, 2020, cnbc.com. Accessed October 10, 2023.

Jiang, Steven. "Global death toll from coronavirus exceeds 2,100." *CNN*, February 19, 2020, cnn.com.

Paulson, Michael. "Broadway, symbol of New York resilience, shuts down amid virus threat." *New York Times*, March 12, 2020, nytimes.com. Accessed October 11. 2023.

Paulson, Michael. "Broadway usher tests positive for coronavirus." *New York Times*, March 11, 2020, nytimes.com. Accessed October 10, 2023.

Siddiqui, Usaid. "Coronavirus outbreak 'getting bigger': All the latest updates." *Aljazeera*, 28 February 2020, aljazeera.com. Accessed October 10, 2023.

Scipioni, Jade. "Health and wellness White House advisor Dr. Fauci says handshaking needs to stop even when pandemic ends—other experts agree." *CNBC*, April 9, 2020. Accessed November 14, 2023.

Zollo, Paul. "Behind the song: 'Hurricane' by Bob Dylan." 2020, https://docs.google.com/document/d/1QitJ713y9_98Fb5mpSt1sRQVydrJYl84-nYDBfeFbDY/edit. Accessed October 8, 2023.

Chapter 6

Small Business Administration (SBA), 2021, http://sba.gov. Accessed October 12, 2023.

Olmstead Environmental Services. https://olmstedenvironmentalservices.com.

Sands, Roger. "Broadway: The engine that helps fuel new York City's economy." *Forbes*, 2023. Accessed October 12, 2023.

United States Environmental Protection Agency. "Section 18 emergency exemption requests and coronavirus (COVID-19)." *epa.gov*. Accessed October 12, 2023.

Chapter 7

"Coronavirus Rumor Control." *FEMA*. Accessed November 16, 2023.

Dickstein, Morris. "How song, dance and movies bailed us out of the Depression." *Los Angeles Times*, April 1, 2009. Accessed October 17, 2023.

Forster, Victoria. "Maine wedding gives half of the guests coronavirus, outbreak leads to 177 Covid-19 cases and 7 deaths." *Forbes*, 2020. Accessed February 10, 2024.

Howard, Jacqueline. "A herd immunity strategy to fight the pandemic can be 'dangerous,' experts say. Here's why." *CNN*, 17 October 2020. Accessed November 16, 2023.

Kaneda, Toshiko, and Carl Haub. "How many people have ever lived on Earth?" *Population Reference Bureau*, prb.org. Accessed November 14, 2023.

Kennedy, Mark. "Why Broadway is waiting 4 months to reopen—and why it has to be all or nothing." *NBC*, May 11, 2021. Accessed November 16, 2023.

Lunden, Jeff. "Broadway shows can reopen in May, but that doesn't mean they will." *NPR*, May 3, 2021, npr.org. Accessed October 17, 2023.

McPhee, Ryan. "2020 Tony Awards put on hold as coronavirus pandemic causes Broadway shutdown." *playbill.com*, March 25, 2020. Accessed October 15, 2023.

Office of the New York State Comptroller. osc.ny.gov. Accessed November 17, 2023.

Paulson, Michael. "Unemployed Stage Actors to Face New Health Insurance Hurdle." *New York Times*, October 1, 2020. Accessed October 16, 2023.

Paulson, Michael. "When the show doesn't go on: Broadway is rattled by covid
     cancellations." *New York Times*, 2021. Accessed October 31, 2023.
Playbill. "AEA makes 'historic move' to help professional actors get health coverage
     more quickly." *Playbill.com*, November 6, 2015. Accessed October 16, 2023.
Russo, Gillian. "Broadway reopening continues, with 'Hamilton,' 'Wicked,' 'The
     Lion King,' and more." *New York Theatre Guide*, newyorktheatreguide.com.

PERMISSIONS

ACKNOWLEDGMENTS

Writing a book takes an enormous amount of time, and I'd like to thank my husband Mark Subias for giving me all of the time that I needed.

Special thanks to my entire *Girl from the North Country* acting family, who gave great amounts of their own time to this book. Through our interviews, I got the rare opportunity to meet each of them all over again, and I'm grateful for our lunches, coffees, and Zooms.

Thank you to Tristan Baker, Charlie Parsons, Aaron Lustbader, and Conor McPherson for giving me their blessings to write this book.

Profound thanks to Jeff Rosen and Marc Cimino/Universal Music Publishing.

Eternal gratitude and thanks to Dom O'Hanlon at Methuen Drama for taking this book on and for giving me encouragement in my sloggiest moments as well as incisive notes on multiple drafts.

Thank you to my agents Dan Milaschewski and Byrd Leavell.

Thank you to the Public Theater, especially Heidi Griffiths and Jordan Thaler for casting me.

Thank you to my sweet loves Dashiell and Laney and Lulu and Archie for making my life so meaningful.

And thank you to my family. I dedicate this book to memory of my cousin Elizabeth Almond Cook.

Finally, thank you to Bob Dylan. On behalf of everyone everywhere, thanks Bob.

INDEX

*Indicates an interview; **Indicates an email.

accompanist
  downtown 11–12
  touring the UK 3–4
acting
  as a career 140–1
  over-emotional 85–6
Actors' Equity Association (AEA) 17
  safety standards** 198–9
AEA see Actors' Equity Association
"All Along the Watchtower" (Joe,
    Marianne, Company) 139
Almond, Todd see individual entries
Almond, Travis 139, 224, 226
Altman, Robert 175
Anderson, Laurie, "The End of the
    World" 114
anger 9, 119, 175
Atim, Sheila [Marianne Laine] 51, 72,
    244
  on Bob Dylan 43
  glass-of-milk question* 106–9
  Laurence Olivier Award 10, 43, 54,
    109
  offers 45
  playing Marianne* 103, 105–7
  premiere production rehearsals* 43,
    45–7, 49, 56
  "Tight Connection to My
    Heart" 41, 46–8, 103,
    106–8*
  transfer to Broadway* 72
  working with Conor 41
audiences
  empty seats 52, 215
  London previews 51
  New York previews 117–22
auditioning 49

Baker, Simon (sound designer) 125
Baker, Tristan (commercial producer)
    10, 244
  Broadway League* 204
  choosing The Public Theater*
    67–8
  closing 120, 238
  Conor McPherson 42
  fall opening** 201–2
  idea for production* 19–26
  Lucy Hind* 38
  Old Vic Theatre 49–50, 52, 54, 70
  opening night 123
  previews* 49–50, 53–4
  Runway Entertainment 18–19,
    33–4
  September return** 202
  transfer to Broadway* 70, 72,
    145–6
  working on the script* 34–5
  working on the sound* 36, 38
  a year on** 198
"Ballad of a Thin Man" (Orchestra)
    62
BAM see Brooklyn Academy of Music
Bareilles, Sara, Waitress 74
basketball 57
Bassett, Angela 127
Bates, Colin [Gene Laine] 209
  playing Gene* 209–10
Bayardelle, Jeannette [Mrs. Neilsen]
    220, 244, 246–7
  Artie Gaffin* 82
  casting at Gibney Studios 73
  Covid at the Belasco Theater*
    173–6, 180–3
  Covid on the plane* 170–2

fixing the play* 119–20
interpreting Bob Dylan* 100
meeting Bob Dylan* 128–31,
    136–8
"month-long break"* 185
Omicron variant* 228
post-Covid feelings* 223–4
prophecies 9, 126, 180–3
reading at the Public Theater*
    15–17, 56
reviews* 124–7
Rock of Ages 84
Tony award nomination 15
transfer to Broadway* 144–5
Bean, Shoshana 87
Beautiful: The Carole King Musical
    26–7
Belasco, David 64
Belasco Theater 173–4
    Covid at 174–6, 178–9
    going back 178–9
    see also Broadway
Berman, Ashley (company manager)
    184, 199–200, 228
    Cobra health insurance** 200
    September return** 200–1
    summer return** 199–200
Billington, Michael 53
Binder, David
    transfer to Broadway* 70–1
    see also Brooklyn Academy of
        Music (BAM)
Blood, Jennifer (swing/Elizabeth Lane)
    159, 225–8, 244, 247
    Omicron variant* 225–7
    triumph 227
Blood on the Tracks 94, 184
bodies, awareness of 234
Bond, Justin Vivian Mx. 12
Boston, national tour 241–3
Brancato, Jeff (assistant/production
    stage manager) 178, 192,
    227–31, 244
    Artie Gaffin* 82, 84, 122, 149–50,
        160
    Broadway reopening** 217–8
    Colin Bates** 209
    Covid at the Belasco Theater*
        180–1, 183–4

first preview* 117
Matt McGrath** 162
"month-long break"*** 185
Omicron variant* 225–6
opening night on Broadway*
    157
Brantley, Ben, *New York Times* reviews
    53–4, 68, 123–5
Broadway
    dreaming of 3–5
    experience of 9–10
    houses 8–9
    off and on 5–6
    opening night viii 9–10, 157–9,
        185
    performing on 9, 177
    transfer to 143–50, 153–6,
        159–62
    see also Belasco Theater
Broadway Advocacy Coalition 211,
    237
Broadway, Covid closure
    another year of 207
    Cobra health insurance 200
    Equity health insurance 200–1
    see also Covid pandemic
Broadway, Covid Omicron 214,
    224–9
    anxiety for 229–34
    shows cancelling 227–8
Broadway, Covid reopening 212–4
    anxiety for 216–7
    audiences low 219, 221
    capacity restrictions 212
    Pass Over (Nandu) 216
    post-Covid feelings 219–24
    post-depression 215–8
    protocols 211–2
    September return 200–1
    "Show must go on" 210–1
    summer return 199–200
    versus economics 203–8
Broadway curtain number, "Pressing
    On" 164
Broadway ethos 210
Broadway League 203–5
    Little League 205–6, 213
Broadway lights, for Artie Gaffin 160
Broadway show ends 238–40

Brooklyn
  design shop clerk 155
  filming in 81
  harmonica lessons 111
  train to 154
Brooklyn Academy of Music (BAM)
  70–2
  see also Binder, David
brunch feasts 9, 82, 122
Burke, Elias (character) see Elias
Burke, Mr. (character) see Marc
  Kudisch
Burke, Mrs. (character) see Jeannette
  Bayardelle
Burns, Scott Z. 124

Cage, John 41
Caplan, Liz (vocal coach) 169
cast
  at The Public Theater 76–9, 84–9
  love for 145, 149
casting
  at Gibney Studios 73
  at The Public Theater 73–6
Catullo, Patrick 73
CCM 87–9, 157, 167
Central Park, Delacorte stage 13
Charles, RuPaul 9
Clinton, Chelsea 127
Cole, Matt 36
Coleman, Ben, transfer to Broadway**
  156
College-Conservatory of Music at the
  University of Cincinnati see
  CCM
Comer, Jodie
  Laurence Olivier Award 70
  Tony Award 70
Cordero, Nick 208
Covid pandemic 5
  at the Belasco Theater 174–6,
    180–4
  on the cruise ship 176–7
  herd immunity 206
  high-fives 177–8
  Jeannette Bayardelle* 170–6
  not in America 162
  on the plane 170–2
  recording the 187–9

show closures 158
  workdays 206
  see also Broadway, Covid
Cranston, Bryan 70, 127
Croft, Jay 176
Cuervo, Alma 16
Cullen, David 92
Cuomo, Andrew (New York Governor)
  212
Curtis Brown agency 21

Dame Edna: The Royal Tour 37
deBessonet, Lear 13
depression, Covid pandemic 9
deus ex machina 212
disabilities
  Cost of Living (Majok) 235
  Elias (character) 236
Disney Theatrical Group 203
Dostoevsky, Fyodor, The Brothers
  Karamazov 58
Draper, Kate (character) see Caitlin
  Houlahan
"Duquesne Whistle" (Elias)
  casting 13
  damaging the voice 163
  Elias death 6, 110, 135, 176
  Georgia Gatti* 41
  high notes 18, 116
  Jeff Brancato* 162
  Lucy Hind* 163
  performing 55–6, 174, 240, 242
  Rachel Stern* 128
  rehearsals 88–9
  video 194–7, 244
Dylan, Bob 3–7, 9–10, 239–40, 242–3,
  246–7
  America 90
  approval 33
  catalog rights 35
  Christian era 27, 64–6, 164
  Conor McPherson* 22–4, 27, 40,
    65, 69, 164, 238
  Duluth 25, 62, 139
  Empire Burlesque 108
  ghost hovering 26
  hymnist 48
  interpreting 89–102
  interview 25

lyrics 217
Mare Winningham* 90
Matthew Warchus* 34
meeting 128–40
My Own Version of You 91
Nick Marston 25
Oskar Eustis* 66–9, 71
playing for 134–5
reading the play 24–5
sending the albums 26
Sheila Atim* 43, 46
Simon Hale* 36, 89
The Times They Are a-Changing
    (musical) 20
Tristan Baker* 19–23, 67, 202
working on the sound 47

Ebert, Gabriel 216
Edwards, Anthony 130, 137, 160,
    212–13, 227
going on as Doc Walker* 245, 247
Elias (character)
    Boston tour 241–3
    breakfast scene 61–3, 78
    death of 6–8, 110–1, 175–6, 236
    disabilities 235
    "Duquesne Whistle" *see* "Duquesne
        Whistle"
    entrance 59–61
    experience by Marco 234–35
    harmonica 111–2, 134–5
    playing 64, 78, 85–6, 113–4
    rake on stage 210
    speaking about 236–8
    violence 110, 114, 117–8
emails 197–202
    see also individual emails
Ensemble Theater of Cincinnati 87
Equity health insurance 200–1
Eustis, Oskar 14, 55, 77, 124, 131,
    145
    Black Marianne* 103
    choosing The Public Theater*
        66–9
    Conor McPherson 67
    fixing the play* 121
    interpreting Bob Dylan* 89, 95–6
    meeting Bob Dylan* 132–3,
        135–6

Old Vic Theatre 68–9
opening night on Broadway*
    158–9
reviews* 128
transfer to Broadway* 70–2
Everett, Bridget 12

faith 166–7
family, violence within 112, 234
fear 9
    empty seats 52, 215
    Omicron 225, 232
    reopening 224
    slow train 11
    transfer to New York 84
Federal Emergency Management
    Agency (FEMA) 206
Fishbein, Elliot (physical therapist)
    169–70
fixing the play
    Colton Ryan [Gene Laine] 119
    Conor McPherson (playwright)
        118
    Jeannette Bayardelle 119–20
    Robert Joy [Doctor Walker] 121
Foresight Theatricals 125
"Forever Young" (Elizabeth, Company)
    40, 52, 77, 137, 243
Frayn, Michael, *Noises Off* 140
Frost, Sue 205
funding, Old Vic Theatre 34

Gaffin, Artie (stage manager) 9
    breakfast feasts 77, 114
    Broadway lights dimmed 160
    cast at The Public Theater** 86–7,
        89
    death of 160
    first preview** 116
    holding for the house 127
    meeting** 79–84
    opening** 122, 126
    rehearsals** 118
    second preview** 117
    transfer to Broadway** 149–50
    tree in memory of 137
    understudies** 141–2
Gatti, Georgia (theatrical producer)
    37–8, 41, 43, 52, 68

Old Vic Theatre 36
premiere production rehearsals*
    42–4
previews* 50, 54
working on the sound* 36, 42
Georgia 99
Gerle, Andrew 187
ghost(s)
    of Dylan 26
    in the play 64, 84
    playing Elias 7–8, 110, 176
    in the theater 4, 9, 37, 64
"Girl from the North Country"
    (musical)
    advert in London 4
    awards *see* Laurence Olivier
        Awards; Tony Awards
    plot 10–11, 238–40
    as a radio play 44, 48
    see also Hard Tale of Winter;
        individual entries; play
Givens, David (director of
    photography) 196–7
glass-of-milk question 41, 48,
    103–9, 114, 117
    Kimber Elayne Sprawl [Marianne
        Laine] 108–9
    Shiela Atim [Marianne Laine]
        106–9
    Tom Nelis [Mr. Perry] 105–6
Gray, Amber 187
Griffiths, Heidi 11
Guettel, Adam 58

Ha, Jin 16
Hackett, Mandy (associate artistic
    director) 55, 129, 150
    choosing The Public Theater* 67,
        69
    Covid at the Belasco Theater* 183
    meeting Bob Dylan* 131–6
    reading at The Public Theater* 56
    transfer to Broadway* 144–6, 148
Hale, Simon (musical arranger/
    orchestrator) 10, 244
    Broadway curtain number "Pressing
        On"* 164–5
    Conor McPherson 42
    "Duquesne Whistle" 55

Grammy nominations 36
interpreting Bob Dylan* 89–90,
    93–6, 102
Luba Mason* 80–1
Marianne vocals* 108
Old Vic Theatre 37, 94
setting the songs 98–100
"Slow Train" 60
Spring Awakening 36
"Tight Connection to My Heart"
    47
Tony award 246
working on the sound* 36–7
Hanukkah prayers 9, 91
Hard Tale of Winter 29–30, 32, 34–5,
    57–9
Haring, Keith, *Radiant Baby* 66
harmonica 110–2
    playing for Bob Dylan 134–5
harmonium, orchestration 94
Harris, Aleshea, *What to Send Up
    When It Goes Down* 207
Harris, Matthew Frederick 76, 143
"Has Anybody Seen My Love"
    (Marianne, Company) 103,
    106–7
heartbreak 7, 9, 76, 141
Heating, Ventilation and Air-
    Conditioning (HVAC), Covid
    safety protocols 199
Hedwig and the Angry Inch 87
Henderson, Shirley [Elizabeth Laine]
    42, 47–8, 51–4, 76, 100, 244
    interpreting Bob Dylan* 96–7,
        101
    Laurence Olivier Awards 10, 28,
        54
Life During Wartime 28
Like a Rolling Stone 94
"Moaning Myrtle" 28
premiere production* 45, 47
previews* 51
transfer to Broadway* 72
working on the script* 28–9, 31,
    33
working on the sound* 39–41
herd immunity 206
Heylin, Clinton 24
Trouble In Mind 65

Highland, Chris 11, 13, 73
    casting at The Public Theater** 73
    Old Vic Theatre 73
Hill, John Michael 216
Himberg, Philip 58
Hind, Lucy (choreographer) 244
    approach 38–9
    cast at The Public Theater* 84–5
    changes for Broadway* 163–4
    Covid at the Belasco Theater*
        181–2
    interpreting Bob Dylan* 97,
        100–1
    "Like a Rolling Stone" 99
    Luba Mason* 120
    Old Vic Theatre 38, 50
    premiere production rehearsals 44,
        48
    previews* 50, 52
    reviews* 123–5
    "Tight Connection to My Heart"
        41–2
    working on the sound* 38–9, 41
Hinds, Ciarán [Nick Laine]
    casting 42–4, 46
    premiere production rehearsals
        42–4, 46–8
    previews 50
Houlahan, Caitlin [Kate Draper] 74,
        231, 244
    casting at The Public Theater*
        74–6
    I Want You 140
    meeting Bob Dylan* 129, 135,
        140
    post-Covid feelings* 222
    transfer to Broadway* 143–5, 147,
        160–1
Humphries, Barry 37
"Hurricane" (Joe, Marianne,
        Company) 139, 174–5, 180–2,
        220
HVAC see Heating, Ventilation and
        Air-Conditioning

"I Don't Know About You" 188–9
"I forget that there's a sky above
        Manhattan" 12–13
"I Want You" (Gene, Kate) 140, 231

"Idiot Wind" (Joe, Marianne,
        Company) 184
intellectual property (I.P.) 19, 26
interviews, setting up 10, 244–7
"Is Your Love in Vain?" (Mrs. Burke,
        Mr. Burke, Company) 7

Jackson, Shirley, We Have Always
        Lived in the Castle 53–4
Jenkins, Daniel 16
Joe's Pub 11–12
"Jokerman" (Marianne, Mrs. Neilsen,
        Mrs. Burke, Elizabeth, Kate,
        Company) 37, 233
Joseph, Rajiv 58
Joy, Robert [Doctor Walker] 76, 83,
        182
    Artie Gaffin* 82–3
    cast at The Public Theater* 85–6
    fixing the play* 121
    interpreting Bob Dylan* 100
    post-Covid feelings* 223
    transfer to Broadway* 162

Kritzer, Leslie 87
Kudisch, Marc [Mr. Burke] 7, 244–5
    Aiden Wharton* 232
    bagel brunch 122
    bodies 234
    character 16
    "Duquesne Whistle" 55–6
    fishing scene 112
    interpreting Bob Dylan* 89
    Jeannette Bayardelle* 185
    Luba Mason* 78
    playing drums* 95, 110–1
    playing Mr. Burke 61
    post-Covid feelings* 219
    reading at Gibney Studios 73–4
    reading at the Public Theater* 14,
        16, 55
    Signature Theater 14
    Thanksgiving scene 240
    violence 113–4, 227
Kuhn, Judy 16–17

LaChiusa, Michael John 14
Laine, Elizabeth (character) see
        Henderson, Shirley

Laine, Gene (character) *see* Ryan, Colton
Laine, Marianne (character) *see* Atim, Sheila; Sprawl, Kimber Elaine
Laine, Nick (character) *see* Ciarán Hinds; Jay O. Sanders
Lapine, James, *Sunday in the Park with George* 92–4
Lappin, Steve 19
Laurence Olivier Awards
  Conor McPherson 21
  five nominations 54
  Jodie Comer 70
  Leopoldstadt (Stoppard) 70
  Sheila Atim 10, 43, 48, 109
  Shirley Henderson 10, 28
Lee Williams, Chelsea [ensemble/ Marianne Lane] 76, 170, 182, 194, 209, 230, 244
  cast off-Broadway* 77
  health issues* 190–3
  interpreting Bob Dylan* 99–100
  meeting Bob Dylan* 132
  *Oklahoma!** 190–2
  post-Covid feelings* 222
  reviews* 127–8
  transfer to Broadway* 147, 149
Legacy Robe ceremony 157–8
Les Misérables
  aspirations for 3, 215
  Broadway 57–8, 207
  Cameron Mackintosh 54
  Cosette/Judy Kuhn 16
  In My Life 17
  "one day more. . ." 80
  reading/re-reading 19, 166–7
  Sondheim Theater 19, 26
"License to Kill" (Reverend Marlowe, Joe, Mrs. Neilsen, Marianne, Company) 40, 60
"Like a Rolling Stone" (Elizabeth, Company) 77, 93–6, 99–193, 220
Little League 205–6, 213
Lloyd Webber, Andrew 206
  The Phantom of the Opera 92–4
London creative team 10
  see also individual members
love, turns to violence 112

Lustbader, Aaron (general manager) 222
  after the pandemic 198, 202, 219
  Covid safety protocols 196
  national tour 2024 241
  off to Broadway 125, 145–7
  Omicron variant* 224
  opening night 183
  post-Covid feelings* 219
  reviews* 125
  transfer to Broadway* 145–7
  uptown traditions 164
Lynch, David 246

McCollum, Kevin 205
McElvaine, Robert S., *The Great Depression: America* 62
McGrath, Matt [Reverend Marlowe] 168, 208, 238, 244
  A Streetcar Named Desire 162
  Broadway reopening* 216
  joining on Broadway* 162
  joining on Broadway 159
McKean, Michael 16
Mackintosh, Cameron 54, 206
McPherson, Conor (director)
  approach 45
  Artie Gaffin* 82–4
  choosing The Public Theater* 68–9
  glass-of-milk question* 109
  and Lucy Hind 125, 163–4
  Mandy Hackett 131–2
  and Marco Paguia 234, 236–7
  Old Vic Theatre 37, 52
  play closing 238, 245
  play in London 4
  play in New York 5, 61, 63
  premiere production rehearsals* 44–5
  "Pressing On"* 164–8
  previews* 50–3
  reading at the Public Theater 13, 17–18
  reviews* 123–4
  *Seafarer** 42
  Simon Hale 164
  sound of the songs 93–4
  *The Night Alive** 42

The Weir 37
    transfer to Broadway* 71
    working on the sound* 37–40
McPherson, Conor (director) and
        actors 41–2, 46–7, 77, 118–9
    Anthony Edwards 245
    Austin Scott 165
    Caitlin Houlahan 74
    cast off-Broadway* 77–8
    Coltan Ryan 74–5, 119
    Jeannette Bayardelle 171, 180–1
    John Schiappa 85
    Kimber Elayne Sprawl 87–8, 108
    Luba Mason 73, 78, 80–1, 120–1
    Mare Winningham 101–2, 118,
        130, 136–8
    Robert Joy 86
    Sheila Atim 106–8
    Shirley Henderson 39–40
    Todd Almond 3, 37–8, 113–4, 167,
        169–70, 196, 202, 232, 236, 242
    Tom Nelis 105
McPherson, Conor (playwright) 10
    character 10, 22–3
    Dublin 21
    fixing the play 118
    idea for the production* 20–5
    original concept 44–5, 47, 51
    story of the play 238–40
    working on the script* 26–36, 65
McPherson, Conor (playwright) and
        Bob Dylan 24, 40
    choosing Christian albums* 26–42,
        65, 164, 166, 238
    interpreting* 90, 92–3, 96–9
    setting the songs 95–100
Madame Bovary 9, 20
Maine
    buying the house 186
    living in the house 187
    summer in 186
Majok, Martyna, *Cost of Living* 235
Malloy, Dave, *Moby Dick* 105
Marlowe, Reverend (character) *see*
        McGrath, Matt
Marsh, Matthew Dean 121
    Romeo & Juliet (musical) 121
Marston, Nick (agent) 21–3
    idea for the production* 22–3, 25

Mason, Luba [Mrs. Burke] 7, 60, 78,
        88, 110, 114–5, 120, 168, 170,
        174, 181–2, 217, 220, 226, 234,
        240, 244
    Artie Gaffin* 81
    cast off-Broadway* 78–9
    casting at The Public Theater* 73–4
    fixing the play* 120–2
    interpreting Bob Dylan* 91
    Omicron variant* 228
    post-Covid feelings* 221
    rehearsals* 80–1
    transfer to Broadway* 160
Matias, Or (music director), reading at
        the Public Theater* 14–18, 55
Mayne, Ben (understudy) 111, 141,
        142–3* 244
meeting Bob Dylan
    Caitlin Houlahan 129, 135, 140
    Chelsea Lee Williams [Marianne
        Lane] 132
    Colton Ryan [Gene Laine] 129
    Jeannette Bayardelle 128–31,
        136–8
    Mandy Hackett (associate artistic
        director) 131–6
    Mare Winningham [Elizabeth Lane]
        130–1, 136–9
    Oskar Eustis 132–3, 135–6
    Rachel Stern 132
    Scott Sanders (audio engineer)
        131–2, 135
Mendez, Lindsey 197
Meyers, Lynn 87
Mitchell, John Cameron 12
moving on 198
Moynihan, Dessie
    Omicron variant* 228–9
    transfer to Broadway* 145–6, 148

Nebraska, childhood 3–4
Nederlanders, The 204
Neilsen, Mrs. (character) *see*
        Bayardelle, Jeannette
Nelis, Tom [Mr. Perry] 238, 244
    glass-of-milk question* 105–6
    interpreting Bob Dylan* 92
    playing Mr. Perry* 76, 106
Noël Coward Theatre, transfer to 54, 70

Nwandu, Antoinette Chinonye, *Pass Over* 216

Old Vic Theatre 49–50, 69
  Chris Highland 73
  Conor McPherson 37, 52
  funding 34
  Georgia Gatti 36
  Lucy Hind 38, 50
  Matthew Warchus 10, 30–1, 33
  Oskar Eustis 68–9
  rehearsals 42
  script 29
  Simon Hale 37, 94
  transfer to Broadway 68, 73
  transfer to Noël Coward Theatre 54, 70
  Tristan Baker 49–50, 54, 70
  workshops 35
Olivo, Karen 87
Omicron infection
  Colin Bates 230
  Mare Winningham 224–8
  Todd Almond 229–30, 232
opening night on Broadway
  Jeff Brancato (assistant/production stage manager) 157
  John Schiappa 162
  Oskar Eustis 158–9
  play in New York 157–9
  throwing away flowers viii, 9–10, 185
opening night parties 221
over-emotional acting 85–6

Paguia, Marco (music director) 234–7, 244
  experience of Elias* 234–7
  interpreting Bob Dylan* 98–9
  post-Covid feelings* 223
  rehearsals with Todd Almond 88–9
Papp, Joseph 11
Parker, Alecia (Broadway producer/general manager)
  Omicron variant* 228
  reopening after Covid* 212–4
Parsons, Charlie 18, 33
parties 9
  opening night 221
Pavlovic, Carmen 206

Perry, Mr. (character) *see* Nelis, Tom
Pittu, David [Reverend Marlowe] 16, 56, 244
  fishing scene 112
  leaving* 159
  Mare Winningham 137
  over-acting 78
  on the play* 121
  reading at Gibney Studios 73
  reviews* 126–8
play in London, Old Vic Theatre 49–50, 69
play in New York
  Duluth 25
  film of 245
  opening night at The Public Theater 122
  opening night on Broadway 157–9
  plot 10
  return of 199–201
  signs of working 41
  story of the 238–40
play scenes
  act two 112
  first 103–9
  fishing 112–3
  Thanksgiving 110–1, 223–4
post-Covid feelings
  Aaron Lustbader (general manager) 219
  Austin Scott [Joe Scott] 222–3
  Caitlin Houlahan 222
  Chelsea Lee Williams [Marianne Lane] 222
  Jay O. Sanders [Nick Laine] 219–20
  Jeannette Bayardelle 223–4
  Luba Mason 221
  Marc Kudisch 219
  Marco Paguia (music director) 223
  Rachel Stern 221
  Robert Joy [Doctor Walker] 223
  Scott Sanders (audio engineer) 221
"Praising God" 59
premiere production rehearsals
  Ciarán Hind [Nick Laine] 42–4, 46–8
  Georgia Gatti (theatrical producer) 42–4
  Lucy Hind (choreographer) 44, 48

Matthew Warchus (artistic director) 48

Shiela Atim [Marianne Laine] 43, 45–7, 49, 56

"Pressing On" (Mrs. Neilsen, Company) 52, 77, 196, 220

Broadway curtain number 164

keep faith 166–8

previews, London 49–54

previews, New York 115–6
   audiences 117–22
   fixing the play 117–22

production
   choosing Christian albums 18–26
   designers 36–42
   idea for 18–26
   jukebox musicals 19
   premiere 42–9
   results 42–9
   tickets 49–54

props, glass-of-milk question 41, 48, 103–9, 114, 117

Public Theater, The
   choice of 66–9
   downtown 6
   reading at 11–18, 54–6

racism
   Broadway Advocacy Coalition 211, 237
   violence 237

rake workshop 210

reading at The Public Theater 11–18, 54–6

rehearsals 8
   after Covid 208–14
   Gibney Dance Center Manhattan 15
   with Marco Paguia 88–9
   Old Vic Theatre 42

Reichard, Daniel 66–7

Reilly, John C. 31

religion, in the play 65

religious experience 7–8, 64–6, 118, 180, 196

reviews 122–8
   Ben Brantley New York Times 53–4, 68, 123–5
   Helen Shaw Vulture 216–7
   J.C. Trewin Observer 123

Roberts, Justice John 127–8

Ronane, Jessica (casting director) 39

Rooney, David 235

Rosen, Jeff 19–20, 24–5, 136, 139

Rubin, Barbara 184, 225–6, 232–3
   Omicron variant* 225, 232–3

Rudin, Scott 205–6

Runaway Entertainment 18, 33

Ryan, Colton [Gene Laine] 74, 140–2, 168, 244
   Artie Gaffin* 83–4
   cast at The Public Theater* 85
   cast off-Broadway* 76–7
   casting at The Public Studios* 74–6
   fixing the play* 119
   interpreting Bob Dylan* 94, 100
   leaving 209
   meeting Bob Dylan* 129

Ryan, Kate Moira 58

Sanders, Jay O. [Nick Laine] 168, 231, 244
   joining on Broadway* 161
   joining on Broadway 159, 161
   post-Covid feelings* 219–20

Sanders, Scott (audio engineer) 129, 176, 244
   interpreting Bob Dylan* 91
   meeting Bob Dylan* 131–2, 135
   post-Covid feelings* 221
   "Saved" 27

SBA see Small Business Administration

Scandalios, Nick 204

Schiappa, John [ensemble] 76, 85, 244
   Legacy Robe 158
   national tour** 247
   opening night on Broadway 158* 162

Schumacher, Tom, reopening after Covid* 203–8, 213–4

Scott, Austin [Joe Scott] 60, 139, 185, 221–2, 244
   Covid at the Belasco Theater* 180–3
   Hamilton 161
   joining on Broadway* 159–62
   "month-long break"** 185
   Omicron variant* 226–7
   playing Joe Scott* 165–6

post-Covid feelings* 222–3
reopening after Covid* 211
Scott, Joe (character) see Scott, Austin
Scott, Sherie Rene 119, 140
Seller, Jeffrey 205
Semon, Housso (swing)* 233
"Señor" (Elias, Kate, Gene, Company) 6, 217, 231
Shalloo, Jack 13
Shaw, Helen, Vulture review 216–7
Shields, Brooke 216
Shuberts, the 204
Shuttered Venue Operator Grant 214
Sibley, John (audio) 225
Side Show 36
"Sign on the Window" (Mrs. Burke, Company) 55
sleepwalking 168, 187–9, 202, 208
"Slow Train" (Reverend Marlowe, Joe, Mrs. Neilsen, Marianne, Company) 10, 27, 60, 65, 136
Small Business Administration (SBA), Office of Disaster Assistance 214
Smith, Rae (costume/scenic designer) 125
Sondheim, Stephen, Sunday in the Park with George 92–4
songs, sound of 93–4
songs (Almond)
    "I Don't Know About You" 188–9
    writing 58–9
songs (Dylan)
    "All Along the Watchtower" (Joe, Marianne, Company) 139
    "Ballad of a Thin Man" (Orchestra) 62
    "Duquesne Whistle" (Elias, Kate, Gene, Company) see "Duquesne Whistle"
    "Forever Young" (Elizabeth, Company) 40, 52, 77, 137, 243
    "Girl from the North Country" (Company) 999
    "Has Anybody Seen My Love" (Marianne, Company) 103, 106–7
    "Hurricane" (Joe, Marianne, Company) 139, 174–5, 180–2, 220

"I Want You" (Gene, Kate) 140, 231
"Idiot Wind" (Joe, Marianne, Company) 184
"Is Your Love in Vain?" (Mrs. Burke, Mr. Burke, Company) 7
"Jokerman" (Marianne, Mrs. Neilsen, Mrs. Burke, Elizabeth, Kate, Company) 37, 233
"License to Kill" (Reverend Marlowe, Joe, Mrs. Neilsen, Marianne, Company) 40, 60
"Like a Rolling Stone" (Elizabeth, Company) 77, 93–103, 220
"Pressing On" (Mrs. Neilsen, Company) 52, 77, 164, 166–7, 196, 220
"Señor" (Elias, Kate, Gene, Company) 6, 217, 231
"Sign on the Window" (Mrs. Burke, Company) 55
"Slow Train" (Reverend Marlowe, Joe, Mrs. Neilsen, Marianne, Company) 10, 27, 60, 65, 136
"Sweetheart Like You" (Mrs Burke, Mrs Neilsen, Company) 170, 174
"Tales of Yankee Power" (Elias, Kate, Gene, Company) 6
"Tight Connection to My Heart" (Marianne, Company) 41, 46–8, 103, 106–7, 210, 220
"True Love Tends to Forget" (Mrs. Burke, Mrs. Neilsen, Company) 138, 170–71, 174
"Went to See the Gypsy" (Mrs. Neilsen, Company) 90
"What Can I Do for You?" (Mr. Burke, Joe, Company) 112, 238
Sony Music 19
Sprawl, Kimber Elayne [Marianne Laine] 10, 244
    Austin Scott* 183, 222, 226
    Barbara Rubin* 233
    cast at The Public Theater* 87–8
    CCM 88–9
    glass-of-milk question* 108–9
    interpreting Bob Dylan* 91
    Jeannette Bayardelle* 144
    "License to Kill" 60

playing Marianne* 105, 108, 161
reopening after Covid* 211
reviews* 127
"Tight Connection to My Heart"
    41, 103, 107*, 210, 220
transfer to Broadway* 149, 161
video-shoot 195–7
working with Conor 41
Stanley, Elizabeth 14, 177–9
    Covid on Broadway* 177, 179
    high-five 177
Stern, Rachel [ensemble] 76, 134, 244
    interpreting Bob Dylan* 99, 102
    meeting Bob Dylan* 132
    post-Covid feelings* 221
    reviews* 127–8
Stone, David 205, 214
Stoppard, Tom, Leopoldstadt 70
Subias, Mark 58, 89, 187
Sundance Institute Theatre Program 58
"Sweetheart Like You" (Mrs. Burke,
    Mrs. Neilsen, Company) 170, 174

"Tales of Yankee Power" (Elias, Kate,
    Gene, Company) 6
Terrell Dunford, Law (swing) 159
Thaler, Jordan 11
Tharp, Twyla, The Times They Are
    a-Changin (musical) 20
Theater Mitu 153
"Tight Connection to My Heart"
    (Marianne, Company) 41, 46–8,
    103, 106–7, 210, 220
Tony Awards
    Best Musical 146
    ceremony 128, 134, 195, 217, 221,
        238
    ineligibility for 195
    Jodie Comer 70
    Leopoldstadt (Stoppard) 70
    Lindsey Mendez 197
    Matthew Warchus 33
    postponing 195
    rehearsal 246–7
    Sam Gold 76
    Simon Hale 94
    Twyla Tharp 20
Tony Awards, nomination
    Amber Gray 187

Amy Herzog 76
announcements 195
Colton Ryan 209
Conor McPherson 21
Jeannette Bayardelle 15, 90
Lear deBessonet, Into the Woods
    (Sondheim) 13
March Kudisch 14
Mare Winningham 90
transfer to Broadway
    Aaron Lustbader (general manager)
        145–7
    Artie Gaffin (stage manager)
        149–50
    Caitlan Houlahan 143–5, 147,
        160–1
    Conor McPherson (director) 71
    David Binder 70–1
    Jeannette Bayardelle 144–5
    Kimber Elayne Sprawl [Marianne
        Laine] 149, 161
    Mandy Hackett (associate artistic
        director) 144–6, 148
    Mason, Luba 160
    Oskar Eustis 70–2
    Robert [Doctor Walker] 162
    Shiela Atim [Marianne Laine] 72
    Tristan Baker (commercial
        producer) 70, 72, 145–6
transfer to New York, Old Vic Theatre
    68, 73
Trentalange, Chiara (swing) 159
Trewin, J.C., review in Observer 123
triumph 9
    Jennifer Blood 227
"True Love Tends to Forget" (Mrs.
    Burke, Mrs. Neilsen, Company)
    138, 170–1, 174

understudies 141–3
United Talent Agency 11

vacation swings 229, see also
    individual cast members
violence 9
    Elias 110, 114, 117–8
    racist 237
    turns to love 112
    within the family 112, 234

voice
damaging the 163, 165–6
vocal coaches 168–70

Walker, Doctor (character) see Joy, Robert
Walton, Bob (understudy) 139, 142
Wankel, Bob 204
Warchus, Matthew (artistic director) 96, 244
Artie Gaffin** 83
Conor McPherson 28, 44–5
interpreting Bob Dylan* 96–7
Old Vic Theatre 10, 30–1, 33
Olivier awards ceremony 48
premiere production rehearsals* 48
previews* 50, 52
Tristan Baker* 68
working on the script* 30–5
working on the sound* 41–2
Ware, Samantha 16
Watt, Kirsten, opening night on Broadway 157–8
Weissler, Barry 205
"Went to See the Gypsy" (Mrs. Neilsen, Company) 90
Wharton, Aidan (swing/Gene Laine) 229–33, 241, 247
Omicron variant* 229–33
"What Can I Do for You?" (Mr. Burke, Joe, Company) 112, 238
Wilde, Oscar, The Importance of Being Earnest 85
Wilder, Thornton, The Long Christmas Dinner 44
Winningham, David 94
Winningham, Mare [Elizabeth Lane] 9, 241, 244–7
Broadway reopening* 217
cast at The Public Theater* 86
cast off-Broadway* 77
clothes 100–101
Conor's speech 238–9
Covid infection* 224–8

fixing the play* 119
Forever Young 137
House Event 212
interpreting Bob Dylan* 90–1, 94, 98–9, 102
Jeannette Bayardelle 144
late-night scene 60
Like a Rolling Stone 94, 98–100, 102, 114, 220
meeting Bob Dylan 129, 130–1*, 136–9*
playing Elizabeth 64, 76
previews* 118
reopening after Covid* 211
Tony Award nomination 90
tree for Artie 169
Wolfe, George C. 66
working on the script
Conor McPherson (playwright) 26–6, 65
Matthew Warchus (artistic director) 30–5
Shirley Henderson [Elizabeth Laine] 28–9, 31, 33
Tristan Baker (commercial producer) 34–5
working on the sound
Conor McPherson (director) 37–40
Georgia Gatti (theatrical producer) 36, 42
Lucy Hind (choreographer) 38–39, 41
Matthew Warchus (artistic director) 41–2
Shirley Henderson [Elizabeth Laine] 39–41
Simon Hale (musical arranger/orchestrator) 36–7
Tristan Baker (commercial producer) 36, 38
workshops, Old Vic Theatre 35
Wyatt, Kirsten 157–8

Zhao, Chloé, The Rider 139